The Image Revisited

The Image Revisited

Luc Tuymans IN CONVERSATION WITH

Gottfried Boehm, T.J. Clark & Hans M. De Wolf

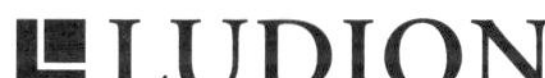 LUDION

7 How to Secure the Value of an IMAGE as an IMAGE in Times of Political Turmoil?
Hans M. De Wolf

14 The Budapest Sessions

92 The Basel Sessions

165 Abschied und Gegenstand: An Intermezzo in Brussels

166 The Brussels Sessions

257 Basel: The Conclusive Conversation

273 Index

279 Photographic Credits

280 Colophon

How to Secure the Value of
an IMAGE as an IMAGE
in Times of Political Turmoil?

About ten years ago, a vast European reform named after the beautiful Italian city of Bologna was on everybody's mind in the academic world. For all those involved with education and the arts, there was simply no way to escape the massive implications of the process designed to ensure comparability in the standards of higher scholastic qualifications.

In retrospect, it is hilarious to consider that such an important matter – finding out what kind of balance would in the future connect different fields of human knowledge as the one represented by the university and the art world – was left in the hands of six captains of industry and two university rectors who were given complete "carte blanche" from European leaders. If history has proven that some astonishingly stupid decisions can be made within the most respected and impressive framework, then this reform qualifies as a glorified example. The inspired decision of the "Negotiators" was to copy the blueprint of the American academic system and to apply it to all the existing European models, including those – such as art academies and polytechnics – that, for good reasons, had maintained a separate, practice-based status since their inception in the 19th century. Overnight, those institutions were forced to wake up to a new regime that was no longer defined by style, creativity and skills. From now on, their central key value had to become the notion of RESEARCH. The fact that nobody could come up with a workable definition of what exactly was meant by "research in the arts" did not matter.

Ten years ago many of us were indeed on full alert and highly suspicious about the reform. We did not understand what kind of game we would end up with, nor where the ball with which we were expected to play was. In all honesty, this was also the case for several well-meaning academics in charge of implementing the reform. They were abandoned in an unknown field where they had to operate in an atmosphere of uneasiness because even the best among them were faced with their inability to determine according to which criteria the so-called "research in the arts" could be validated.

I would like to keep in mind this particular period in time because it was very short (the process went on for less than two years) and yet it was during those days that some people from both sides – including me – still believed that, if we wanted it, we could have used the dynamics imposed by the reform to do something completely different.

Deep in ourselves we knew how risky it would have been to abandon Kant's position that there can be no common ground between art and science; however, in hindsight, we must admit that we all were seduced by the situation's potential. For most people in the art world, universities were little-known but powerful and well-established devices… Where did that interest come from, with universities suddenly starting to charm all kinds of artists?

The book you are holding is the result of a series of conversations from that period in time around 2007–2008, when some of us, taking advantage of the fact that almost nobody knew how to orientate themselves in the post-Bologna reality, invented an alternative model inspired by the reform's ambition to do something completely new. Our initial presumptions were clear and simple. We thought that an operation bringing those two worlds together could only be successful if it was based on a deep mutual respect and an honest curiosity for the world of the other.

The case to be proven was that if you brought a "selected" representative of the academic world (here intuition turned out to be a crucial key to success) together with an artist, there should be no reason to believe that something new and interesting could not come out of those confrontations. The meetings we organized between Gottfried Boehm and Luc Tuymans were our first test case and they led to this publication.

We are still fascinated today by the intrinsic quality of the talks as well as the boldness with which Luc and Gottfried left their intellectual comfort-zones looking for alternative perspectives – these conversations have aged better than any wine. However, we cannot yet say if the book represents a paradigm shift in regard to the way art and science can co-exist in the post-Bologna reality, or if it will just be a rare exception of good practice in an environment that would now be marked by lack of resonance and intellectual poverty.

In retrospect, it is surprising to see how rigorous and pure those conversations were, as if they *almost* represented the promise of the higher intellectual universe we were all longing for, while at the same time the social tissue holding it together was rapidly degenerating into the mess we experience today, partly as a result of reforms such as the one we call "Bologna".

The reason why the alternative formula we developed has stood so firm with time has certainly to do with the fact that, in principle, the entire responsibility for each project lay in the hands of those who cared about its content: the artist and his academic partner. Luc's and Gottfried's engagement in such a project stands out as a tribute to our organization, just as the assumption that after the time spent together, the artist would return to his studio to take care of his business again and the academic would do exactly the same, in a renewed atmosphere of respect and affection for each other's field of knowledge without altering the core principles of their respective occupations.

Instinctively I already knew by then – and that's what made me act – that this would become a critical point of the reform: would we have been able to maintain a model in which the institutions were not needed as such and that could guarantee a standard of mutual respect, and whereby neither of the fields of knowledge involved would be submitted to the other one? Would we have been able to engender and to introduce, rapidly enough, new forms of consciousness and alertness that could protect an old and glorious field of human expertise such as the arts under those new circumstances – a self-referential field that had always found itself at the forefront of our idea of identity? "This is where we come from", Tuymans claimed during a lecture at Harvard University in 2009 while showing us a picture of the "Arnolfini" painting by Jan van Eyck. Have we indeed succeeded in making our approach a valuable alternative to the Bologna reform? We were driven by a curious mix of fear and hope in those days. There was hope, because we were fully engaged in completely new forms of engendering knowledge that were inspiring and promising (this book serves as their illustration); there was fear because we knew that the climate was not good.

If, during those early days of the reform, an artist such as Luc took a serious interest in the opportunities brought forward by our newly developed methodology, in reality that involvement never made him move out of the parameters of his activity as an artist. He was not available for "academization", as it would be called later on, and that was the price we had agreed to pay. What we all had in common was the understanding that our engagement was not institutional. What brought us together was a sincere concern for the future status of the arts in our society as well as enthusiasm for the uniqueness and originality of the formula we were about to apply. And it worked.

This particular attitude (however legitimate it might be) helps to explain why our initiative would never produce the necessary energy to stop another movement engendered by the same reform and that would soon hold the whole field of higher artistic education in an iron grip. What could have been predicted with the introduction of the reform eventually became a reality: suddenly a group of mediocre individuals would come forward in their brand-new outfits as RESEARCHERS, and there was nothing that could be done to stop them because they had the institutions on their side. Those people – most of whom the art world had never heard of – were willing to fill in all the BLANK SPOTS created by the reform which the universities, busy with the responsibility of turning the reform into a hard reality, had been so afraid of. In fact, it would result in one of the most monstrous intellectual deceits in recent memory. Most universities had little or no idea of the real value and respectability of what they were embracing; they were not disturbed by the fact that they implemented a new field of research in the complete absence of criteria and workable instruments of valorization; the only issue that truly relieved them was the fact that these new boys and girls from the "research in the arts" were mercifully ready to commit themselves to the most traditional forms of academic output. Suddenly the first "Journal of Artistic Research" entered the picture and all was good.

Ten years have gone by since this all started, and now that the positions are clear, we can only come to the conclusion that the reform has led to a profound divide. All the respectable artists that were around in the early days of the reform, such as Luc Tuymans, have turned their back on the academic world again, while on the other hand a vast grey zone has materialized under the umbrellas of university-controlled institutions, wasting massive amounts of money in the name of "research in the arts". And the boys and girls responsible have been prudent enough to avoid any light being shed on what they have been doing while implementing their abject little plan. That is what umbrellas are good for.

So, one of the most splendid results of the Bologna Process became the creation of an ALIAS in regard to the place where real art is produced, discussed, studied and negotiated: a parallel art world with no connections to the "real" art world, with infamous "PhDs in the arts" that have, in fact, zero respectability. If, by accident, valuable artists have obtained that degree, the chance that they will mention it on their CV is close to zero.

Some projects need a resonance box of their own in order to be truly understood and appreciated. Confronted with that cocktail of institutional blindness, irresponsibility, cowardice and mediocrity known as the Bologna Process, the project that you are now about to discover will hopefully shine as a pure antidote. The conversations between Luc Tuymans and Gottfried Boehm, moderated by myself, are exemplary because from the very beginning all participants approached the artworks and ideas they were interested in with a fresh mind. Two independent and highly original individuals made the intellectual capital they have stored over the course of the years available for discussion and confrontation. The new format we tested for the first time in front of six paintings by El Greco in the Szépművészeti Múzeum in Budapest, set free a new type of collective energy.

Luc Tuymans brought in a whole set of insights directly related to his undisputed craftsmanship as one of the most original painters of his generation, including all the subtleties that derived from it. However, that was only one aspect of his contribution. The painter speaking his mind about painting was regularly interrupted, corrected and provoked by the intellectual inside him who, in an almost rebellious way, insisted on making his various points, and bringing up ideological, political and social interpretations otherwise hidden. The combination of these two positions operated as an expression of absolute AUTHORITY that invited little counter-response and that was driven by a dialectics of rupture – Luc comes across as someone who tends to dismiss most of the outside world as hostile and ignorant until the proof of the opposite has been clearly established. While this might be experienced as a mark of arrogance, it is in fact the expression of a creative mind's complete submission to the higher goals the discussion deserves; goals that his exceptional mind is willing to reach at any price. In the end, he IS the accomplished painter in the room and that brings us to another element that needs consideration. For instance, when Luc talks about an early masterpiece by Manet, all the painting's layers will be analysed within minutes and in such a profound way that we are all reminded that making a good painting is not the same as executing a recipe. Tuymans speaks critically and respectfully about the work of a COLLEAGUE with the authority of a PEER, as if he had seen him just a week before.

There is something splendid about Gottfried Boehm's personality – so different from that of an artist – and that has contributed in no minor part to the exceptionality of these conversations. Gottfried has a rare talent for steadily investigating the subjects of discussion in order to find moments of "co-intelligence" with his partner. He is not interested in self-affirmation, but he is rather a servant of a higher cause. (In that, his dedication was no less genuine than Luc's.) "Co-intelligence" in this case means a state of mind in which all ideas and convictions – existing and new ones – have to be submitted to reconsideration over and over again in light of what might emerge in a new discussion. This activity operates in a reflective and conscious way because the field of references it is connected to is rich and complex. Yet, those arguments never represent that particular field of references as such. They are the result of a combination of things happening at the very same time as the discussion taking place. This position is a combination of open-mindedness and lack of defensiveness with no other ambition than to learn. It may be that this time, in a completely different way and in the presence of the artist, this method might reveal how an IMAGE really functions. Gottfried's observations not only reflect the best practice within academia – they also transcend into new fields of experiences. Of course, he approaches art on a more theoretical basis, brilliantly shifting from the image as a workable unity to a variety of details, hidden elements and symbolic meanings, only to return to the work as a conclusive IMAGE again. What struck me was the fact that many of his interventions would end with a question mark, as if he felt that it might still be too early to convert one of his reflections into an opinion. Doubt and curiosity form an intense alliance in Gottfried's thinking.

It might come as a surprise to many, but Gottfried's and Luc's different styles started to intertwine spontaneously and strengthen each other from the first Budapest conversations. Gottfried's references would allow Luc's convictions to function within a new and enriched context where they would obtain a relevance they had never had before. These dialectics often led both of them to conceive on-the-spot "answers" to questions they had never thought before, which brings us to a last paradox. In many aspects this methodology, while we were in the process of experimenting with it, seemed new and refreshing. As far as we knew, a project such as ours had never been executed before. Now that we can appreciate the final result, it is hard to overcome the impression that we might have revivified something ancient at the same time, something that once existed and that we forgot: the possibility of a complex and almost holistic world-view in which all kind of knowledges deserve a place, and in which the artist and the academic belong together. It is the same paradox that might help to understand why our experiment would not be challenged even when, for the last couple of sessions, we invited Timothy James "T.J." Clark to join us in the debates. His contribution enriched further a constellation where each element could have a legitimate position.

Ten years have gone by since that day when the Bologna Process was solemnly launched and implemented. In normal circumstances this anniversary would be considered an occasion to celebrate as well as to draw a first comprehensive balance of all the benefits and the points that should be rectified in the future. However, all remained quiet on the artistic research's front. Very quiet. Could this be understood as the ultimate proof that deep inside ourselves we all know that there is little or nothing to celebrate? Perhaps we should take this moment as an opportunity to open the debate again. In this case, we cannot think of a better publication to do so than the collection of conversations you are about to read.

Hans M. De Wolf

The Budapest Sessions

The first of the two Budapest sessions took place on a cold Monday afternoon in January 2008. The choice of Budapest as the place where this experiment would start was not an accident. In December 2007 the Hall of Art (Műcsarnok) had opened Tuymans' first major retrospective in Central Europe, an event that had dominated the city cultural agenda at the time. Situated in the monumental Heroes Square (Hősök tere), the Hall of Art is faced by the even more dominant building of the Fine Arts Museum (Szépművészeti), a powerful testimony of the former ruling local bourgeois class and its aspirations. Luc Tuymans had visited the museum as a young man in the 1970s and he still had overwhelming memories of his first confrontation with six paintings by El Greco that are part of the collection. He often recalled how influential this experience had been for his education as a painter, and the arrival of his own retrospective exhibition in the building in front of the museum had a special importance for him. This episode reminds us of the fact that regardless of what course history might take, all art by definition came into being as contemporary art when it first emerged.

For this experiment, I had established some simple rules. Our conversations would be filmed and recorded separately in order to develop an autonomous view that would not interfere with the conversation as a whole, avoiding the aesthetics traditionally associated with the practice of documentary-making; filming could by no means interfere with the course of the conversation, the only objective being to obtain a reliable document of what had been said; the artist and his academic partners would avoid doing any research work in advance that could influence the discussions in front of the art. At the beginning of the talks Gottfried Boehm went so far as to confess that he had even refrained from studying the catalogues on the oeuvre of Luc Tuymans sent to him by the artist's office. On that Monday afternoon, at 2.30PM, the experiment started. The museum was closed to the public and, very soon after being shown to the rooms, we were left to ourselves in the most ideal situation for our purposes. Our early conversations obviously took place in the El Greco room and they continued, without any interruption, in the rest of the museum until closing time.

The next morning, we met at the Műcsarnok for our second session. Here, our mindset was somewhat different. We had exchanged the universal canon of Western art for a comprehensive presentation of the work of a contemporary painter internationally acclaimed as one of the most influential of our times, and the privilege of being welcomed by the master himself. Needless to say, those conversations would become a detailed survey as well as a discovery of Luc's art at the same time. However, as the reader will find out, this session did not end up being merely monographic. It was clear that the debates that had taken place the day before had opened a new type of mental space that we would share and never leave again, the final conclusion being that no oeuvre, no matter how powerful and original it might be, can exist and truly be understood without a larger context. In art, there is no such thing as progress.

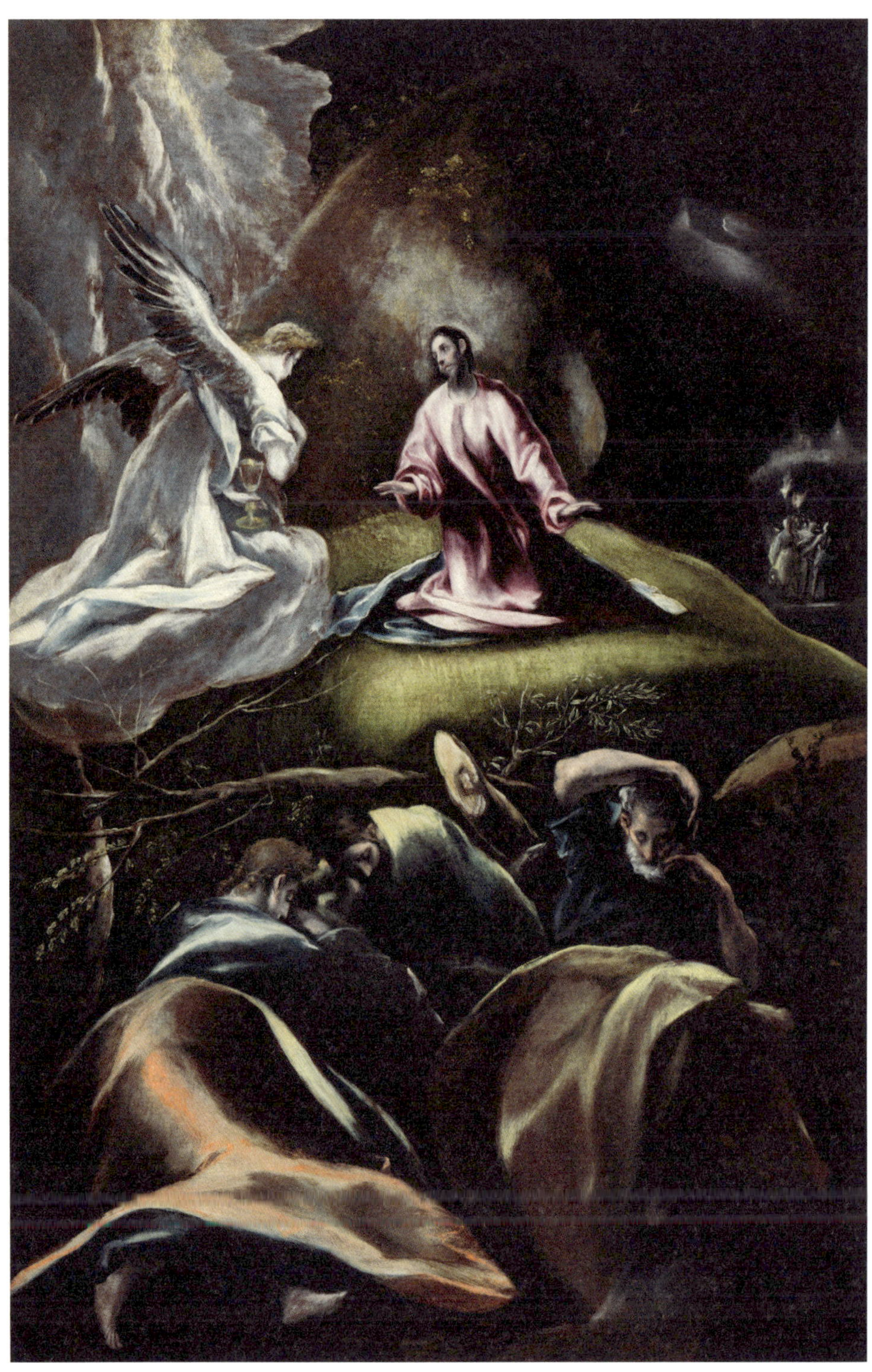

1 EL GRECO, *The Agony in the Garden*, c. 1610–14

Oil on canvas, 170 × 112.5 cm

Szépművészeti Múzeum, Budapest, INV. 51.2827

Gottfried Boehm (GB) | Hans M. De Wolf (HDW) | Luc Tuymans (LT)

LT I would like to start our conversation by talking about El Greco's[1] *The Agony*. It's a painting that has always functioned as a "memory image" for me, in the sense that it becomes even more meaningful when it's no longer in front of me. I think that *The Agony* becomes more animated in our memory as opposed to the animation that you see in the large-scale cinematic sequences of Rubens, for example. There is a concept of centralism – where the centre of this image is – that has always struck me.

GB The verticality of the composition suspending the narration and the concept has always played an important role in my experience of the painting. It is impossible for us to act in a vertical space – we only act horizontally. In other words, this vertical arrangement subverts any reference point and yet you can still see what's going on and appreciate the story that is being told. And this also strengthens another aspect, which is the huge apricot-brown area in the lower left half. It reveals how a painting can manifest itself on a basic level and depart from the narrative it describes.

HDW I find the term "visibility" very important here. These paintings look very different when you're standing right in front of them than from a distance.

1 El Greco, born Doménikos Theotokópoulos (1541–1614), was a painter, sculptor and architect of the Spanish Renaissance. The nickname "El Greco" (The Greek) was a reference to his Greek origins. His emotional painting style vividly expressed the passion of Counter-Reformation Spain.

LT Also, the paint is applied in layers, and the way that this line overlaps really forms the centre of the painting. In my paintings, there's always a breaking point. A painting may first appear to be vertical, but at the same time it slides down in the corner. It makes me think of deconstruction, because it is almost abstract. I don't mean that it is working within the idea of abstraction, but it represents this sense of "withholding" information that Mr Boehm spoke of earlier. While the narrative is there, it is split and appears fractured, and that's deconstructive.

HDW Could it be said that narratives were obligatory at this time?

LT Well, El Greco was on trial twenty-five times during the Inquisition. He had to defend himself and the elongation and distortion of his figures. He argued his case pretty rationally, and that's interesting. Of course, I also wonder how the paintings were received in their time.

GB He was operating on two levels, which is perhaps related to our present-day perceptions…

LT He's incredibly modern but I also find similarities with other painters. Tintoretto and El Greco both worked for Titian. It's interesting to see how the most harmonious painters, at the end of their lives, worked to destroy the very same harmony they have been associated with for that long. From the beginning, El Greco had a way of eliminating the model. When you compare the areas of shadow with later painters who make a very economical use of the line, such as Velázquez, you see that El Greco is very different. His forms are more atmospheric.

GB What always interested me about El Greco are the sudden changes of direction. As soon as one's gaze enters the painting for the first time, there is a sudden bend, and one looks towards the top. We find this repeated in individual gestures like Christ's hands in relation to his body, which is anatomically inconceivable – you can't position your hands that way. This makes the painting take on a life of its own, and that's when I find that a heated temporal pace enters the picture. These sudden twists articulate temporality – time becomes visible, with vehemence and immediacy. This is something that is being emphasized or interpreted at a narrative level.

HDW What would you say about the radiance of the angels?

LT I think that in the area where Christ turns – or doesn't turn – towards the angel, a ghost-like form presented as a purely ideal encounter appears.

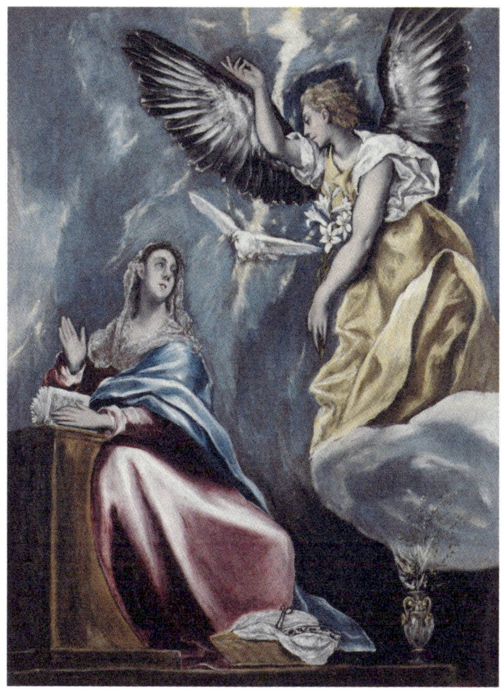

2 El Greco, *The Annunciation*, c. 1600
Oil on canvas, 91 × 66.5 cm
Szépművészeti Múzeum, Budapest, INV. 3537

But, above all, what has always shocked me is how the painting takes on a life of its own through these aspects of unrealistic hand positions. In the end, there are these orange areas that create the feeling of a cut-out, a collage, which is reinforced through the temperature of the colour scheme.

HDW El Greco has a very specific way of mixing colours.

LT I think that the pace at which he worked was also entirely new. I can't think of another painter who painted so fast. At the same time, like every good painting, none of his paintings seem too literal or manufactured. El Greco leaves empty areas in order to introduce perspective – like the green one in the middle or the empty one at the top. They work as interior and exterior spaces at the same time.

HDW *The Annunciation* seems less dynamic.

LT *The Annunciation* is less dynamic in the sense that there is a flatness in the rendition of both angels. *The Agony* has an extra dimension that doesn't seem to exist in *The Annunciation*.

GB I understand what you mean. On the other hand, I think it's tremendous how such a delicate subject like the conception of the Saviour is entirely unimaginable in this composition. The metaphor of the dove, the beam of the light, and the gesture, which at the elbow relates to a vertical line and the wing, is visually very powerful.

LT Yes, but ultimately, in my opinion, it has the wrong dimensions. I find that the dense composition of such a cathartic moment would perhaps have been better without the dove. I think the dove's head was painted before the background and was elaborated later on, as the central point of the painting covers up the energy flow and the communication between the two figures. The whole painting revolves around that, and the rest is just filling, so the format becomes a bit off-putting because the small size of the dove's head creates a discrepancy in relation to the other figures. The dove is too real in comparison, so there's no balance. In that sense, I find it a bit like an exercise.

GB Perhaps the dove has the function of redirecting the attention of the viewer. It highlights the lightning flash descending, and at the same time, through its suggestion of depth, the three-dimensional quality of the painting. It looks like an actual dove, it represents something of this world. It's about empiricism, tangibility…

HDW That has to do with the contrast between the religious and the empirical. Ultimately it is a conflict, although not a painterly one.

LT This conflict is presented on a visual level though. El Greco is one of the few painters who approached this subject in a very specific way. In *The Agony,* this feeling is not particularly present in the overall arrangement, or in the painting style, whereas in *The Annunciation* I feel that the form of the image is inappropriate. The painting *Saint Andrew,* for example, is a descriptive painting. There is a diagonal line that runs through the painting and continues – or disappears – into the corner. But there is also a painstaking awareness of materials.

HDW The colours are strange. They don't complement each other.

LT The green area is very interesting, as well as the way that the blue and the reddish brown spread throughout the whole composition – including the beard. What really interests me here is the bottom of the beard. I find it very modern. When I look at a picture I always try to figure out how it

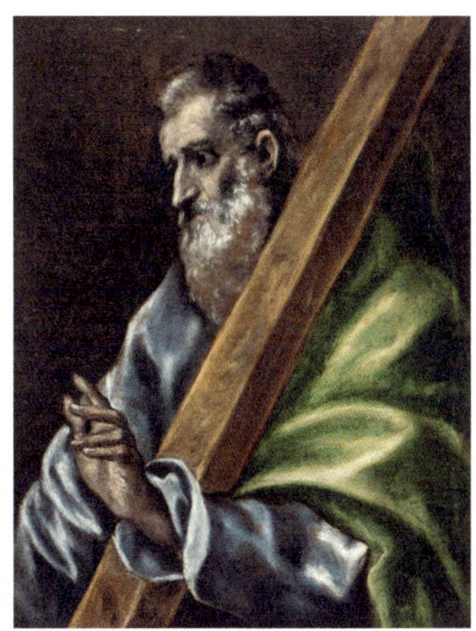

3 El Greco, *Saint Andrew, c.* 1610–14
Oil on canvas, 70 × 53.5 cm
Szépművészeti Múzeum, Budapest, inv. 51.800

was painted. For me, it is about what was painted first – and I don't mean the idea, the drawing or the preliminary drawing. I'm talking about the first stroke, the first mark. I think that *The Agony* is incredibly interwoven in its execution. Everything blends perfectly. It was clear from the start what was important. It's beautiful that it still exists, and that we can look at it.

GB When I look at these paintings, I find certain areas particularly striking. We have already discussed the verticality of *The Agony*, but in my view the severed branch in the middle is another notable spot. It obviously plays an important role within the whole composition, even if I still haven't understood completely what that is.

LT I think the severed branch alludes to the physical agony – the injury and the pain. It is the moment when it becomes clear that something is about to happen, and I find that the form is intertwined with the story. There are these elliptical forms that El Greco uses quite a lot, where the subject almost withdraws from the main theme. It has a certain lyricism. Formally it's quite a different story – the scene doesn't seem frozen due to the speed of the painting process.

HDW I find it interesting that this is the point where the two perspectival levels begin to separate. It could be also that this is a metaphor for violence: the tree is a living organism that's been severed by force, so what is depicted is the emotional gap between Christ, who is suffering, and the apostles, who have no clue of what is going on.

LT As I mentioned earlier, it is clear that the movement is sort of collaged and arranged as though under a dome. It almost feels as if the image is protected by a vitrine, which is why the figure is at the centre of the composition and the green area and the severed branch actually sticks through there. To me this is another interesting thing about El Greco: the idea of territory, and how for the first time he actually makes a topographical

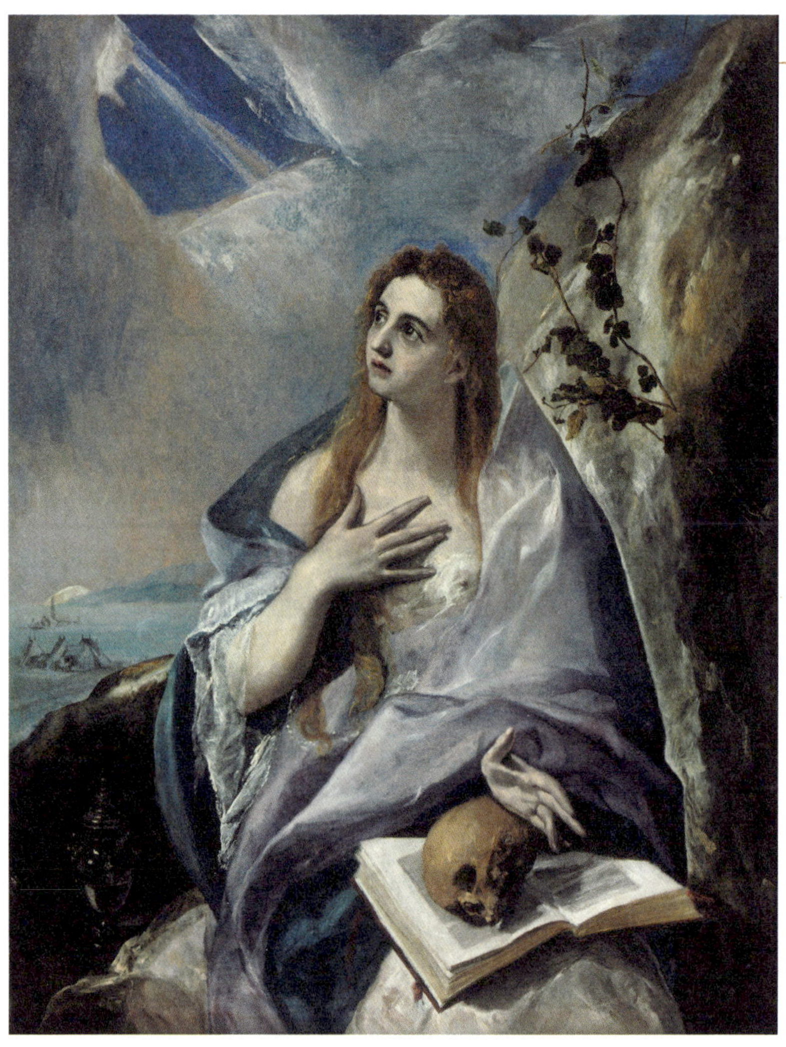

<u>4</u> El Greco, *The Penitent Mary Magdalene*, c. 1576–77
Oil on canvas, 156.5 × 121 cm
Szépművészeti Múzeum, Budapest, inv. 5640

recognition of the painting. He was also the first painter who painted a landscape without a human figure in it, as in *View of Toledo* [1599–1600]. In a painting like this you sense how interior and exterior mix. There is a kind of transformation, and it's clear that the branch is actually a theatrical feature, as is the line in *The Annunciation*, or the diagonals in *Saint Andrew*, which is repeated again and again.

HDW What disturbs me most in *The Agony* is the cloud on which the angel travels. If you look at it for too long, the world starts shrinking. To me this is a fairly flat part of the painting. In *The Penitent Mary Magdalene* the landscape is constructed in a completely different manner than the sky. Again, the idea of voluminosity and withholding is simultaneously carried out here, but not openly. The sky is actually built around the figure like an atmosphere. The way the upper portion is painted was very unusual for that period, isn't it?

GB Partly. Although I think you can find something similar in the work of Paolo Veronese, especially the colours. I don't know whether you're interested in Veronese, but if you ask whether anyone had paved the way for this phenomenon, then there are certain things that come directly from him, like the apricot shade here, or this strange lilac and turquoise – the turquoise is like a Veronese sky.

LT In *Mary Magdalene* it is clear that the field of vision continues beyond the painting, almost to the point of becoming laden with pathos. But what interests me most about this painting, aside from the way in which the sky is painted, is what's happening with the head of Mary Magdalene. From the line beneath the chin, the head doesn't add up to much – it's almost entirely passive and expressionless. The breast is also very interesting. El Greco captures it as if it's something flowing, like the sky. The whole bottom area with the cloth is very constructed and completely controlled, and then further up the painting disappears more and more, and the sky doesn't rescue it either.

HDW The sky has energy, and there certainly is a religious dimension that we somehow always tend to forget.

GB The energy occurs at various levels: it has to do with the light, with the organization of colour, and with what we discussed earlier about movement, speed and time. Luc just introduced the term "pathos". That's an interesting word because generally it has a negative connotation, although in this painting it's somehow on the edge. But aren't all these paintings full of pathos? For example, when I see how the angel in *The Annunciation* is full of gesture, how the whole body becomes a gesture, upwards, downwards, staying in its place – its flowing appearance is full of pathos. But we agree that here it feels right, it's organized.

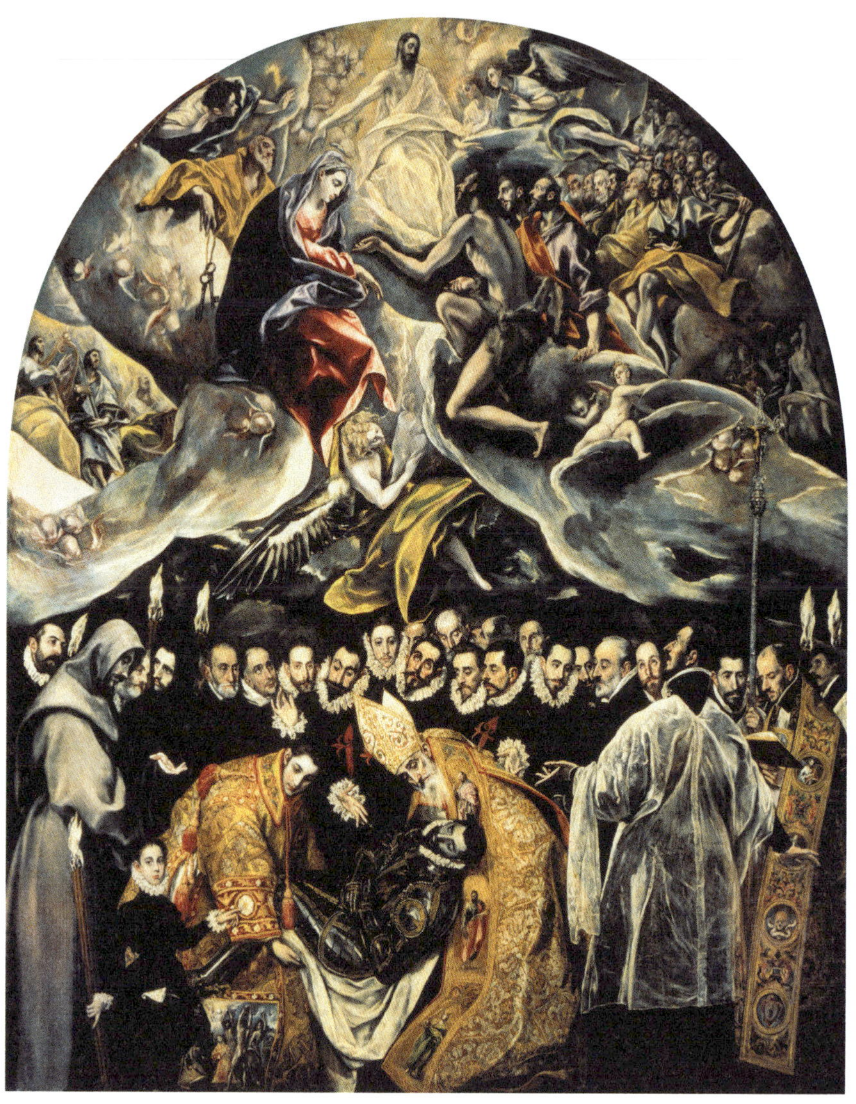

5 EL GRECO, *The Burial of the Count of Orgaz*, 1586–88
Oil on canvas, 480 × 360 cm
Church of Saint Tome, Toledo

LT Yes, but it's also about the way you look at it. When it really works well, as in the *Burial of the Count of Orgaz*, there is pathos, but it operates in a state of tension – there is a split. But when it appears as pure pathos, then it reaches a point where it no longer works. That's why I think he walks a really thin, dangerous line. *Saint James the Less*, for example, is all about the background, but it's also about what's hidden behind it. Of course it is a later painting, but it's clear how conventionally it is painted in comparison with other paintings. It is in fact a study, and it's interesting to see how

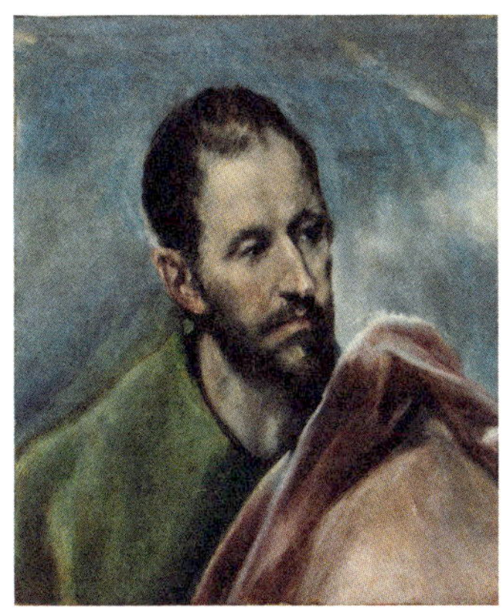

6 El Greco, *Saint James the Less*, c. 1600
Oil on canvas, 49.5 × 42.5 cm
Szépművészeti Múzeum, Budapest, INV. 9048

precisely the story is represented, how economically the whole thing is conceived – and here we get much, much closer to Velázquez and to a completely different, thoroughly unique approach. There had to be a certain amount of spirituality, but at the same time, that's one of the expressions/roles that El Greco also performed. Here he performs less. *Saint James the Less* is different from the rest of his production.

HDW There's quite clearly an issue with perspective that he just didn't come to terms with. The diagonal doesn't sit right with the space…

LT The perspective is not so essential here. The depiction is portrayed as reality without mimesis, so you don't really think about it. In fact, the idea of representation or imagination doesn't really play a part here. On a purely technical level, you can see what El Greco was capable of as a painter, and you can see that even more clearly here than anywhere else. In terms of quality, of all his paintings this is perhaps the one that I personally value most in terms of pure painting. It was painted around 1595 after Rubens' stay at the Spanish court, and if you compare it to Velázquez, you can see the effect Rubens had on Velázquez. Velázquez's paintings were fairly rigid before then.

GB Since you mentioned the perspective in this painting, I love the intersection of the movement from the lower right to the upper left with another one from the lower left to the upper right. They cross at the tip of Mary Magdalene's nose.

HDW … they cross like that twice in the space behind.

LT Yes. Again, the sky functions as a background, but that also happens all around the figure. The question is: what is the relationship between foreground and background? It's not clear at all with El Greco. The way the sky functions almost as something solid. Unlike other painters, he probably did not paint from the back to the front. And regarding the light, the classic method was for the brightest parts to be the least dense in handling, so the luminosity and translucence of the paintings was arrived at quite differently.

The sky seems more substantial than the figure in the foreground. And there's real depth in this painting, which is something that preoccupied me earlier – the idea of a funnel that almost sucks you into the painting, and yet the painting actually goes into different directions and then moves vertically, which has a really big impact in purely physical terms as well.

GB My reading of the *Mary Magdalene* painting is that the book is open and set aside, the skull is set aside, and both are delicately balanced. The whole scene is held together only by a hand. At a representational level, everything is held together by the body tension working in this way in this very specific moment.

LT Yes, that's why this part of the painting is very important. If you look at her hands, the size of her hand on her breast seems monumental in comparison with her face, and is isolated from the rest of the body. And her other hand, which is arranged in a completely different perspective, establishes an equilibrium in the painting. I can imagine that El Greco used a real model for the body, but not for the face. It's quite clear how the focus is on the bottom of the composition. It is about the significance of this instability, of holding a balance, the insecurity of life or however else we might interpret this. The composition is almost arranged like a still life, and actually taken even further. The painting was perhaps built up more from this perspective. That's understandable too, because there is this sharp break, indicated in white, next to the body of Mary Magdalene.

GB Do you read it as a landscape, as a rock, as drapery or as a tent?

LT In purely representational terms it is a landscape. However, I read it more as material. For example, if this middle left area wasn't there and the sky was shaped differently, then there would be nothing to indicate a landscape. I don't think that the idea of representing a rock or the volume of the stone was something that El Greco was very interested in. What shocks me is the incredibly exact and precise, almost photographic, manner in which the book and the skull have been rendered, which I suspect are the main concern of the painting.

GB Is the painting built up traditionally, from the back to the front, or is it painted in another way? In purely technical terms, I assume that he started with a primer and prepared the ground as the support. How do you see this as a painter?

<u>LT</u> That's also how I see it – an obvious technical procedure. El Greco primed the canvas and then probably made a preliminary drawing, because this clearly isn't a detail, but in fact a painting that he composed and assembled. But I do think there is a quality of pure obsession and painting's own physical necessity that ultimately determines itself. It means that, while painting, you've got a certain "attention span", that of course doesn't always encompass the whole composition. More importantly, the painting process itself is instinctive – it follows its own logic. Even if an image is pre-conceived, the actual process of painting shapes things quite differently.

<u>HDW</u> Do you mean that the initial concept is constantly being altered during the painting process?

<u>LT</u> Yes, and this holds true for every painter and for every painting. Of course, other painting processes exist, but not during this period. We are not looking at Flemish Primitivism, for example. This painting evokes a certain form of dilettantism. What makes El Greco an important painter is his modernity, and above all his dilettantism and the idea that the painting isn't – or isn't intended to be – absolutely finished. As a viewer, on a purely visual level, we can directly engage with his paintings. They are not finite images, but elude you; their format and colouring are very difficult to remember. This is why they make such an impression on me. Despite their extraordinariness, sense of pathos and nearly theatrical catharsis, you could easily walk past them. You could interpret that as a superficial impression, but in our memory and with distance, it completely changes shape. I believe that this is one of the fundamental components of painting. Time is another interesting aspect. There's an idea of something very specific happening at a certain point in time that, for me, is basically what constitutes painting.

<u>GB</u> That's an interesting point. With the El Greco paintings in the Prado, for example the monumental *Baptism of Christ*, I recall a certain kind of ongoing syncopated rhythm, like in a jazz piece, a "tchack" that trembles. It is all about time.

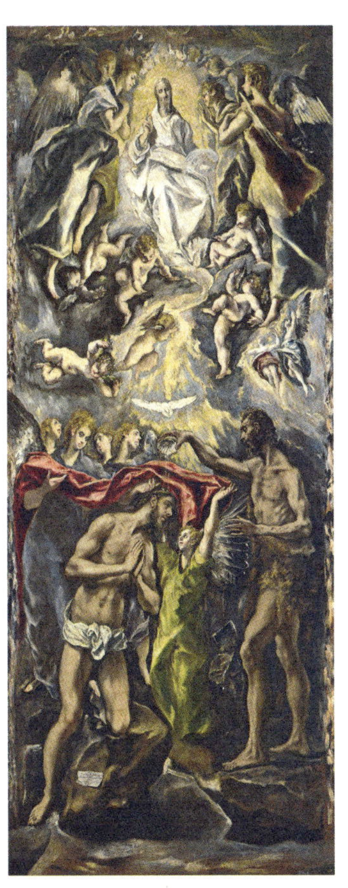

<u>7</u> El Greco, *The Baptism of Christ*,
c. 1597–1600
Oil on canvas, 350 × 144 cm
Museo Nacional del Prado, Madrid,
INV. P000821

LT I like El Greco. Not so much for the elements that I, as a painter, make use of in my own work, but more for what I dislike. I don't like it when a painting isn't "soundless", or when the movement can be shaped. That's why in this reversal it was unexpectedly shocking, because I suddenly saw that many of my own objections were refuted simply by their physicality and by understanding that there are different possibilities after all. And as I highlighted earlier, these aren't even El Greco's most important paintings. Those in Toledo are another story.

HDW Well, these painters didn't paint with retrospective exhibitions of their work in mind. Showing too many El Greco paintings together actually misses the mark.

LT And that's why it's so interesting to see a group of his paintings brought together and contextualized. This did not happen at the time.

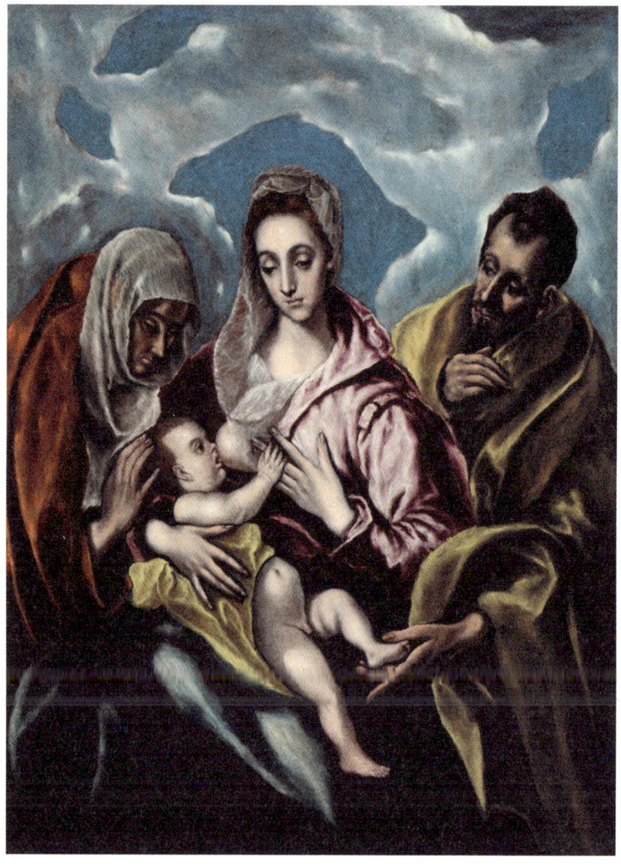

8 El Greco (Workshop), *Holy Family with Saint Anne*, c. 1600–09
Oil on canvas, 38 × 103.5 cm
Szépművészeti Múzeum, Budapest, inv. 50.755

hdw The *Holy Family* is a strange work.

lt It has all the characteristics of an El Greco, but it is obviously "in the style of". It's great to see his work next to a painting produced by his school.

gb It uses his formulas, but…

lt The intensity isn't there.

gb There's no electricity flowing through it.

lt In painting, the intensity of the image is of tremendous importance, and is impossible to imitate stylistically. I think there are different kinds of intelligence, and that you can also be intelligent with your hands. If you start thinking too much, then it's translated in terms of style and the intensity is lost. This is the case with El Greco. It's not just an attitude, it's a force of habit more than anything else, and he persisted with it almost physically, and obsessively. Despite the fact that he was well-read, there is also a level of ignorance present.

hdw It would be interesting to compare El Greco to a very fine Zurbarán painting, which would reveal a depth that we don't find in the former.

gb What I always find exciting about El Greco is that – and this has something to do with the intelligence of the hand – time and time again he succeeds in extracting a kind of fury and vibrancy from a particular theme, subject-matter or figure that moves beyond materiality, narration and expression, and grants them a force that you can't escape if you open your eyes. That is really fantastic.

lt I think that the concept of revelation plays a tremendous role in each painting too. The idea of dilettantism is very interesting in this context because this is what makes him essentially modern: the elongation of the figures, the direction and deconstruction of the image. If you look at these paintings from a certain distance, they all move in different directions and don't connect with one another. They each open up a different field of vision – one moves down diagonally, another one upwards, and so on. Initially, when standing in front of them, you have the impression that the paintings are standing still. That's what I mean by animation – as soon as you enter the room, the paintings seem to move, even though they're immobile. This is important – they give shape to ideas around movement in an almost manic way that can be grasped from a distance. There is a level of

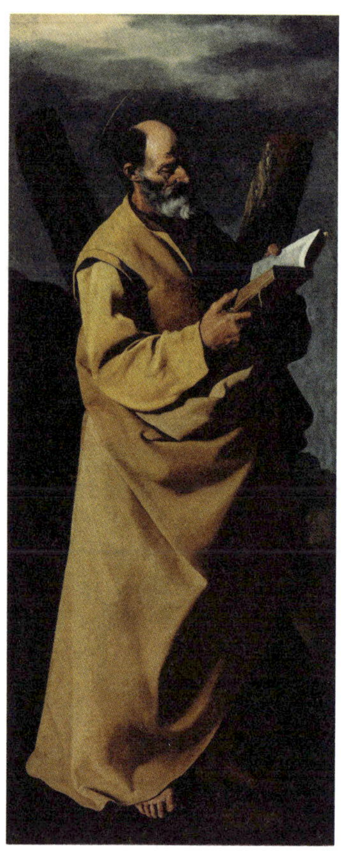

9 Francisco de Zurbarán, *Saint Andrew,*
c. 1635–40
Oil on canvas, 146 × 61 cm
Szépművészeti Múzeum, Budapest, inv. 50.749

flatness and less modelling to the resultant image, but that was the product of a very specific decision, which, in itself, was new.

HDW A very unusual decision.

LT Yes, it's an idiosyncratic decision for which El Greco was inherently criticized because it was perceived as unconventional to the point of heresy.

HDW Perhaps we should look at another Spanish painter.

LT Shall we look at Francisco de Zurbarán[2] or Velázquez first?

HDW Let's begin with Zurbarán's *Saint Andrew.* There's an evident sense of great confidence, right?

GB Perhaps we ought to focus on the cross, which is closely linked with the pose of the figure. Traditionally, the cross symbolizes St Andrew's suffering and life,[3] but what I find remarkable in this painting is how the cross is linked to the apostle's body and the internalized pose of his figure engaged in reading. It's not an external attribute. Instead, it strengthens his pose in visual terms, which is presented in a state of preoccupation. The light source at the top is interesting, his bald head, his book…

LT This painting has a very clear objective – we know we're meant to look at the book he's reading, and the whole composition revolves around this. The large expanse of St Andrew's robe revealing a bit of his foot emerging

2 Francisco de Zurbarán (1598–1664) was a Spanish painter known primarily for his religious paintings depicting monks, nuns and martyrs, as well as for his still lifes.

3 Andrew had been crucified on an X-shaped cross, or "saltire", now commonly known as a "St Andrew's Cross", supposedly at his own request, as he deemed himself unworthy to be crucified on the same type of cross as Christ had been.

from the drapery serves to anchor the image and reinforces this painting's sense of focus.

HDW Exactly. The book is most certainly the focal point, which we arrive at from the bottom up, but St Andrew and his gaze are composed at the top of the composition and directed downward. And these two different levels intersect at the level of St Andrew's cross.

LT At the same time, there is no sense of intruding on a private moment. Although the painting looks big, its scale is actually a little smaller than 1:1, which helps to create a sense of distance. In terms of pictorial ideology, the shape of the cross behind the figure reinforces existing conventions of spirituality. This is why I initially experienced it as an institutionalized image. The exertion of power through the image is what fascinates me about Zurbarán. I think he must have been very aware of that. I don't know how many of his paintings were made as commissions, but certainly this is an example of one.

HDW After all, he was one of the most important and well-established painters in Seville.

GB And, to a lesser extent, in Madrid too. I'm thinking of the four large canvases depicting the Labours of Hercules.

LT I have no criticism regarding where or how it was painted. Of course at the time, it was a modern work, painted in accordance with the spirit and fashion of the moment, using special lighting effects. By contrast, when I see a painting like *The Hurdy-Gurdy Player* by Georges de La Tour, it's clear that the painter's overly heightened sense of fetishism has taken over most of the image. And in painting, it can be quite dangerous when fetishism intervenes.

GB That could explain the cognitive dissonance in our conversations about pornography, faith and fetishism.

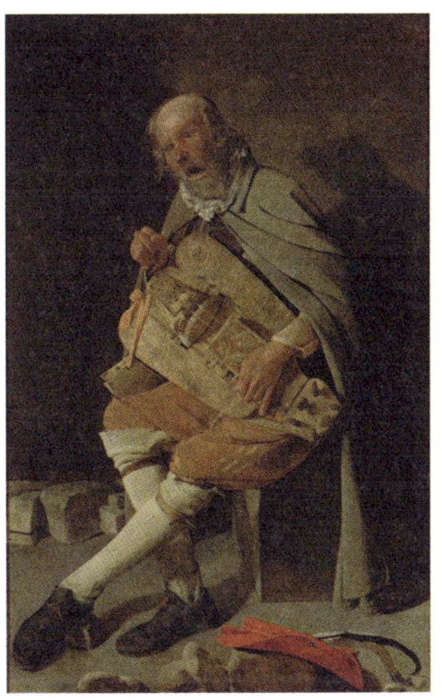

10 Georges de La Tour, *The Hurdy-Gurdy Player*, c. 1631–36
Oil on canvas, 162 × 105 cm
Musée d'arts de Nantes, Nantes, inv. 340

LT Yes, and certainly when bringing the conversations around to our own moment in time. I think Caravaggio was actually the first to have rendered this collision of faith and fetish through flesh. Velázquez remains on a purely erotic level, which, for me, has completely different origins.

HDW I'm not so sure. In *Los Borrachos*, for example, the fleshiness is there in full.

LT Let's return to the painting of St Andrew, specifically his foot. It's painted with total perfection. The landscape is clearly behind the figure, rather than surrounding it, and the figure, of course, completely dominates the foreground.

GB With the cross mediating a bit.

HDW I'm interested in the minimalism of the landscape, there's almost nothing else there. Our sole point of focus is this strong personality.

LT You refer to him as a "strong personality" and that's really the most important point of the painting. You would never say that about El Greco because his intent is completely different. Even in a portrait, he never delivers this same level of psychological impact.

GB Can we get back to fetishism?

LT Yes, actually this whole painting is a fetish: the beard, the light, the cross (that is painted quite differently from the cloth), and the drapery, which, like St Andrew's face (apart from the beard), is almost photographic. The book looks completely real, but the rest of the composition, as it recedes into the scenery, seems imaginary. The act of reading too appears forced, as if it were an adopted or contrived pose. The painting acts as an affirmation: it portrays nothing more than an act…

GB You mean that he's not really reading, just posing and pretending to read?

LT Yes, everything points in that direction. I don't see this painting as a representational image, but as something demanding to be believed. I have an incredible mistrust of it.

GB Although, in terms of views prevalent in seventeenth-century Spain, it could be said that "we're all actors on the world stage".

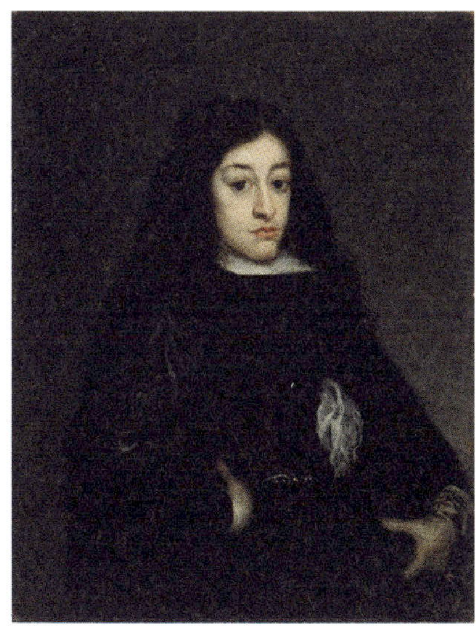

<u>11</u> Juan Bautista Martínez del Mazo,
Portrait of a Noble Youth, 17th century
Oil on canvas, 78.5 × 61 cm
Szépművészeti Múzeum, Budapest, INV. 3838

LT Absolutely, which explains the hypocrisy and morbid attitude towards the world in Spanish painting. I acquired a better understanding of this after my visit to the Escorial.[4] The tour ends at the basilica, where you finally encounter the shining, small square windows behind the sacristy. These are the "closest to God", so to speak. That sums up their whole world-view – the empire on which the sun never set.

HDW I understand what you're saying, but I don't feel the same way. I find myself immediately overwhelmed by this painting by Zurbarán, by the work as a whole.

LT As I mentioned earlier, there are other paintings by Zurbarán, but we're discussing *Saint Andrew*. I recall his impeccable still-life paintings, but there is a folkloric element that intervenes in those.

HDW What do you think of a *Portrait of a Noble Youth* by Juan Bautista Martínez del Mazo? I find it quite fascinating.

GB Del Mazo worked for the King at the same time as Velázquez, right?

HDW Yes, they were both court painters.

4 The Royal Seat of San Lorenzo de El Escorial, also known as "El Escorial", located in the town of the same name, is the historical residence of the King of Spain, and serves as a monastery, royal palace, museum and school.

GB What moves me about this painting is its irredeemable, unspeakable sense of melancholy.

HDW Irredeemable, yes – this best describes it for me too.

LT I think what's important in this work is its affirmation of status, "of a noble youth". I'm not sure if that's the real title, but it is a class that was responsible for its own portrayal, and in doing so, constructed itself for history and for posterity. And then of course they came down with the blues! They had a surplus of time on their hands, enough time for melancholy. I'm more drawn to the mouth and the way that his hand is positioned, suggesting strong self-confidence. There is an almost wan, vulnerable expression in his eyes, which do not look out from the painting, and perhaps they don't even look at the viewer. One eye might be looking at the viewer, but they are painted completely differently…

GB Yes, he's cross-eyed. The way he holds his hand is not realistic. Its position should force his elbow to protrude more towards the front, as in Titian's portrait of Gerolamo Barbarigo with the blue sleeve, which I believe is held in London – but it's strangely inconclusive. In addition, his shoulder seems crippled, as if he's sick or injured.

HDW There's another problem as well – he's a much older child than you would initially think.

GB He's ready to die… all that's left is for him to die.

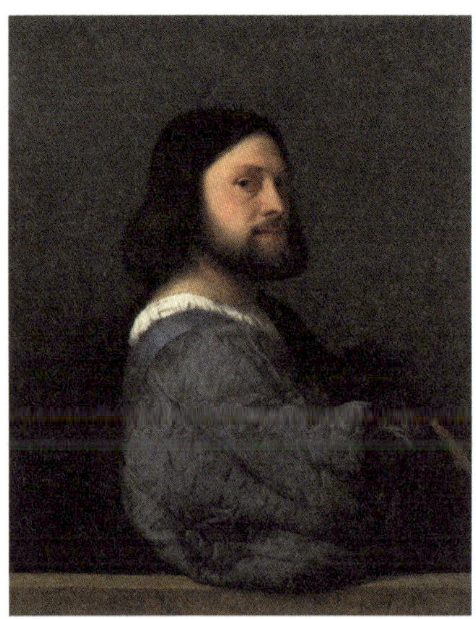

LT For me this painting expresses a certain kind of sentimentality. It's painted in a not uninteresting way – especially the eyes, which I find very well executed. Most of all I'm struck by the melancholy gaze, which is directed back at the viewer and serves to reverse, or even tame, our voyeurism.

12 TITIAN, *Portrait of Gerolamo (?) Barbarigo*, c. 1510
Oil on canvas, 81.2 × 66.3 cm
The National Gallery, London, INV. NG1944

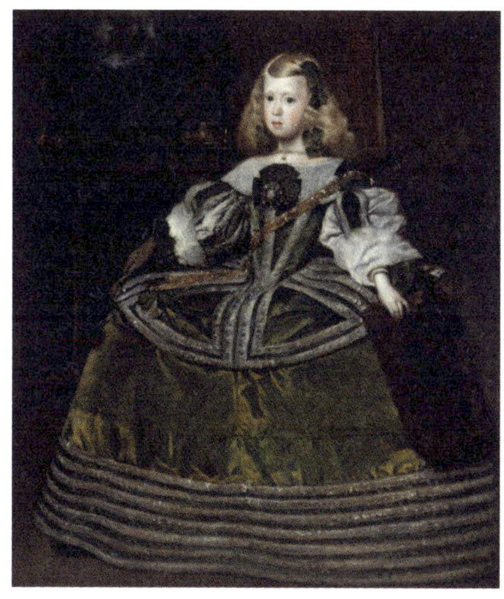

13 Juan Bautista Martínez del Mazo,
Infanta Margarita Teresa in a Green Dress, c. 1660
Oil on canvas, 121 × 107 cm
Szépművészeti Múzeum, Budapest, inv. 6708

HDW But it's the diagonal line that ruins the whole painting.

LT The line is painted very well, so it's perfectly okay. That's the only thing that counts.

HDW I meant that without the eyes this would be just an average painting.

LT You mentioned that he's cross-eyed. Perhaps this was done deliberately.

GB This strange position of the eyes, which reveals an element of ambiguity in the person's intentions, perhaps is really the crux of the whole painting. The sitter gazes outwards, but also looks away, or inwards…

LT And back from the inside to the outside – an entire psychology unfolding.

HDW In this way the painting holds up a mirror to society with a noble's personal drama, doesn't it?

GB And it's the costume of the Spanish court…

HDW This is another painting by del Mazo.[5] As a child, Princess Margarita Teresa was given away in marriage to her maternal uncle Leopold I, the Holy Roman Emperor. Every year King Philip IV of Spain would send a

5 Del Mazo was Velázquez's son-in-law and succeeded him as court painter to King Philip IV of Spain. Because his style was derivative of Velázquez, it is difficult to attribute paintings to del Mazo with any certainty and there is a tendency to credit him with works considered to be not good enough to have been painted by Velázquez himself.

painted portrait to the court of Vienna to keep Leopold apprised of how she looked and was developing. A series of portraits of Margarita Teresa hangs in the Kunsthistorisches Museum in Vienna.

LT It's difficult to see in this light, but this is an early painting by Velázquez.

GB Painted while he was still in Seville.

LT You can see how stiffly Velázquez painted this, compared with the Zurbarán. It surprises me how much this early period is dominated by a certain kind of stiffness. As I see it, this isn't Velázquez yet – there is a lack of the economy, the stance, or the personal engagement that led him later to fix a position. In this example, he doesn't adopt a standpoint vis-à-vis the painting. He's still assembling it. This is why the six months that Rubens spent at the Spanish court were so incredibly important to Velázquez. Afterwards, his paintings became more animated as he began working more quickly, with a wider range of colours, which he eventually limited and reduced again. We could call this painting "reduced", but not like Zurbarán's, which is pure or minimalist in its expression. Here, everything is evenly distributed and defined, and that petrifies the painting. There's no life in it. I would actually walk past this painting by Velázquez. It's not something that really interests me… except perhaps the eyes of the woman who's pouring the wine. But what's the relationship between the two talking men? Again – this is like St Andrew holding the book unread.

HDW It's a model. You can see here Velázquez experimenting with models that had been introduced earlier by Caravaggio.

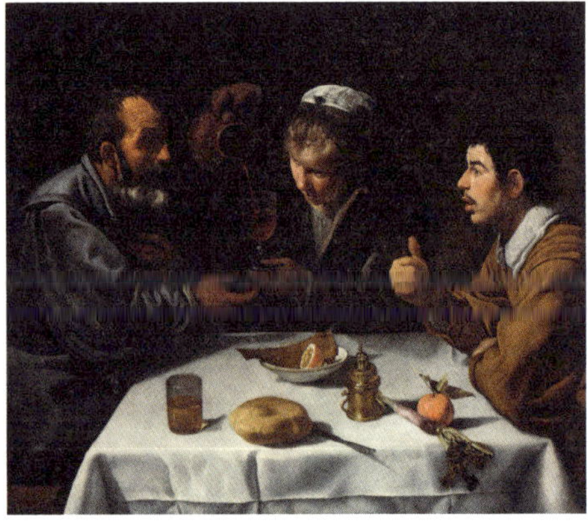

14 DIEGO VELÁZQUEZ, *Peasants at the Table (El Almuerzo)*, c. 1618–19
Oil on canvas, 96 × 112 cm
Szépművészeti Múzeum, Budapest, INV. 3820

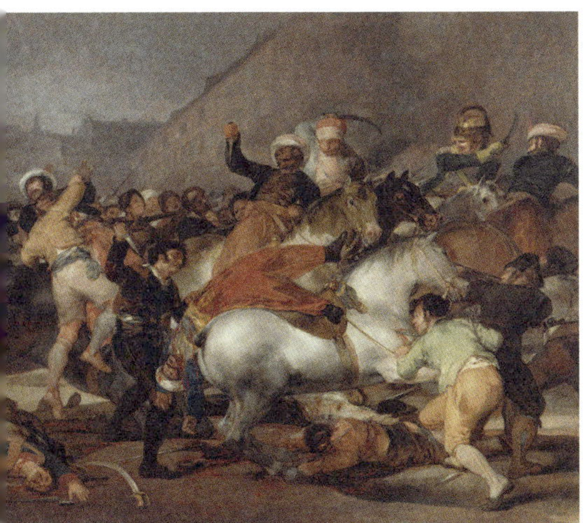

15 Francisco Goya, *The Second of May 1808 in Madrid (The Fight against the Mamelukes)*, 1814
Oil on canvas, 268.5 × 347.5 cm
Museo Nacional del Prado, Madrid, INV. P000748

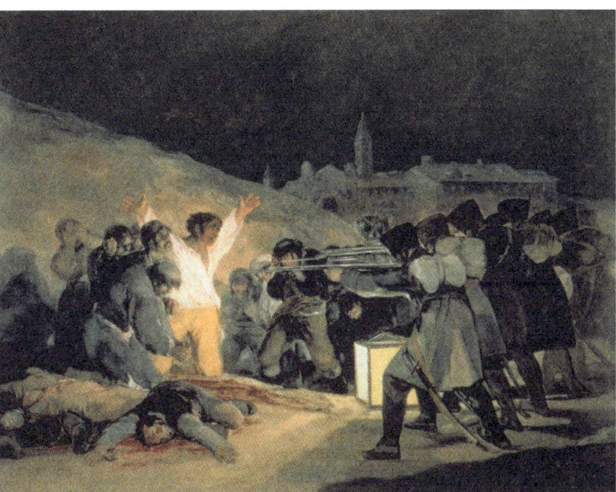

16 Francisco Goya, *The Third of May 1808 in Madrid (The Executions)*, 1814
Oil on canvas, 268 × 347 cm
Museo Nacional del Prado, Madrid, INV. P000749

LT The influence is evident. Of course the Zurbarán painting right next to it is actually more interesting.

GB But going back to Velázquez, Luc, you used the word "assembled". *Peasants at the Table (El Almuerzo)* is made up of three paintings: the man on the left, then the woman pouring from the jug, which is the strongest one in my opinion, and, finally, the young man. You can see how it's assembled by the individual elements on the table, all of which are too close together. Basically, it's the reproduction of a pictorial composition.

LT It's similar to the *Supper at Emmaus* [1601] by Caravaggio and also reminds me of the fake by Han van Meegeren, because again it's composed around a table. It's not a relevant painting. And when you look at the painting from a distance it almost disappears. It becomes more abstract.

HDW Let's go to the four Goya paintings. The most interesting is this *Scene from the Spanish War* painting. It was painted in 1810, four years before the famous "May" paintings [*Second of May 1808* and *Third of May 1808*].[6] I find its undefined shimmering very impressive.

6 *Second of May 1808* and *Third of May 1808*, both now held in the Prado, were painted by Goya in 1814, after the artist had written to the regent, Cardinal Luis de Bourbon, expressing a desire to create works commemorating the events that had taken place during the Spanish War of Independence (1808–12) from French occupation.

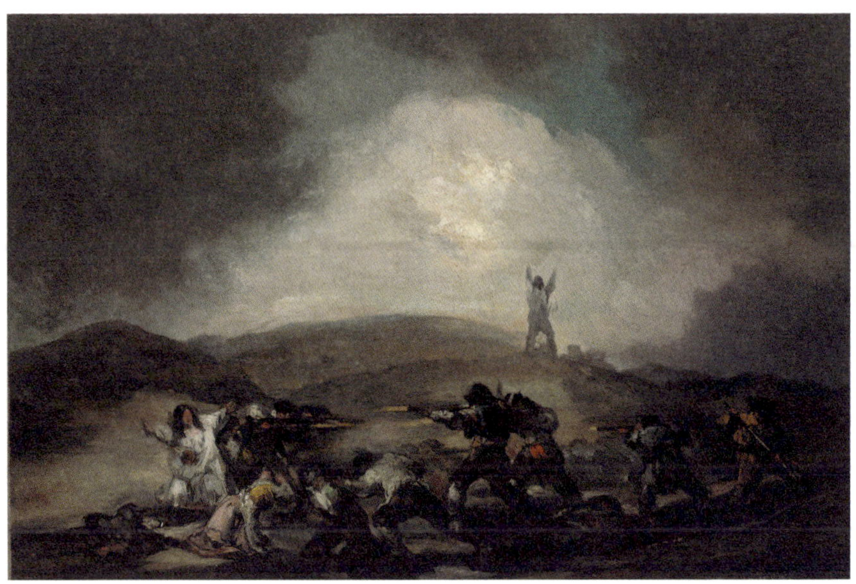

17 Francisco Goya, *Scene from the Spanish War of Independence*, after 1808
Oil on canvas, 69 × 107.5 cm
Szépművészeti Múzeum, Budapest, INV. 4121

LT What impresses me about Goya is his handling of the ground, the gravity. Of course there's romanticism in its presentation and handling but the nostalgia, the fetish and the romanticism all become pure horror. I also think that aspects of journalism were deployed, and it's not surprising that the painting quickly acquired political significance. Of course, this period of terror goes hand in hand with a certain type of composition and painting speed, the necessity for efficacy with which these paintings were produced. The entire landscape is within the horizon… there's no verticality here, only a horizontal, almost diagonal, picture plane. You can feel how the volume of the bodies and the gravity weigh down on the ground, almost extending beneath it. The 'plumpness' of the figures, and the concept of mutilation, which is actually painted and depicted in an almost picturesque way, is also what I find so interesting in the "May" paintings.

HDW It's a bit Promethean, isn't it? As if the figures have emerged from clay.

LT And the faces are very unrefined.

GB I also find that the ground is absolutely crucial. If you look closely, the ground rises, and then whoosh! It's an abyss, not topographical.

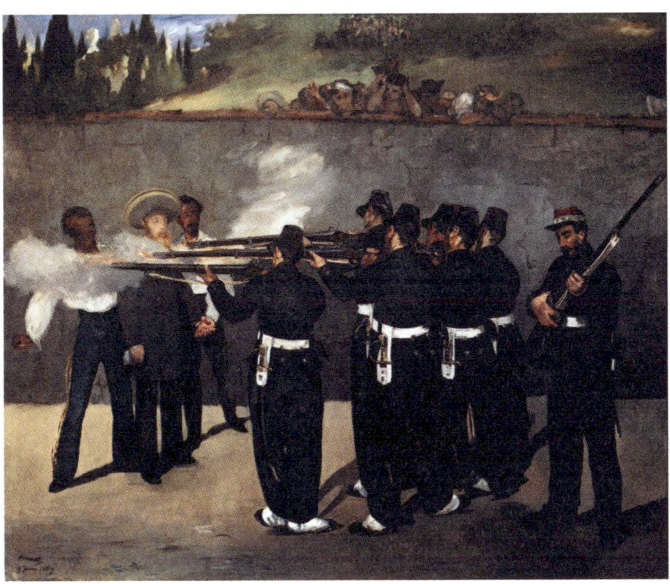

<u>18</u> Édouard Manet, *The Execution of Maximilian*, 1867
Oil on canvas, 252 × 305 cm
Kunsthalle, Mannheim, INV. M281

<u>LT</u> It's like being in a gorge – you can't crawl out of it. A sense of claustrophobia develops within the landscape, and even though the sky has a dramatic quality, it's unlike the dramatic skies of El Greco. The drama here is related only to what's happening in the scene – violence. Violence is the real motif.

<u>GB</u> And the lack of firm ground – there's no common ground to stand on. If you try to estimate the distance between this curve or between the figures, you can't measure it optically, there's a complete caesura in the painting…

<u>LT</u> Just like the wall in various versions of Manet's *Execution of Maximilian*, here the observer is standing behind the wall and behind it, lies another abyss.

<u>HDW</u> What also impresses me about Goya is that naked violence acquires physiognomic expression for the first time.

<u>GB</u> But they're also actually swept up in the violence. It's like a current sweeping through the figures. They're not perpetrators, but a kind of collective…

HDW It dominates their physiognomy – specifically the way their legs appear. Only Goya painted like that.

LT Bruegel as well, but the idea here is that there's a repetitive force that increases the violence. Goya probably didn't think highly of other people. He witnessed these atrocities and, of course, they made a strong impression on him and changed his life. This was the first time that he took a political standpoint – not in terms of an ideological outlook, but in terms of art. In the same way that Manet and Géricault tried at certain points to give their works this kind of charge. Goya was living amidst total chaos, and he painted with this awareness in mind. Everything was moving around him and the blind speed with which he captured this is incredible. This is why the ground, or the lack of it, is totally embedded in the painting. This is not a Courbet. While it's not Realism, it's still pretty truthful. Unlike St Andrew reading the book, this is actually happening.

HDW Are you referring to the glow at the top of the painting?

LT The glow is actually a figure without hands, possibly mutilated, almost the remains of a figure, lifting his arms up to heaven.

GB Perhaps he's lamenting?

LT … Or has lost hope.

HDW Could it also be the expression of madness?

LT … of madness or something else. It's clear that whatever it is, it's not good.

HDW I mean madness in the sense that the significance of the image can no longer be grasped…

LT Yes, and this is what interests me about Goya – the violence is invested with lyricism and voyeuristic complicity. It is a completely new concept. He's interested in the forms, the movement, the force, and mutilation as the painting's focal point, and it's not so much on the political level. There are not very many pictures in which blood is translated that literally in terms of paint. The same is true of gunfire.

GB What about the red, the yellow and the blue?

LT Those are points of reference that control the rhythm of the action.

19 FRANCISCO GOYA, *The Water Carrier*
(La Aguadora), c. 1808–12
Oil on canvas, 68 × 50.5 cm
Szépművészeti Múzeum, Budapest, INV. 760

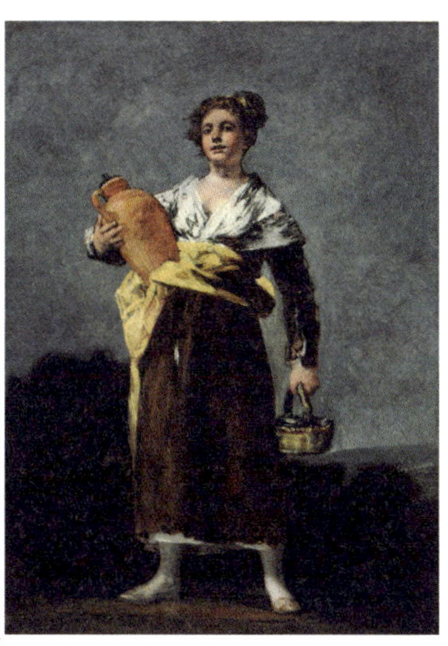

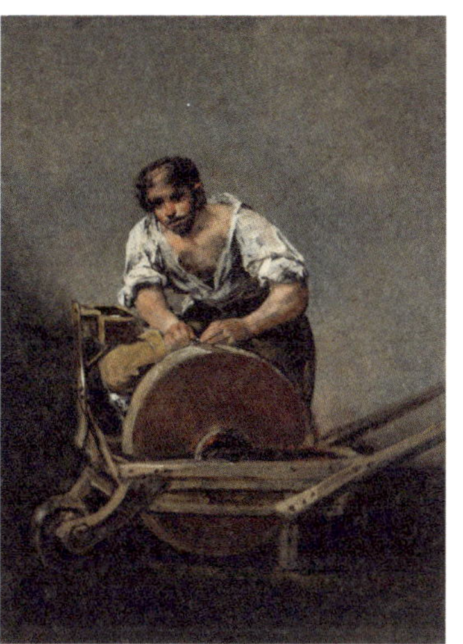

GB Markers?

LT Yes, because you can't be sure whether or not this is blood…

GB It's certainly paint…

HDW We already discussed pathos with El Greco. In this work, the pathos isn't weakened when it goes over the top, with figures that have realistic expressions.

LT If there's a weakness anywhere, then it's in the lower left corner of the painting where the pathos acquires a kind of pornographic aspect – of necrophilia.

HDW A mother clasping her child in her arms…

LT Moving on, it's nice to see these two portraits of workers – real peasants, depicted with thick noses and expressive, but totally foolish, faces. Who they are is not so relevant. It's only about the action..

GB The vase and the basket in *The Water Carrier* are typical allegories that are usually loaded with significance. But here, there's nothing. He has ruined the allegorical apparatus. The paintings are empty and hollow.

LT But fabulously painted – her neck is absolutely sharp. What has always fascinated me about Goya is that, initially, he had a very flat way of painting and then, at a stroke – boom! There's certainty. For example, the water carrier's feet and slippers actually conflict with the rest of the painting because they're painted so finely.

GB The position of the woman's legs, with both soles on the ground, is also interesting. You don't stand like that normally. By contrast, look at how the man in *The Knife-Grinder* is standing, with one leg supporting his weight. Her weight is distributed equally on both legs, which turns the lower part of her body into a kind of plinth…

20 FRANCISCO GOYA, *The Knife-Grinder*
(El Afilador), c. 1808–12
Oil on canvas, 68 × 50.5 cm
Szépművészeti Múzeum, Budapest, INV. 763

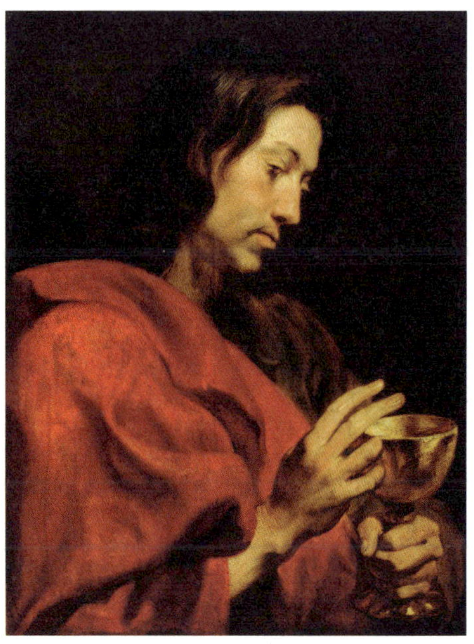

21 Anthony van Dyck, *Saint John the Evangelist*, c. 1618–20
Oil on panel, 64 × 51 cm
Szépművészeti Múzeum, Budapest, INV. 6377

HDW Isn't that connected with the weight she's holding?

LT No, it's connected with the ground, similar to the way it's painted in *Scene from the Spanish War of Independence*. It's an interesting point because it occurred to me right away that the gaze is horizontal, even though these paintings move upward and the activity is largely contained at the bottom (he's leaning over the grinding wheel). What's remarkable is the difference between how their bodies and their clothes are painted. The clothes cover bodies that are transitory. I find this very exciting.

HDW Goya clearly wasn't a humanist at that time.

GB Perhaps a disappointed humanist.

LT I think that that moment in history was pretty decisive. It was a raw point in the epoch when everything changed, and Goya produced a series of paintings that were completely different from what was expected. They were part of reality and of course this made reality palpable. There's a pictorial exorcism in Goya's work which continues right up to the "Black Paintings" – I don't think it can be explained in any other way.

GB That's a good point.

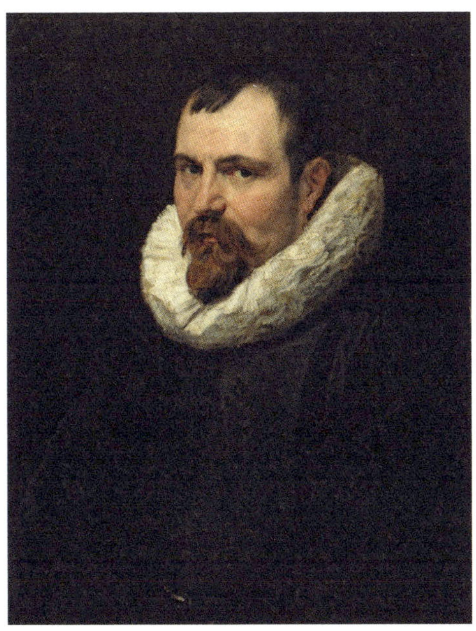

22 Anthony van Dyck, *Portrait of a Man, c.* 1617–20
Oil on panel, 66 × 51 cm
Szépművészeti Múzeum, Budapest, INV. 1136

HDW Well, now I'd like to leave Spain and move on to Flanders.

GB Following in the footsteps of earlier misery…

HDW No, to earlier Antwerp and van Dyck.[7]

LT What I find interesting about van Dyck, compared with Rubens, is the particular style and way in which the bourgeoisie and its psychology are revealed in his paintings, especially in the portraits. You can see it in *Saint John the Evangelist* in how his hands are presented, and how the eyelids and the mouth are stylistically completely different to Rubens. Rubens' painting acquires a certain robustness, but here there is a gentleness and refinement. This refinement was almost a way of life, but with Rubens it appears more as a mythological guise. With van Dyck, a new physicality asserted itself, which I find very interesting in relation to his portraits, for example, in *Portrait of a Man*. The figure's head, the way the moustache moves, his gaze – to me that St John is almost too beautiful.

7 Sir Anthony van Dyck (1599–1641) was a Flemish Baroque artist who became the leading court painter in England, after great success in Italy and Flanders.

GB I've always had the same problem with van Dyck. I find there is much more immediacy in the portraits of Frans Hals.

HDW I disagree. Van Dyck painted this whole series while he was in Genoa and what really impresses me about these works is the enormous amount of black paint used. Within all of these paintings there is only one spot of light, and this is so powerful. That portrait is among them, and I find it a virtuoso painting. I agree with you that it's virtuosity in paint. It doesn't have any literary or mythological foundations. Van Dyck is not an intellectual; he's a doer.

GB Well, but then psychology would have to come into play to hold it together in order to be successful.

LT A really good portrait or drawing by van Dyck demonstrates a psychological depth of feeling. Whether it happens to interest you or not, you arrive at a completely different view of the subject than you do with the pure physique of a painted portrait by Rubens, for example, which is an affirmation, a fact, a depiction of the sitter's status. The sense of insecurity in van Dyck's sitters is a completely different matter, and I find it interesting how psychology and the unknown come first. I'm not sure whether he was well-read, but he was certainly intelligent. His experience was completely different with regard to his environment. He was younger than Rubens, and different from most of his contemporaries. With Rubens everything was clear. He wasn't someone who hesitated. Van Dyck hesitates, but he does so with style and elegance, and that's what Rubens lacks.

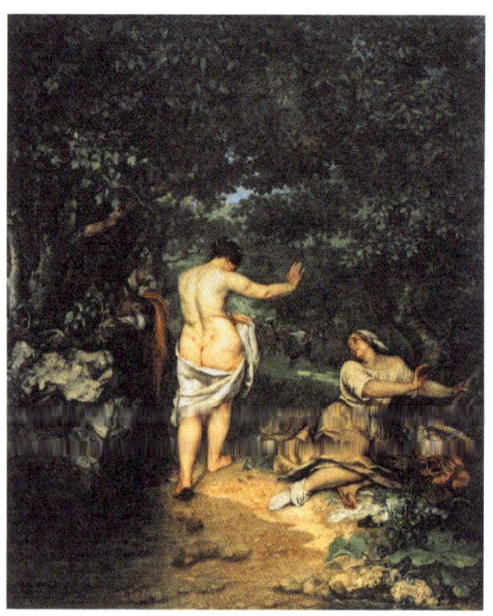

HDW Let's move on to Courbet's *The Wrestlers*. Courbet submitted this painting to the Salon of 1853, along with *The Bathers*, and while it didn't provoke a scandal like *The Bathers* did, I find it an interesting painting.

LT The figures are isolated, "plonked down" into the landscape…

23 Gustave Courbet, *The Bathers*, 1853
Oil on canvas, 227 × 193 cm
Musée Fabre, Montpellier, INV. 868.1.19

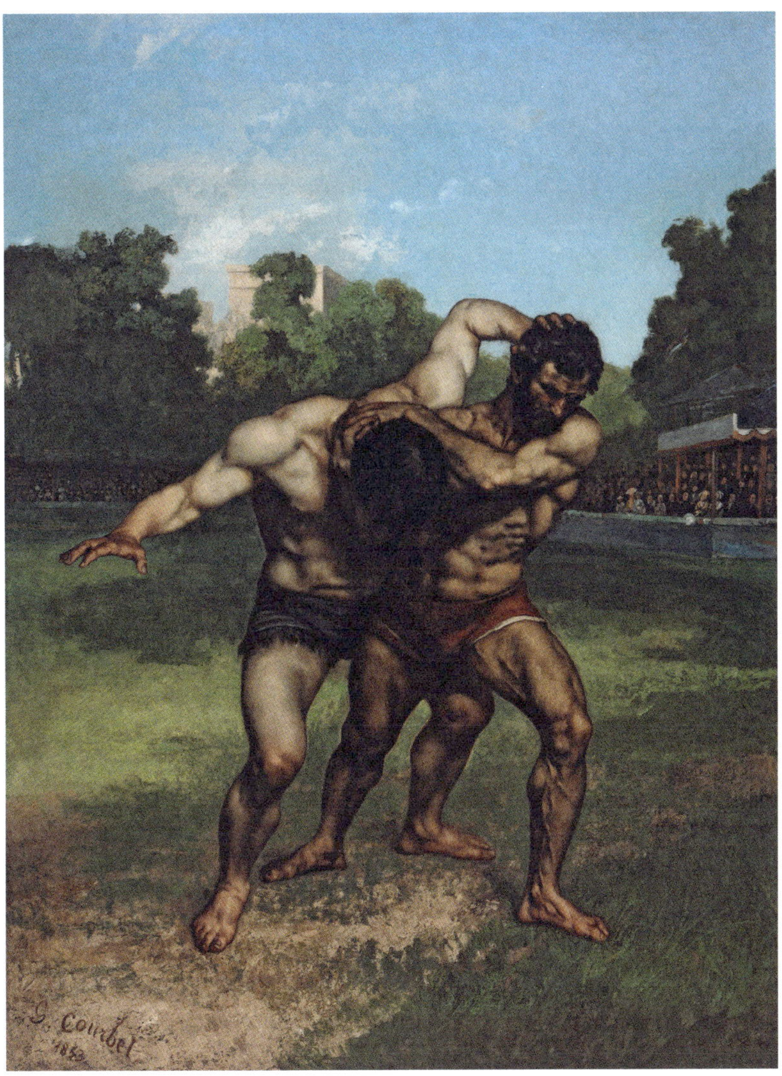

<u>24</u> Gustave Courbet, *The Wrestlers*, 1853
Oil on canvas, 252 × 198 cm
Szépművészeti Múzeum, Budapest, inv. 502.b

<u>hdw</u> Perhaps you see it differently, but I'm interested in its subject – shame, or shamelessness. A bourgeois crowd is watching two naked men grappling with each other until one of them falls over.

<u>lt</u> That's the idea of pornography, but that has always existed. I'm struck most of all by the detachment of the landscape. The collaged nature of the

image and the uncertainty of the location – is it set in the outskirts of the city, or by the Arc de Triomphe? – remind me of Manet's *Le Déjeuner sur l'Herbe* [1863]. The sky also lacks specificity because it's actually too blue.

HDW The way in which the two male bodies are shown interlocking is not particularly clever.

LT The figures might be more or less anatomically correct, but their forms are overly exaggerated and, compared with the landscape, feel "cut and paste".

GB To me, Courbet's painting conveys a strong sense of fatality. Two people are engaged in an extreme effort, yet there's no real context or aim – it's not even sport. In sport there's always a sense that someone must win – it's a contest. But in this work, the bodies dissolve into a series of individual, straining muscles.

LT Especially the two men's legs, with their veins, which are much more interesting than their heads. It's a shame that the head of the wrestler on the left contributes nothing. He isn't a person – it really is just about a useless exercising of strength.

GB An empty display.

HDW What about the spectators? Why are these people interested in this kind of thing?

GB The point to make about the spectators is that they're actually much too far away. They can't see anything at all – they're a hundred metres away and lined up like puppets. As a suggestion of voyeurism it doesn't work and this is a weak aspect.

LT I actually think that the way the scene is depicted is to make us, here and now, the voyeurs, and to be part of the public. This is why the landscape is not endless, but is closed off by the building or a triumphal arch. We create a circle around the figures and this formation turns them into captive animals. A sense of violence emerges, which basically boils down to a fight to the death. While the realm of sports in *The Wrestlers* is endowed with a mythological context, the same applies to the notion of the arena, of encircling, of territory. This is made clear in the painting but visually, it doesn't seem to work. As a painting or illustration it does, but I miss the spatial element. There's absolutely nothing spatial in this work.

GB The term "collage" hits the nail on the head.

LT Courbet wasted an incredible amount of time on the muscles and corporeality, but the light isn't right. It's studio light, and you would never see this light outdoors. Then there's the grass, which is also painted pretty oddly. It's a typical Salon painting, produced for the Salon, and I think its significance is also commercial – this is a painting that is selling itself. It's a large-format work, which was important, and the subject-matter is in fact mythological, but couched in a form that is very contemporary. There is no ambiguity.

HDW I find Courbet here very enigmatic, but I don't know to what extent he deliberately intended this voyeurism, which is, in fact, ours.

LT What disturbs me most is that the figures are standing in the centre of the composition. Imagine if the hand of the wrestler on the left almost touched the frame. This would have resulted in a completely different impression.

HDW Courbet's personality was shaped by politics. I've always been struck by how much of an anti-intellectual he was. He rejected every kind of academicism, every form of organized knowledge, on principle, even refusing to read books. And yet he's obviously an intelligent painter. Luc, how do you see the relationship between knowledge and painting?

LT Each moment in painting has its own pragmatism. Firstly, conceiving the image is very important, but then follows the issue of whether the concept can actually be realized. A number of basic determining factors assert themselves, and yet there is the ambition to try and go one step further each time. It has to be very clear to you what the possibilities are, and I think that knowledge now, compared to that of Courbet's day, bears a very different relationship to pictorial representation. The relationship to appropriation, then and now, has completely changed. Knowledge relating to images has become a different field, which can no longer be defined so unambiguously. Personally, I was very influenced by Ernst Bloch's *Die Ästhetik des Vor-Scheins* [The Aesthetics of Anticipation; 1974] and Robert Musil's *The Man without Qualities* [1943], because they offered a foundation and conjured up a number of images. With Courbet, it's knowledge confirmed in the fatalism of the period – think of Emile Zola's writing where the determinism of a society developed into claustrophobia and took on material forms. This also happens in the paintings of Manet, in particular, in his use of colour. Courbet's painting *The Origin of the World* [1866] is one of the most powerful statements about this relationship. There's a psychological intelligence that you can sense, a certainty, and because of that, a certain determination, and aggression. It's incredibly aggressive. That's what strikes me above all, the painting's hardness and aggressiveness, which isn't just to do with the body but is a specific mentality. I sense this especially in Courbet and it struck me in the exhibition in Paris, where it became clear to me that I'd never realized before how incredibly aggressive his work was.

HDW The times were also very violent.

LT Quite, and he responded pretty directly to that.

HDW This is the moment in which the contract between artists and society breaks down. It's the period of *La Bohème*, of Proudhon, and Fourier – a moment in time where the industrial revolution that had brought forward a powerful bourgeoisie would culminate in a brutal rupture with all the social classes that had suffered from this new industrial climate. Artists inspired by the first socialist thinkers would consider themselves no longer in the service of society, preferring to live in conditions of financial restraint instead.

LT Yes, that whole world of thought is present. Conversations today are completely different and, in that sense, you might say that a certain kind of romanticism appeared for the first time, the individual's decision to expand the range of subject-matter.

HDW Here are three landscapes by Courbet.

GB Cézanne said that Courbet painted like a mason.

LT As if made from stone, but I also find that each painting has a sense of devouring, like *La Grande Bouffe* [aka *Blow-out*; 1973]. I'm both interested and irritated by this aspect of Courbet. Maybe that's what makes him interesting?

HDW We should return to that, but I'm currently doing some work on Marcel Duchamp's very difficult and complex love–hate relationship with Courbet.

LT I can understand that. Duchamp was a big aesthete, and Courbet wasn't. There's no aestheticism in Courbet. There's a rawness like the one which is also present in the Goya paintings we've seen. Structurally they are almost

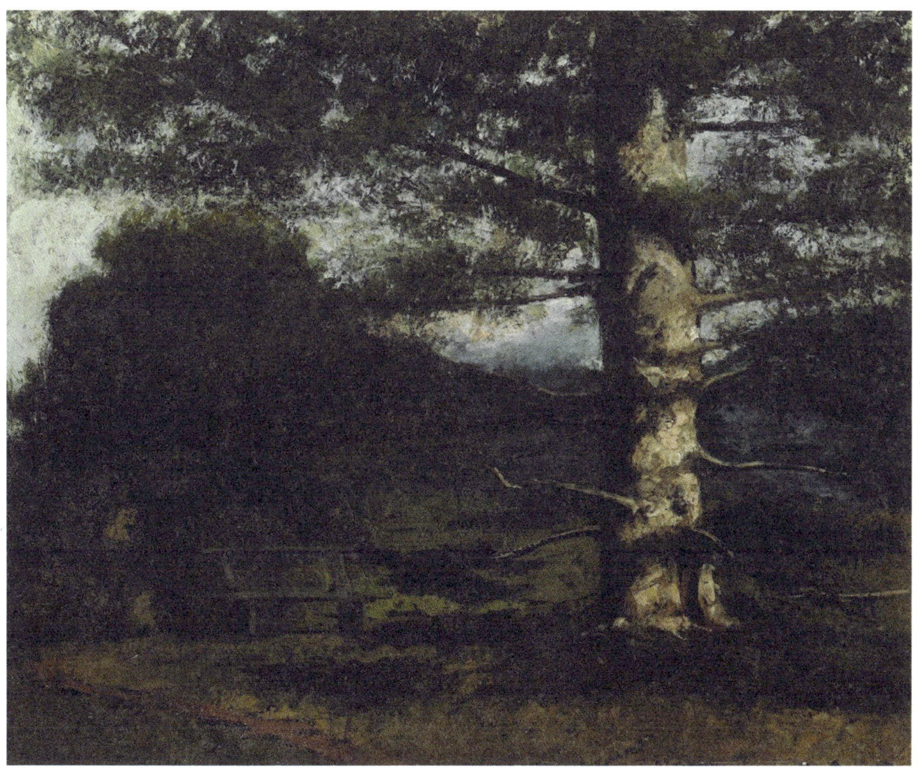

25 GUSTAVE COURBET, *Cedar Tree at Hauteville*, 1868
Oil on canvas, 69 × 89 cm
Szépművészeti Múzeum, Budapest, INV. 438.B

the same, but with a completely different mentality. Courbet's is even more brazen because there's no lyricism that could shape it. The environment has disappeared. Even to relish nature has become an act of defiance – the idyll has been removed. It's a non-idea, a world without idylls.

HDW It's brutal.

LT Yes, defiant, brutal, and that's his strength.

HDW Conversely, it's Manet's strength that he's not brutal at all.

LT In comparison with Courbet, you could say that he's of course gentler. But it's also gentler in comparison with Manet's early painting. This brutality later ends up in a different bourgeois environment. The "haute bourgeoisie" – but with brains and a very clear stance and great sadism – for which the raw material is introduced here.

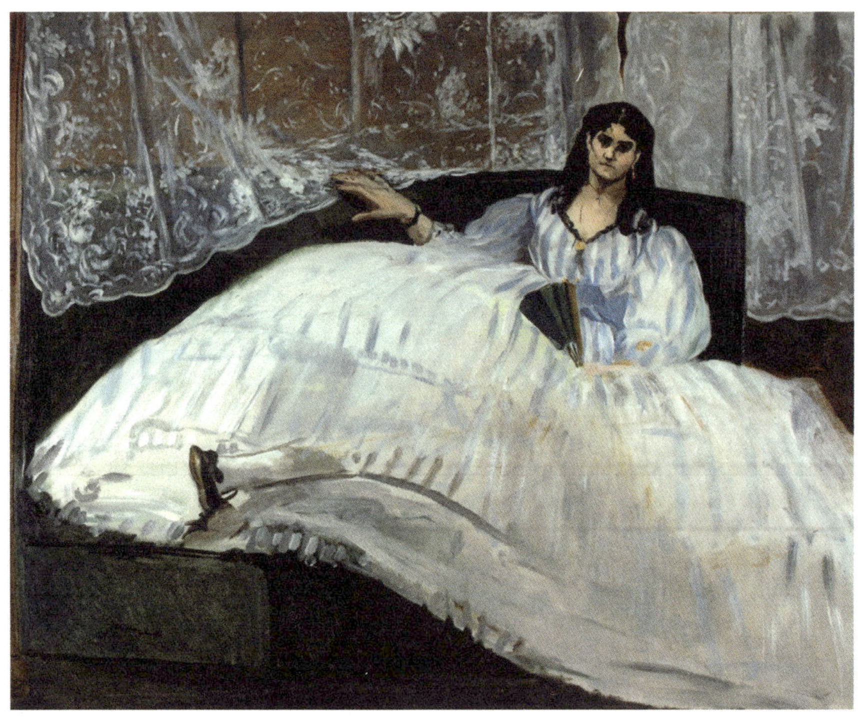

26 ÉDOUARD MANET, *Lady with a Fan*, 1862
Oil on canvas, 89.5 × 113 cm
Szépművészeti Múzeum, Budapest, INV. 368.B

HDW That's another one of those political statements.

GB Perhaps we should mention that with Courbet, defiance and realism are presented at the same time as a set of available facts – that's what the world is like.

LT Yes, that's important. I also find it interesting how this particular blue is constantly repeated. What has always fascinated me about Manet is his approach, and not just its implementation, but the directness of his handling and contrasts. There are many Spaniards, like Ribera, who pass over contrast, and then it doesn't work any more. Instead it almost goes right to the very limits of fading in and out. In *Lady with a Fan* it doesn't occur as much as in *Olympia* [1863], where it plays a principal part, but we also have the trivialization of the subject. The woman's hand is much too big in relation to her head. On her wrist she wears what looks to be a watch, or maybe it's a bracelet? And then there is her foot, which is almost that of

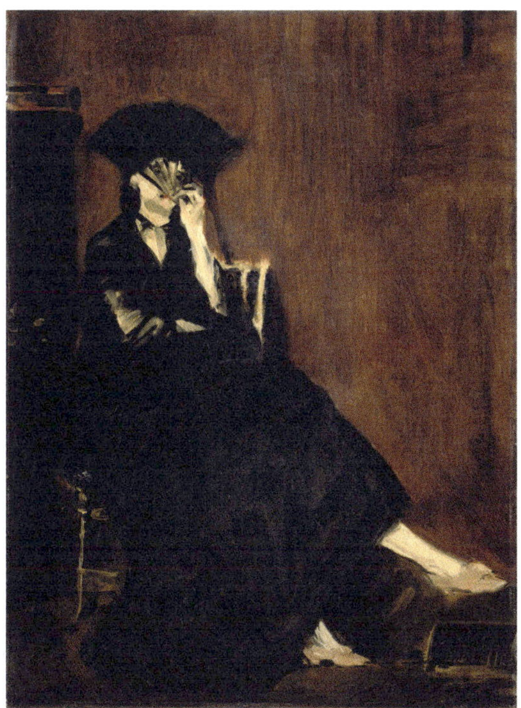

27 ÉDOUARD MANET, *Berthe Morisot with a fan*, 1872
Oil on canvas, 60.4 × 45.2 cm
Musée d'Orsay, Paris, INV. RF 1671

a young girl. The painting is totally split, with the sofa that goes over the edge and the curtain that hangs across it. This serves to not only draw the viewer into the painting, but to be compromised by it.

HDW It's the old *Olympia* story.

LT But it still plays a part in all his best paintings.

HDW For me the painting is about visibility. What is visibility? What do we see? I find it interesting that the central element, the fan, actually belongs to this culture. With this fan you can make yourself invisible, but you can also spy on things and see them. There is a painting by Manet that I value very highly – the portrait of Berthe Morisot – in which she hides herself completely behind a fan. It's one of the most complex and beautiful paintings about behaviour. Of course you're right that this picture is about a relationship, one that goes way beyond the portrait.

LT The woman's leg in *Lady with a Fan* is one of its most interesting aspects – it doesn't seem to belong to her body, to the dress, to the painting as a whole… It's anatomically impossible. At the same time it is an eroticizing device because of course the rest of her is all hidden beneath the drapery – she's reclining on the sofa so is proffered to us. This is made clear by the curtain, which shuts out the outside, situating the viewer as accomplice, and at the same time suggests an external world that exists behind her hand – rendered too big – and the watch which evokes temporality. All this was probably not painted in a precisely premeditated way, but it's a mind-set. Manet's faces are usually incredibly composed and assembled, almost sculptural, and imbued with knowledge. The lady's face recalls Velázquez in its realism – he's a bourgeois Velázquez. Her body, on the other hand, is merely suggested, up until you reach her breasts, where Manet has injected colour and added the fan. This is what the painting is all about. The rest of her body is suggested by her leg, which displays a hint of "come hither". We tend to forget this point, but I find that – starting with Caravaggio – the idea of pornography asserts itself in painting, in the bourgeois condition and in everything that was new, and continues right through to Manet.

HDW The bourgeois factor is what's new, of course. Without it you can't understand these paintings.

LT Well, you can understand the painting in purely artistic terms. You can see that it's incredibly well painted.

GB What we see here though is, basically, pornography thwarted. The game actually defeats itself and is ultimately empty.

LT I think it's mainly the addiction, the obsession with pornography, its return, and as we mentioned earlier, the pointless movements of the two wrestlers. Here you actually get the pointlessness of constant repetition, which is pornographic, a pure abstraction, and is of course a disappointment because it's empty. But it's also about consumption, like smoking cigarettes, or drinking a lot. At the same time that's not the painter's intention. Conscious intentions did play an important role with Manet, in a very wise and intelligent way. When you compare how the theme of consumption, or speed, or the New Society is approached today or during the 1960s, Manet was pretty far ahead of his time.

GB The area where the curtain is open, and the way in which it is opened, is the most important part of the painting. The figure of the lady is a chance suggestion of an act of painting, which unfolds in this magnificent empty area. The edges reveal something of a figure, but meaning is generated by the act of painting itself, not by the figure.

LT There is an element of pornography, the physicality of the painting, its sense of abstraction – or, actually, the possibility of abstraction. Photography was already in use at this time, which led to a renewed uncertainty, and at the same time sexuality is made visible, so that a completely different relationship to pictorial creation emerges. But of course what's important is this almost isolated form in the foreground, which then leads back to a figure.

HDW What you said is very interesting, Mr Boehm, because as Clement Greenberg writes, Modernism had already taken place here. Manet was the first artist to make painting itself the real subject.

GB Greenberg exaggerated here, of course.

HDW Yes, but it's really there somehow.

LT It's more about the statement that every critic or theorist in that hypothetical field is keen on making a discovery. But *that*'s not a discovery. Manet knew perfectly well what he was doing. He sensed it while he was painting and the discovery wasn't an "aha" experience, it was a fact. That's the fabulous thing about Manet, especially during this period – later he becomes much more difficult. But when he holds back with regard to reality and what can be abstracted from it, then you get this dichotomy and an unsettling environment, in which his approach is actually much more apparent than it became later.

I find that Manet surpasses Velázquez in some respect. What I admire though about both of them is the certainty, decisiveness and economy of their painting combined with absolute clarity. Velázquez was more reserved, but with Manet this becomes really obvious.

HDW I feel that there's something of a pictorial compulsion in *Lady with a Fan* and almost all of Manet's paintings.

LT He clearly had a hunger for painting. I can sense it, as I can with Velázquez too. As a painter, you can retrace their steps. The face here is a bit different, the faces are different, they're always focused like this, always turned in on themselves, and there's always this implosion, there's never anything that comes out.

HDW A wonderful painting, isn't it?

LT A really great painting.

HDW Here is also Cézanne's painting *The Buffet*.

GB That's not such a great example of his work. It's too closed in.

LT Painted up … Cézanne is a pretty problematic man.

GB He said an awful lot of things go wrong when he paints, and this is an example. I think it's wonderful to be able to see his failures. He always spoke about failing.

LT I think that when you look at early Cézanne you realize that he had incredible difficulty painting. He was a very stiff painter.

GB Not a virtuoso at all. He was the opposite of gifted.

LT Yes, not like James Ensor…

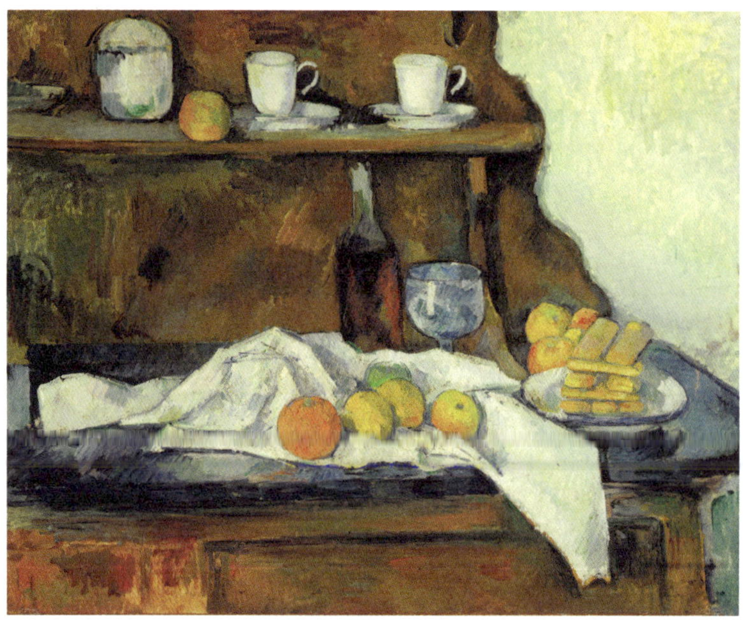

28 PAUL CÉZANNE, *The Buffet*, 1877
Oil on canvas, 65.5 × 81 cm
Szépművészeti Múzeum, Budapest, INV. 371.B

GB …or Manet, or Picasso.

LT Picasso was a pure technician. But Cézanne really had to fiddle about to get something out, and then he created paintings that are outstanding because they show how things can sometimes go wrong. His best work has a quality of openness as if it's made from glass. But this painting hasn't got that at all, it's totally walled up.

Budapest, Műcsarnok Kunsthalle

HDW I'd like to move on and discuss what I believe is the foundation of all painting – the image. What is an image? How does it work? What are the particular characteristics of an image that resonate with us and, as is the case with the El Greco, make us want to discover its identity centuries later? Luc, your paintings make an important contribution to this discourse.

LT In the first gallery of my retrospective here, I have reconstructed a mural from an exhibition in Berlin that shows two hands kneading bread. Despite the difference in size, execution and ground, I painted it in one day, like many of my other works. In a way, the mural acts as a reversal of the smallest paintings in the gallery – the show moves from this megalomaniac gesture all the way down to little paintings of toys. This is the first time that the three paintings, which were conceived as a group titled *Heillicht* [Curing Light], are exhibited together in a museum. Although meant to be a group, I assembled them here based on tactile elements. *Heillicht* is about touch and healing. The first painting had as its source a picture from the 1948 book *My Experiences in Color Photography* by Dr Paul Wolff, which was first published in 1940 as *Meine Erfahrungen mit der Leica … farbig*. He developed a colour printing process during the war for the mass reproduction of colour photographs.

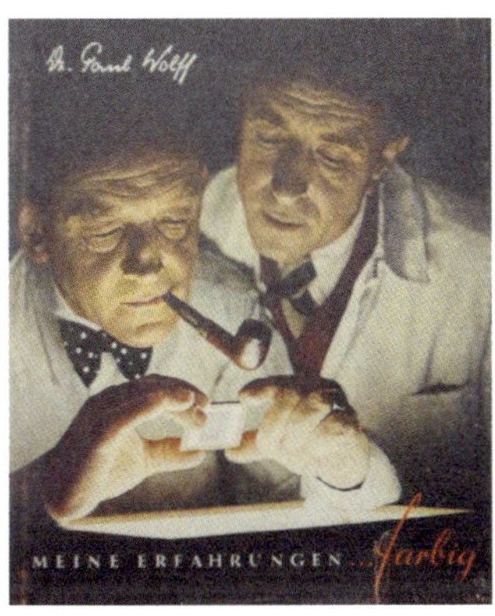

29 Book cover of Paul Wolff, *Meine Erfahrungen mit der Leica … farbig* Frankfurt am Main: Breidenstein, 1940

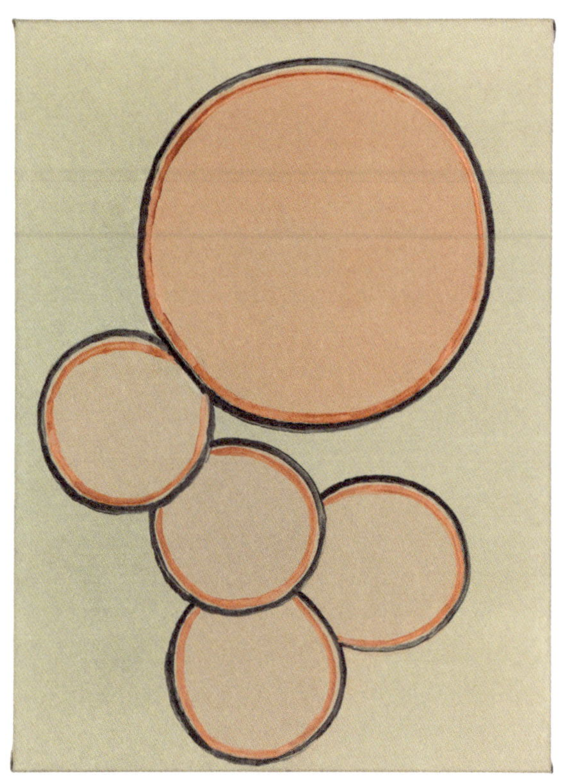

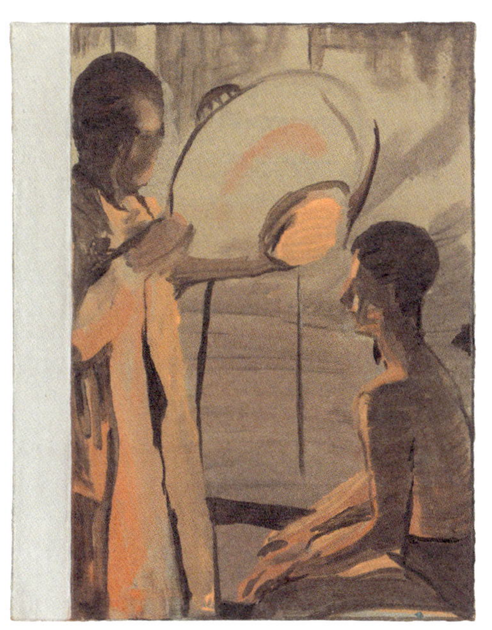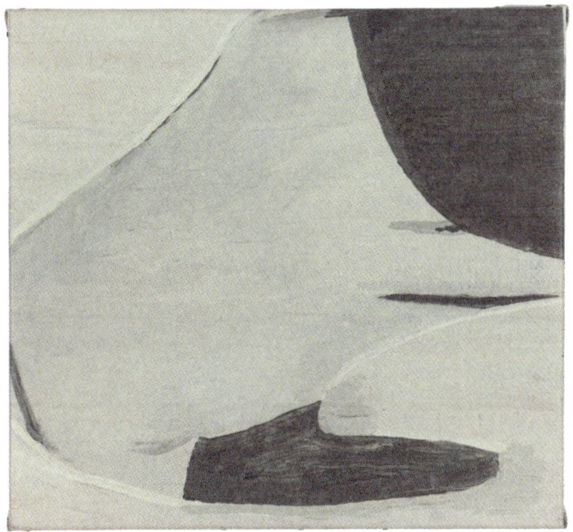

<u>30</u> Luc Tuymans, *Heillicht* [Curing Light], 1991

Oil on canvas, part 1: 85.5 × 63.3 cm;
part 2: 50 × 40 cm; part 3: 40 × 50 cm

Mu.Zee, Ostend

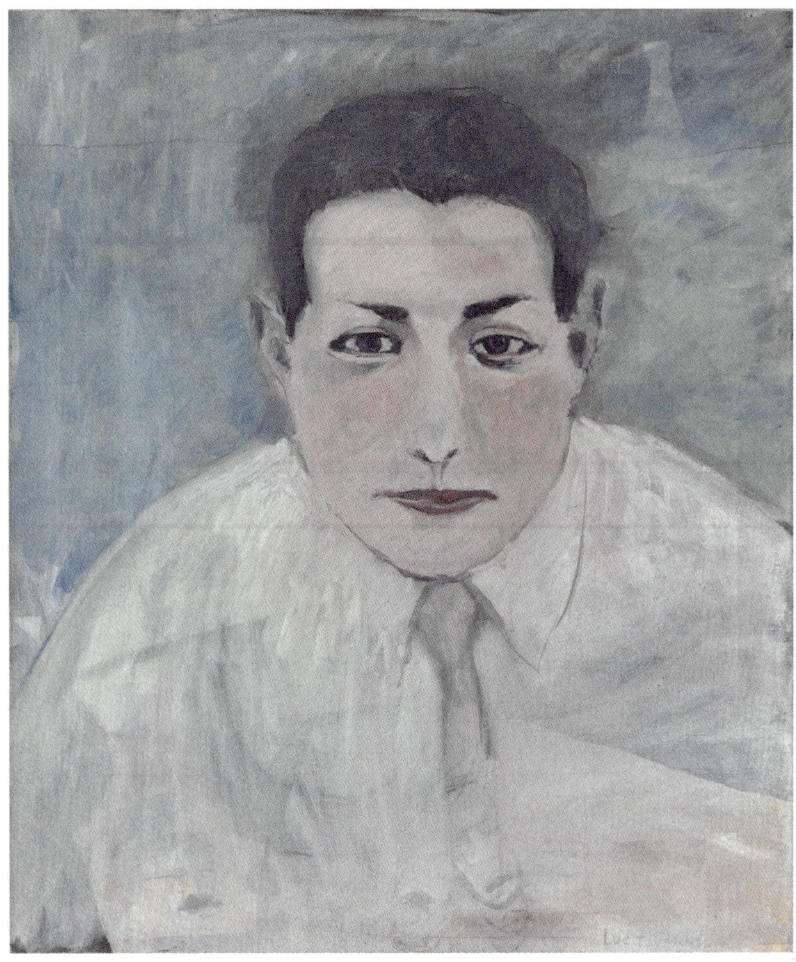

31 Luc Tuymans, *G. Dam*, 1978
Oil on canvas, 70 × 60 cm
Private collection, Antwerp

The Smell is reddish-orange: the colour creates a temperature, a sense of warmth, signifying touch. UV lamps in the painting behind it represent warmth and healing, although it's just a picture of red light from a lamp and the idea is completely abstracted. Unlike the first two paintings, the third one, *Incest*, is painted in cold tones – a stylized hand is reduced to an abstract form, hiding something that you almost can't see but can sense.

HDW In your paintings the image has an identity that doesn't necessarily coincide with photography. For example, understanding the image is very different from possessing it.

LT These works from 1991, along with earlier paintings and film stills, were all produced following a period in the 1980s when I worked exclusively with film. In my opinion, the painting of my mother's brother, *G. Dam*, is important because it's the first autonomous work of this kind – a portrait – and the first painting to engage with the idea of memory or recollection. My mother's brother was killed in the war when his house burned down, and there were no photographs left of him, only an oil painting depicting him in three-quarter view. I painted *G. Dam* from that oil painting in about half an hour. At the time I was fascinated with the photographer August Sander, and the frontal views of his portraits. I like how this painting dominates the gallery – you can't escape its gaze.

HDW What was important about August Sander?

LT The frontality of his portraits, which you often find in painting. The real character of his subjects emerges through these mannered, dishonest postures.

HDW Images are always composed.

LT In other words, it's an image that has been devised. And it's clear that August Sander's photographs were also devised. It's not reportage photography. Like in painting, the motionless quality of the photographs, their sharpness and detail are also important.

GB I should confess that I've never read anything about Luc Tuymans. It was a deliberate decision because I wanted to see the works first with my own eyes and not through the eyes of a critic and his or her writing. That places me in a naïve position now as I would like to start with a remark from the wall text: "It can't be identified immediately". In a sense this is true of all the paintings. You don't immediately recognize Mauthausen or that the portrait is of Luc's uncle. You don't see any of that, but you sense it, and for me, it's crucial that this knowledge is delayed. The image creates a situation in which we're guided towards something visible and that doesn't turn back into conventionality once we know what it is. I'm struck by this

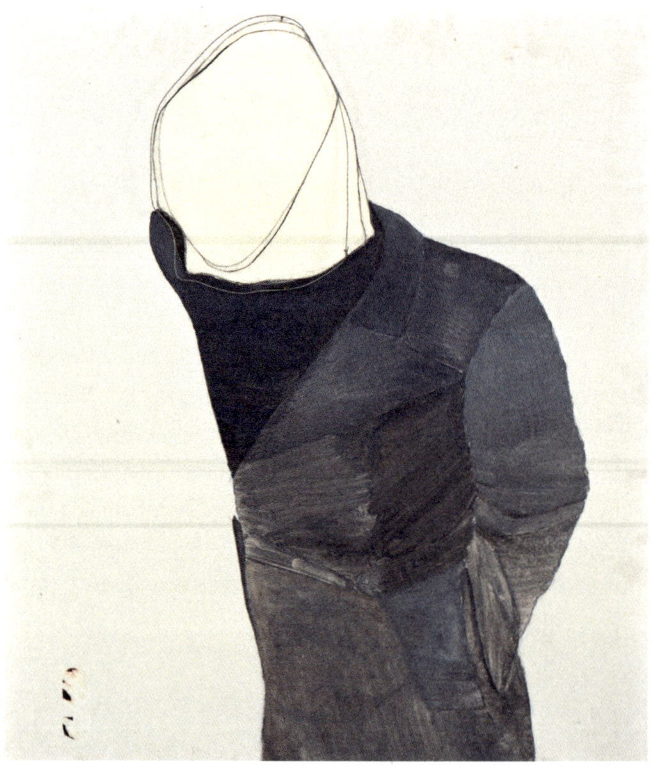

32 Luc Tuymans, *Suicide*, 1975
Oil on wood, paper, iron wire
115 × 100 cm
Private collection, Belgium

cleft between seeing and knowing. Hans, you began by asking what kind of images these are, and what kind of approach to the image this is. The paintings, however differently they relate to reality or draw upon photographs, newspaper cuttings, observations, Old Masters or Morandi, always have a constant searching motion – I'll use that term again because I can't think of a better one. What we see is not simply *there*, but it emerges. I see this as a connection with colour – the image begins to reveal itself, then recedes, and comes back again. This is what I've observed walking around the exhibition, and I'd be interested to find out whether this leads anywhere or whether I'm completely wrong.

LT There's a huge difference between the paintings displayed here and the earlier works. *Suicide* is an early mixed-media self-portrait from 1975, whose

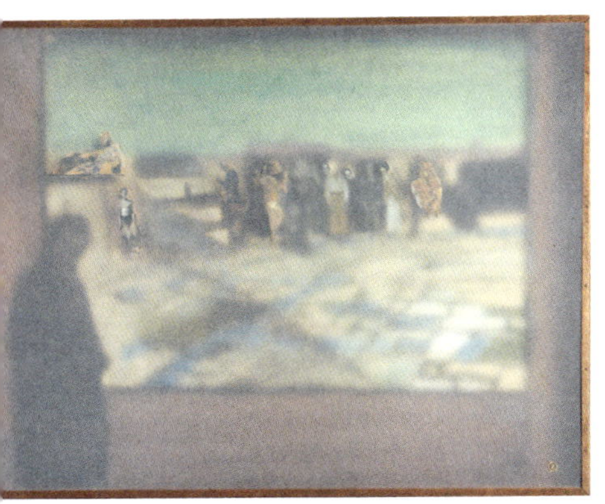

33 Luc Tuymans, *The Arena*, 1978
Oil on paper, tracing paper, photographs,
wood, 60.5 × 78.8 cm
Private collection

painted lines resulted from swinging a light back and forth on a metal cord in my studio, projecting different shadows each time. *The Arena* from 1978 tries to represent an animated film or a film image with focus and blurring. It's a combination of figures clipped from a newspaper, mounted on pieces of wood, which are positioned closer to or further away from the paper screen. It was the first element of a diorama in which the definitive and the in-definitive play a part. It's a kind of combination: part painting, part installation.

GB The "in-definitive" is a good term to begin with. All the paintings have a degree of blurriness, which they need in order to carry out this searching quality we've discussed so that what's visible can emerge from the image and return back into it. This requires a certain amount of oscillation.

LT Unlike Gerhard Richter though, this blurriness is achieved through painting, not by wiping away. The earlier works in the next gallery, such as *Secrets* and *Antichambre* [1985], initially have a graphic quality when you stand close to them. This comes from the tonality, a darkening, as well as the concept of the temperature of a painting. As I mentioned earlier, it's also important how they develop when viewed from a distance. These are huge galleries and yet the small-scale paintings not only stand their ground within this space, but do so even better than the larger ones. We can test this goal of monumentality with the group *Die Zeit*.

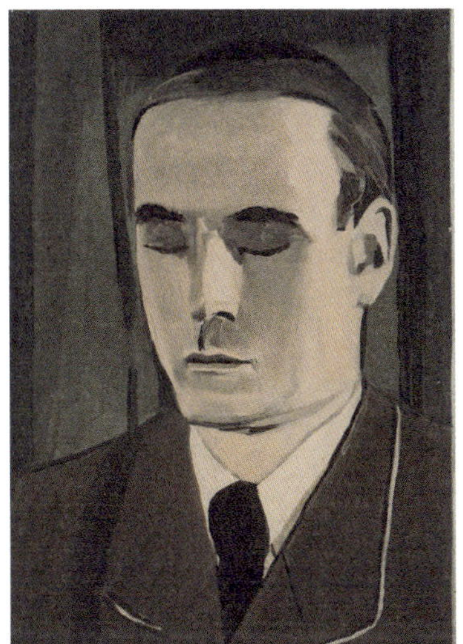

34 Luc Tuymans, *Secrets*, 1990
Oil on canvas, 52 × 37 cm
Private collection

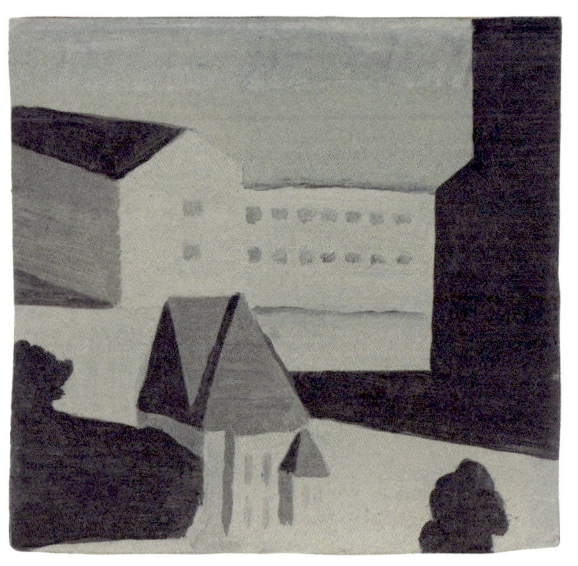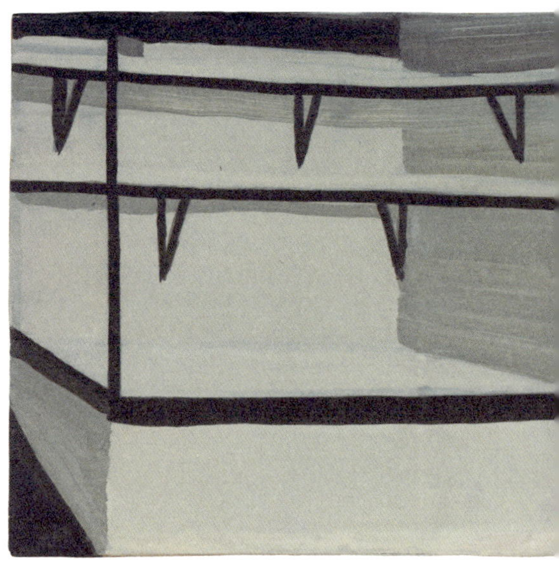

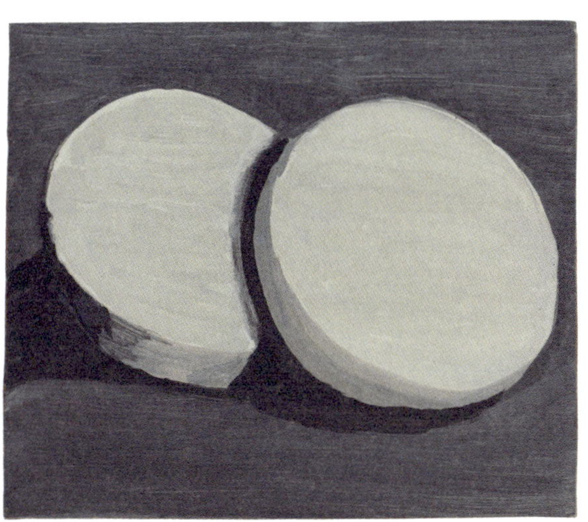 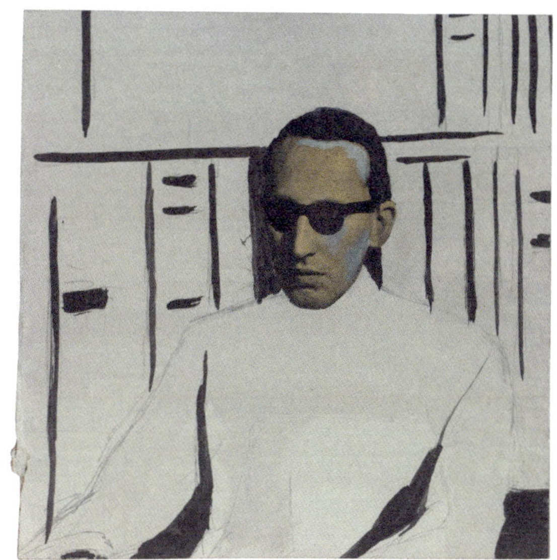

<u>35</u> Luc Tuymans, *Die Zeit* [Time], 1988

Oil on cardboard, part 1: 34.6 × 36.9 cm;
part 2: 36.5 × 35.1 cm; part 3: 31.4 × 36.9 cm;
part 4: 34.6 × 35.1 cm

Private collection

The colour of the floor helps enormously because it almost continues into the painting. Had the floor been black, it would have been a completely different matter.

HDW There's a "contamination" happening between these four paintings whereby the content of each painting is contaminated by that of the others, but you don't know why or how…

LT The series was painted in 1988. At that point I didn't have any canvas, so I painted on very cheap cardboard that I later mounted on wood. Strangely enough, one of the reasons why these paintings are pretty strong is because they aged well. They came about intuitively, based on my fascination with *Pittura Metafisica* and the idea of daylight, the midday hour, the empty space.

HDW *Pittura Metafisica* is a very good point of reference because for Giorgio de Chirico it was a matter of returning to the defamiliarization of the past. But what interests me, Luc, is that I associate these forms with a kind of genetic burden from the 1950s.

LT The paintings are only shadows – they are like puppet images. I consider most of the paintings as objects and, right up to *The Diagnostic View* [1992] – although that's showing a person – they're all derived from this line of thought.

HDW Could it be that every period somehow develops its own morphology?

LT Of course, which is inexplicable in its morphological identity, and therefore acts subconsciously. My question now is: what do you actually think about when you look at one of these paintings? Is it a cinematic experience? Something could be an excerpt from something else – these are exterior spaces, and moving inside, there's a person or a figure, with whom you can identify. Or not. He's wearing sunglasses. The figure in the last row of paintings looks like a doctor or something clinical, and there's an office-like feel because the background – a rough, schematic sketch – could be files or bookshelves. All of these things are pointers in the paintings, and what I like about how they're hanging here is the way in which they dominate the space with a huge monumentality and are presented as facts. Speaking of photography, one of the paintings incorporates a cropped photo of Reinhard Heydrich, cut out from a 1942 issue of *Signal* magazine, a Nazi propaganda periodical, which was glued on with paint and then painted over.

GB Heydrich was chief of the RSHA [Reich Security Head Office].

LT Heinrich Himmler's right-hand man, so to speak. He organized the 1942 Wannsee Conference, where the plans and logistics for the Holocaust – the "Final Solution" – were formalized. The day that he was murdered, he had left his castle in Prague without a police escort, and there has always been a suspicion that Himmler was involved.

HDW He thought that Heydrich would bring about his downfall?

LT Yes, Heydrich was a strong and ambitious guy, and he was actually better-looking than most of the Nazis.

GB He was killed by two parachutists from the Czech army in exile. The English had dropped a few hundred Czech partisan parachutists, and two of them were given the mission to kill him. They took up position on a bend in the road on which Heydrich used to travel to his office in Prague. When the gun of the partisan charged with shooting Heydrich didn't go off, the one standing on the other side of the road threw a hand grenade, but Heydrich didn't die immediately. This sparked a vast campaign of reprisals, including the razing of the village of Lidice, that terrible act of vengeance when all the adult males were executed and most of the women and children were deported to concentration camps.

HDW This portrait of Heydrich is the last painting in the *Die Zeit* series and his eyes are completely obscured.

LT Without being conscious of it, I've painted quite a lot of portraits where the subject is wearing glasses. They fascinate me because they change a face. There is something in a face that makes it instantly accepted as an object, as a form, but in this portrait, of course, it's purely a mask, similar to closed eyes.

HDW It totally dominates the painting.

LT Of course it dominates the painting because you try to find something that you can actually identify with – who is, or was, this person? At the same time you sense that the painting is turned inwards rather than outwards. From a distance it sucks you in and spits you out again.

HDW Is it true that he's wearing fencing clothes?

LT He was wearing protective clothing in the photo, and he wasn't sitting but standing, so the photo was completely different. It isn't really white either – it's actually a shade of grey that I mixed, which generates a sense of depth.

GB I'd like to return to some issues that we've already raised, such as the relationship between painting and photography. In relation to this work, it has something to do with the subject and, more importantly, with the question about the freedom of the photographic gaze. The camera allows you to elevate any segment of the real world to the status of an image. In other words, it's not clear what an image is in relation to a photographic work – and that's what the results actually look like. It seems to me that this has found its way into your painting, and that you've chosen a way of looking, especially in these four *Die Zeit* works, that's not predefined. You've selected one way of looking for this painting, and a different way for another, just as in photographic practice.

LT *Die Zeit* is almost a montage, a selected excerpt, which is very cinematic and probably comes from the four or five years that I worked in film. It's not so much a photographic illustration, but a sequence of images. In that sense there is a difference in the way in which artists used photography in the 1960s to the way I used it later, having grown up with TV in a time when there was a relative lack of experience and an abundance of images. The way the image has been appropriated is interesting. There are two idea-based paintings that have nothing at all to do with reality, whereas the two portraits of Heydrich and Spinattabletten do. The latter depicts the first compressed vegetable tablets that the Germans produced during the war, which later reappeared in the NASA programme, and the painting of Heydrich partially refers back to the printed page, the magazine. The second painting in the series – of the empty store – is like a close-up in film terms. It shows an emptied-out urban plaza at noon. There used to be an inscription in Flemish, "niets in zicht", which means "nothing in sight", but I painted over it.

GB Would it be correct to describe the way in which you activate photography as a means to reach safety vis-à-vis the composition? By this I mean composition in the traditional sense of an image constructed in accordance with a predetermined set of rules, possessing a centre and equilibrium.

Photography, used in this way, relates more to a way of seeing than to content, and it opens up views on to reality that are not predefined.

LT That's correct. The cropped character of photographic images, even of the most classical ones, offers a perspective that is completely different to that of composed images. Photography can emphasize a detail because it's motionless. You can see the way in which some of the paintings were painted. It's a completely different way of painting that engages more with the representation of an existing image, a video still. The lighting and the flattening of the image – how it starts to bleed, and how the graphic aspect, which asserts itself very strongly there, disappears almost completely in this painting.

GB That's part of the subject. Is it a spotlight?

LT Yes. The painting of the light is important, as in *Pharmacy* [2003], where it becomes a self-abstracting fascination.

HDW You also made that the subject of a painting – the one with the slides?

LT Yes, *Slide #3* shows a blank photographic slide that I projected onto the wall and photographed. The effect is akin to a grey Rothko painting. *Exhibit #3* is part of the same group and depicts a sexual encounter between two monkeys. The image comes from a fertility museum in Japan. It has a virile element yet at the same time is pretty violent.

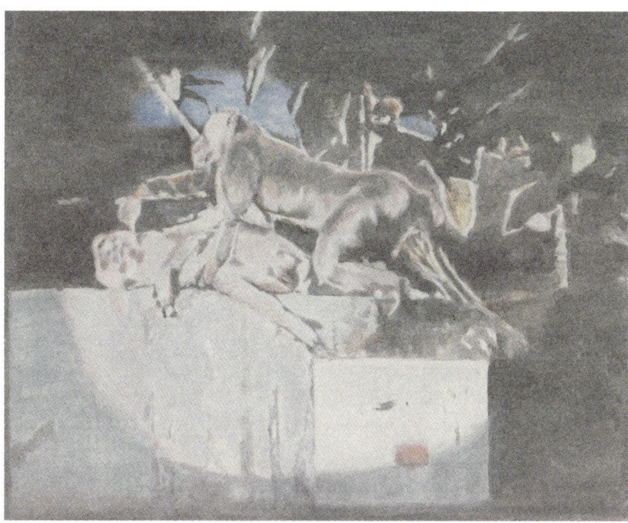

36 LUC TUYMANS, *Exhibit #3*, 2002
Oil on canvas, 111 × 138 cm
Thomas Koerfer, Switzerland

<u>37</u> Luc Tuymans, *Slide #1*, 2002
Oil on canvas, 203.5 × 134 cm
The Amy and Vernon Faulconer Collection
and The Howard Rachofsky Collection

<u>38</u> Luc Tuymans, *Slide #2*, 2002
Oil on canvas, 197 × 135 cm
Private collection

<u>39</u> Luc Tuymans, *Slide #3*, 2002
Oil on canvas, 200 × 159 cm
Private collection

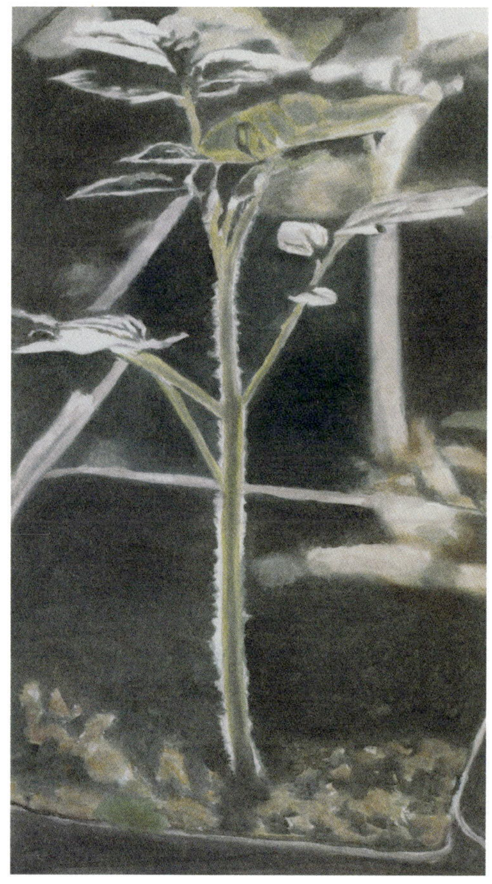

<u>HDW</u> I wanted to ask you about that. What fascinated you so much about this image?

<u>LT</u> I made five paintings about this. At first, I was fascinated by my museum visit. I never take photographs when I'm travelling because I find that it disrupts my memory and is an inadequate form of remembering. So, initially, it was pure experience, but afterwards I discovered a film about the museum and I extracted details from it based on my memory. Then the spotlight appeared, which you don't see when you're there. There are other stuffed animals, including giraffes, which are displayed in sexual positions, pressed together in a very physical way. The monkeys are important

because they are to scale and resemble people: child – baby, human – adult. The sense of physical violation and contamination is quite clear. Speaking of contamination, a painting like *Plant*, which is hung close to the monkeys, is pure construct. Photography was utilized from the beginning – it's a plant that I cut out from paper to scale and then took a photograph of with a Polaroid. It's a construct because it's about the colour, this toxic green that bears no relation to natural plants or to reality. When you no longer see the painting, you only remember the experience of the colour. In this particular case, the plant is merely a trigger for the imagination.

GB I'd like to return to the idea of contamination. Contamination signifies an intervention that affects things in indefinite ways. When a room is contaminated, for example, by UV or X-rays, it affects the whole space in a diffuse way that is often not even visible or direct. This is illustrated very well with *Plant* because the contamination means that everything appears in and under conditions of green, and this green has a tinge that evokes certain temporal and historical contexts. The era of the Polaroid, which is over in a sense, isn't it? The Polaroid is more or less a historical technological process.

LT It still exists – you can buy it. I started taking Polaroids in 1995, and there are several aspects of the process that I find interesting. The film develops like a painting before my eyes. It comes forward from the back until the fullest contrast finally takes shape, then the image is complete. This kind of imprecision is fluid after all. It's not a real photo and it's unique, which is also very important. You can see elements of the Polaroid in *Plant* – in the way it fades, in the violet that appears, and in the bluish light.

HDW I'd like to discuss further your use of colour. The series that we've been looking at – "the contaminated paintings" – is black-and-white until we reach *Plant*, where you have used the Polaroid.

LT I never use black paint. In fact, most painters don't. Every colour that you see here is "van Dyck brown", mixed with red or green, which makes an almost black. If you paint with true black and mix it with white, then it acquires a green or blue tinge, or it becomes a grey, dead colour. Gerhard Richter has painted with black, but that isn't the case here.

GB So that's a chromatic solution?

LT Yes, and it also has to do with the sense of depth. There needs to be a

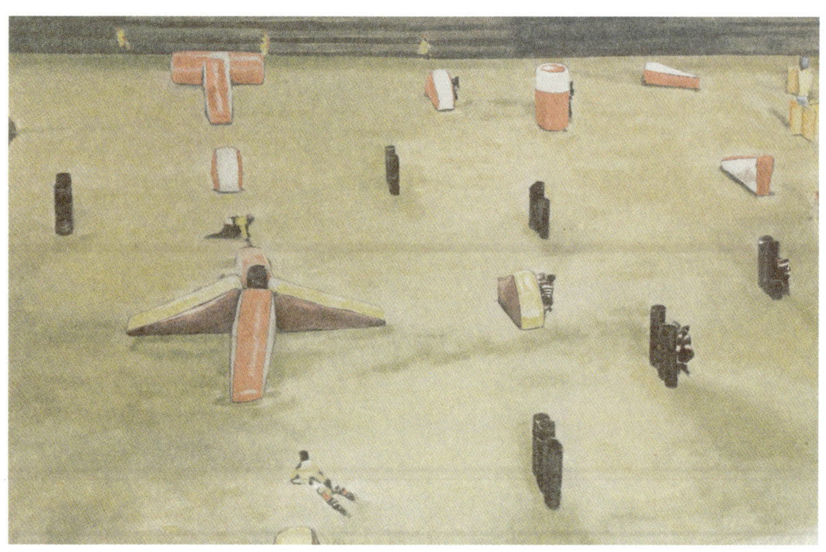

<u>41</u> Luc Tuymans, *Mayhem*, 2003
Oil on canvas, 187 × 291 cm
Hall Collection

warmth and depth in the colour, even if it's formulated as black. If it had really been painted with black, it would have appeared flatter.

GB And would have become isolated…

LT Yes, and then it wouldn't have generated an atmosphere that extends outwards. This applies to the whole series of paintings. It's actually visible, including in the shading, which isn't black of course. Let's move into the next gallery now to view two paintings from my 1995 *Heimat* [Homeland] series. In *Mayhem*, even though there are graphic elements, it's clear that the focal point, subject-matter and way of engaging with painting have changed, seen in the way the figure is just lying there and nearly disappears, and in the three-dimensional, inflated form. The painting was inspired by a paintball contest in a hall in Detroit. Normally, paintball is played outdoors, though for *Mayhem*, I captured it as an indoor scene in this public arena, and the vantage point is from above, looking down.

GB Is the composition derived from a photo?

LT Yes, I took a photo with my wife's camera, mainly because I was so astonished by this scene, which reminded me of a Bruegel painting.

<u>HDW</u> There's something indefinite about this painting – at first there is a relation to toys, but you don't quite know what's happening, which forces you to try and make connections.

<u>LT</u> Because you're looking from above, you see what the figures aren't able to see because they're hidden behind the forms. It's a full view from above – what is hidden is made visible. The game encompasses the whole of the painting. There is also the idea of war as a plaything, communicated through these inflatable plastic forms, which conveys a sense of claustrophobia and paranoia. And the figures themselves are reduced just to signs, to forms.

<u>GB</u> Moving on, I find the head in *Resentment* interesting, almost programmatic. It seems to be related to what we discussed earlier, the idea that a painting delays what it shows, and actually delays it endlessly – we never arrive completely at the thing itself. I think that can be seen clearly here. Presumably this is the reflection of a face on water?

<u>LT</u> No, it's actually a "double image", an editorial dissolving into and out of the image, which is derived from 1970s cinema and montage techniques. In cinema at the time, there was a trend for combining nature and human faces in a rather Romantic way. This painting is part of the *Heimat* series, and it deals with the idea of pathos, which is why it's called *Resentment*.

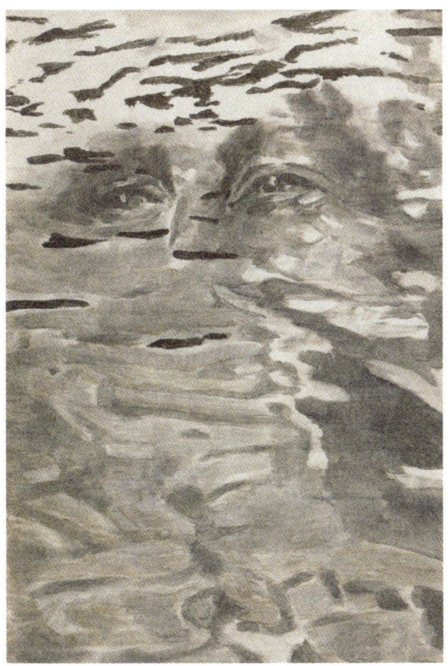

<u>GB</u> What's coming into focus more strongly in these paintings, is a point you made earlier: "I paint pictures out of the indefiniteness of the ground. I paint them from the plane forwards." The importance of the plane, or ground, can be seen very well here. It's so powerful that it doesn't really permit individual elements to take up a position.

<u>42</u> Luc Tuymans, *Resentment*, 1995
Oil on canvas, 94.5 × 63.5 cm
Collection schunck*, Heerlen

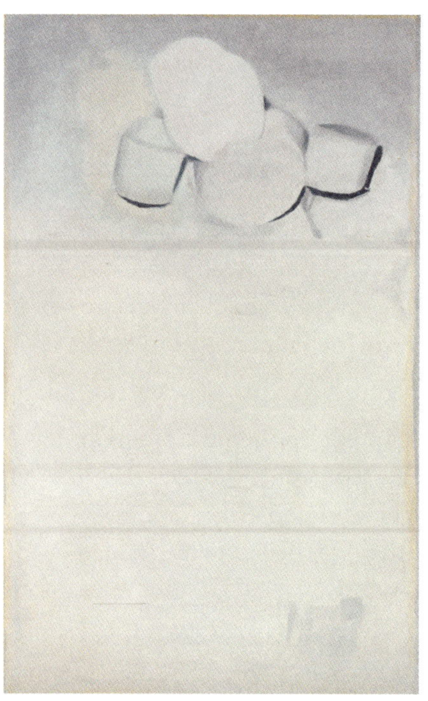

43 Luc Tuymans, *Drum Set*, 1998
Oil on canvas, 194.5 × 121.5 cm
Private collection, courtesy of David Zwirner,
New York/London

HDW What interests me about the ground is that it's in a state of becoming.

GB The ground holds a great deal of power here. After all, it's often painted out, with the pictorial elements built up on top of it and only a small portion is ever revealed at the back. But here, the ground is very much present – it reveals itself and develops.

HDW In my opinion, that's also a result of the different colours. We encounter two new elements in the corners that you can't actually place.

LT Occasionally it's interesting to paint over things like in *Drum Set*, which is a good example of erasure in a picture. It was created from a maquette that I made and glued to a piece of paper, then photographed with a Polaroid. The harsh light at the top of the frame dissolves the drum set into near-abstraction.

HDW How do you work with photographs and still images? Do conceptual images play a part and lead you to make maquettes from them – like in *Drum Set*? What do you find important about the images you use?

LT Firstly, I was fascinated with the drum set as an instrument, but also with the idea of noiselessness, and with formulating that on a smaller scale by reducing the size of the object and representing the photograph at the same time – including the yellowed edges, which are painted and included as a documentation of the process. This emptiness, or the empty area where the painting becomes decentralized, is an important aspect of the painting. You'll notice that there are no paintings hanging in the centre, and this is also important. Some curators want to hang pictures on the centre line because it's a system, although I've made it clear that this is exactly what shouldn't be done. The painting should be decentralized, so that it takes on a life of its own on the wall. When an object is shown properly, it acquires

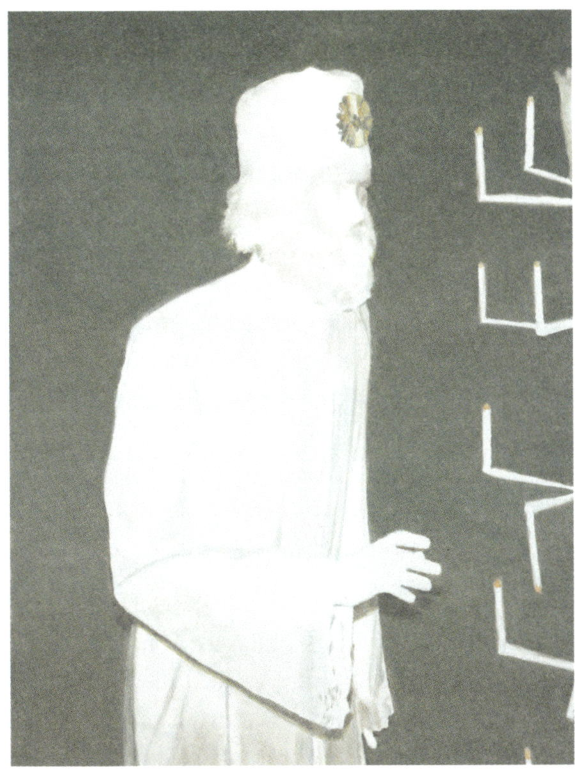

<u>44</u> Luc Tuymans, *The Worshipper*, 2004
Oil on canvas, 192.8 × 147.3 cm
Private collection, Belgium

a certain force and presence, like with *Drum Set*. It is part of the same series as *Plant*, the contaminated painting, and comes from a period of withholding.

<u>HDW</u> Why don't we move to the first gallery with *The Worshipper*?

<u>LT</u> *The Worshipper* came about unexpectedly, as I was researching material for an exhibition about the carnival in Binche where you can find the Musée International du Carnaval et du Masque. It's an international museum of puppets, masks and costumes from Eastern Europe. There, I saw a statue of a costumed man leaning against a wall, which for me took on a life of its own, beyond the carnival setting. The figure struck me as something strangely fanatical, maybe an Orthodox priest. At that time I had my Polaroid camera with me to take pictures of the costumes for my research and I photographed the statue, just like that, and this painting came out

of that image. The camera flash eliminated the shadows so it's impossible to estimate the distance between the wall and the puppet. This gives it a spooky quality, like a focus of worship, which I translated into my painting. When I paint I never use overhead projectors or project images in any way. The format, or size, emerges from working directly on unstretched canvas nailed to the wall. There are some early paintings that were stretched, but I stopped working in that way fairly quickly. Once the canvas is on the wall, I then apply the ground colour. I draw directly onto the wet paint of the ground in a loop – starting in one place and continuing to sketch the whole image in a loop. I'm gauging while I draw, and that's why there's a verticality in the paintings – I have very few horizontal paintings.

GB Do you look at the Polaroid while you're drawing or do you work from memory?

LT I refer to the photograph, it's not from memory. I really check it, and am constantly looking at it from a distance.

HDW For me *The Worshipper* draws part of its strength from the point where the figure's hand pushes across the straight, vertical line of the picture plane.

LT That's the most important part of the painting.

GB Are those candles?

LT It's actually a stylized Christmas tree, made out of wood and painted white with orange dots. In reality, of course, it would be a real Christmas tree.

GB There are a few *pentimenti* which we can see around one of the lines. Can you clarify what they are?

LT Sometimes I make double lines so that an area or object becomes indefinite and out of focus. Here, for example, because the shadow needed to have this transparency. I find shadows very interesting, because it's really impossible to paint a shadow.

HDW I've spent a lot of time studying shadows and I've never got anywhere

LT A shadow is really an inessential colour – it's an atmospheric tinge that has a translucent, ephemeral language. It either disappears or it doesn't, and leaves nothing behind. Here it's motionless and captured as a moment in time.

GB It also represents the thing it's a shadow of – a picture-within-a-picture.

LT And it's a negative print. It's as if the image is emptied, like a piece of gauze or plaster cast, and that cast almost becomes a person. It's like a shell.

GB May I return to the paint structure? So, the ground of the painting, this shade of white, is applied, and then it's built up. Is the brightness that we see generated by the indirect presence of the white?

LT Yes.

GB So then it's actually a reversal?

LT Not quite. I work wet-on-wet. This means that I bring the white – the background – forward, to stop me from moving into contrasts too quickly. Because if you create a huge contrast, you can't go back – it's like when you print something. Try printing white, it's impossible. It should be left blank from the outset – this is a general rule. The lighter shade was all painted first – and thinned out a lot so it goes over the colour of the ground, which it absorbs, and then finally the contrast defines the whole figure.

GB Is that acrylic or tempera?

LT It's all oil.

GB But with wet-on-wet you can only do it once, can't you?

LT No. With tempera of course you couldn't do that, you have to do it in stages, and with acrylic it's difficult because the paint dries very quickly. But with oil it takes days before the paint is dry to the touch, and twenty-five years before it's completely dry. The next work is called *Cinq Anneaux* [Five

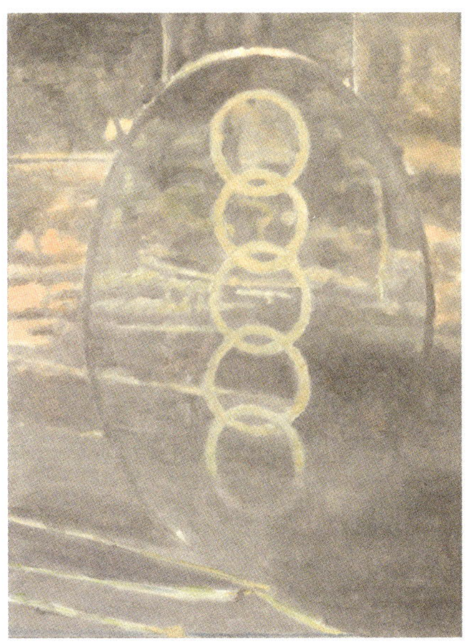

45 Luc Tuymans, *Cinq Anneaux* [Five Rings], 2004 ·
Oil on canvas, 165 × 124 cm
Collection of Brenda R. Potter

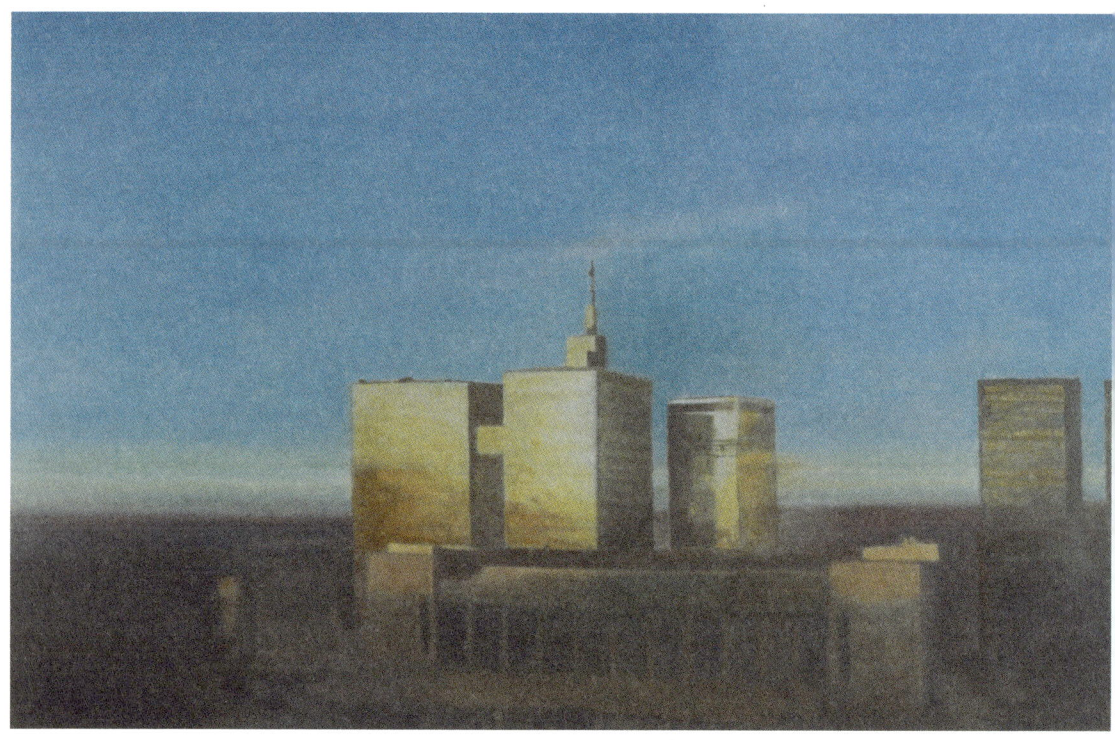

46 Luc Tuymans, *Dusk*, 2004
Oil on canvas, 166 × 260 cm
The ITYS Collection

Rings]. It is the view from a window in a bar at night. The rings are part of the window. It's only about 20 cm high.

HDW I imagine that it would have been logical to paint these rings in a "circling" movement, but instead they're painted using a series of small brushstrokes.

LT In later works the brushstrokes become shorter, which offers a completely different kind of control. I wanted this more nervous brushstroke in order to control the light. It is different from *Dusk*, for example, which is another painting about light, but here I wanted to paint the sunlight.

HDW That's a mirror, isn't it?

LT It's actually the two Belgacom towers near a railway station in Brussels. This painting, which hangs next to the ghostly figure of *The Worshipper*, was made in the wake of 9/11 and features an idyllic late-afternoon scene as twilight turns into night. The twin towers now become almost a threat of something that might happen.

GB Brussels as a Fata Morgana!

LT It is painted differently from *Cinq Anneaux* or *The Worshipper*. It has a certain flattening. I started out as a painter who used quite a lot of paint and in a pretty gestural way. Later I threw it all off in order to give it greater meaning by reducing it. And now I permit myself a more painterly approach again.

HDW When you back away from this painting and look at it from a distance, its effect is very powerful, almost iconic.

LT That's why it was chosen as the "poster child" for the exhibition, because it engages the viewer who is not quite sure what he or she is looking at.

GB That's true. Here we know, or think we know, what we're looking at.

LT The hang of *Dusk* was a very important decision, to avoid placing it directly across from where the light enters the gallery, where *Mayhem* is now hanging.

HDW I live in Brussels so, straight away, it's clear to me what this is a painting of. However, if it were titled *Fort Knox, Texas*, the viewer would have a very different response to it. It bears a kind of urban essence that's very present, and which eliminates the need to associate it with the particular station in Brussels.

LT Exactly. It's called *Dusk* – a time of day. Unlike Edward Hopper's work, it's anonymous both in terms of the viewpoint and the light. It's also a superimposition, which makes it an urban painting, but it could be anywhere. It could also be in an Eastern European context because of the building next to the towers, which has a more classical form.

HDW That's also where the confrontation occurs, isn't it? Those are two very different dynamics that collide.

LT What I enjoyed was creating this intensification of the colour. In *Dusk* I really went for it – bang! – lots of colour.

LT Next we come to *La Correspondance* – the first painting I made after my excursion into film. It's exactly the same size as *Our New Quarters* [1986]

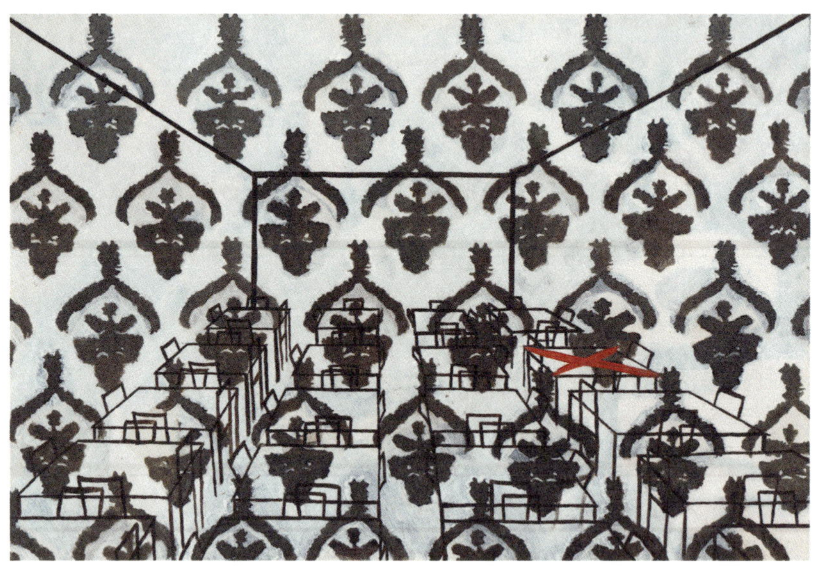

<u>47</u> Luc Tuymans, *La Correspondance*, 1985
Oil on canvas, 80.5 × 120 cm
Collection M HKA – Collection of the Flemish Community

and, like the latter, is based on an anecdote. Between 1905 and 1910, the Dutch author J. van Oudshoorn was active in the diplomatic service. He couldn't afford to bring his wife to join him, so he sent her a postcard every day from the restaurant where he ate his lunch, placing a red cross on the table at which he had just sat. Unlike *Our New Quarters*, which is an image of death, *La Correspondance* stands for eternal presence and homesickness.

Moving on, I don't know what you think when you see it, but *Antichambre* is not a spontaneous composition. The idea came to me after I completed *La Correspondance*. Because of its stylization I started toying with old découpage drawings on very small pieces of paper. Straight away I included the yellow tone in the paint, and incorporated these pencil marks on the paper, so the final work consists of three different colours – that of the pencil, the ballpoint pen, and the ink. It is actually a preliminary drawing for something that I filmed, a room with a hanging chandelier. This was really like an opening for me, because it became possible to enlarge drawings. There's a huge difference between a drawn line and a painted line, and in the earlier period, with *Suicide* or the portrait of *G. Dam*, things became suffocating and existed too much on an existential level. Five years of working with film had provided me with the detachment necessary to develop

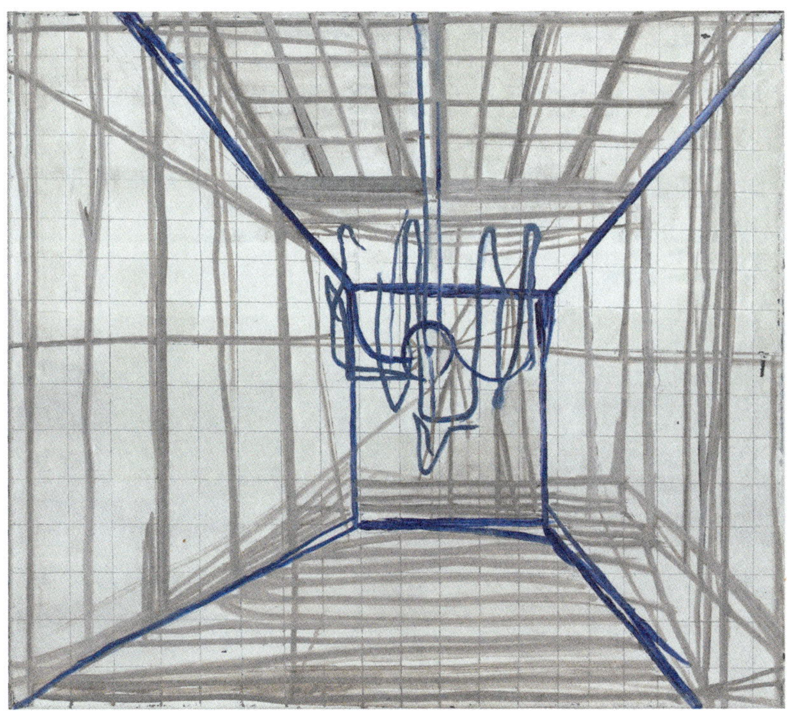

<u>48</u> Luc Tuymans, *Antichambre*, 1985
Oil on canvas, 69.9 × 80.1 cm
Collection M HKA – Collection of the Flemish Community

further. I couldn't have made this shift in 1978 otherwise. Earlier I had
wanted to paint "retrospective portraits", they're almost self-portraits, with
an element of covering-up one's own history. Working in film and developing this idea of causality allowed for the detachment that was necessary to
look towards somewhere else. During my 1992 exhibition at the Kunsthalle
in Bern, I asked a psychoanalyst whether books from which medical students learn how to diagnose from illustrations are still published, and he
sent me a book with the title *Der diagnostische Blick* [The Diagnostic View].
There are ten paintings that came from this book. *Der diagnostische Blick IV*
is the most iconic image within the series, showing a cropped image of a
blue-eyed woman with breast cancer. It is directly related to the images of
toys and eyeballs – the most naturalistic images that, for that very reason,
lack reality. They were the first portraits I painted in a long time. I altered
the position of the eyes in each case so that the person's gaze goes beyond
the viewer and no empathy is established. These are also the first paintings

in which I applied the paint horizontally, creating a grid that makes it impossible for the viewer to enter into the image and its sense of depth. The images become symptoms, bringing about their own trauma.

GB Here it's easy to grasp what you said earlier about the paintings always being objects as well. The conjunction of the subject and the format causes the painting to become an object.

LT The paintings of toys that I made two years earlier, in 1990, are also very important in this regard. Up until that point, I had only depicted spaces – no people, no figurines. All of a sudden, in 1990 I began making these model paintings that were prompted by German model-railway magazines, which also advertise Preisler figures for use in dioramas. Preisler figures are a post-war German product. Inserted into dioramas, they present an ideal world. When something is small, it is easy to manipulate. The series is about megalomania – the attempt to control the world – and is also a response to my fascination for Edward Hopper's paintings. The unnatural staging of people in his work makes his world feel more like a toy to me than a work of art. There's something doll-like about them.

GB By the way, in *Antichambre* – because you asked what we see – I find it very impressive that the projection of the room, which is certainly there, disappears increasingly the longer you look at it. You begin to sense what at first eludes the eye – the emptiness of the room, the space in between, the opening. It becomes perceptible as light or as a mixture of light and shade. It also seems to be the result of how the *quadros* interlock in this grid and in the free construction of various lines that overlap and then actually make what's in between them perceptible.

HDW Absolutely. Although there's another point to add – that it's actually painted using the technique of classical perspective.

LT Yes, it's basically a classical painting. But just as this is a frontal view, there is also an overlay of blue and an intervention in the form of a sign. As you mentioned, the yellowing was very important in the build-up of the painting. This is where the idea of painting the background first, then the foreground, first originated. In *La Correspondance* it was still a mixture of the two, but here there was a clear distinction.

GB But what's at the back asserts itself at the front.

LT Yes, and it's pretty obvious here because the paint is applied much more thickly.

HDW In regard to the portrait, how important is the additional information about the genesis of the painting? In my opinion, it also works independently of that.

LT Yes, of course. I only explained it because it was an important stage that actually formed part of a sequence.

HDW Before I understood what was going on within the painting – whether it's a woman or a man – I sensed a problem that I couldn't put my finger on and I find that very powerful.

LT The image is iconic and the scale is monumental. From a distance, the painting has a stronger effect than *The Diagnostic View III* from the same series, which employs the same compositional system but is completely different in colour. The latter refers to cirrhosis of the liver, meaning that a kind of greyish-yellow tinge creeps into the skin. In *The Diagnostic View IV* it pales. The portrait that I still think is the best though is *The Diagnostic View II*, followed by *Skin Cancer* [1992].

GB In *La Correspondance*, an ornamental structure plays a part. Ornament is a very powerful way of organizing images because it suggests a continuum

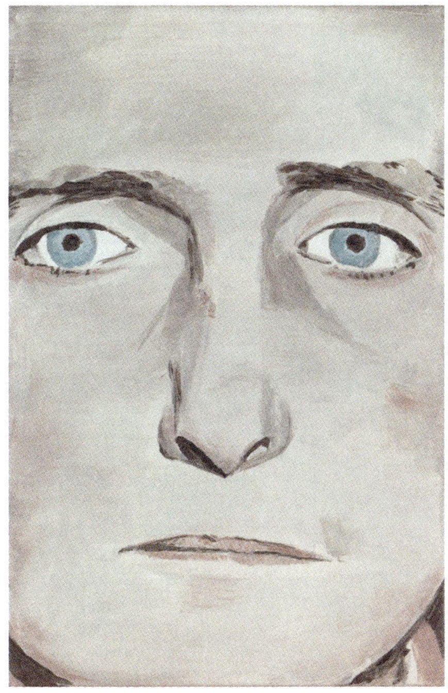

49 Luc Tuymans, *Der diagnostische Blick IV*, 1992
Oil on canvas, 57 × 38.2 cm
Private collection, on long-term loan
to the De Pond Museum, Tilburg

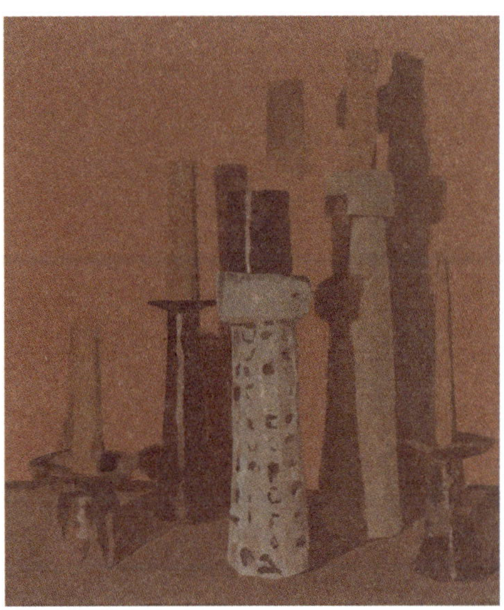

<u>50</u> Luc Tuymans, *Intolerance*, 1993
Oil on canvas, 80 × 70 cm
Private collection

beyond the confines of the image, unlike photography. Did this idea of ornamental structure continue to play a role in your painting?

<u>LT</u> Definitely. There is an interest in drapery and, in *Intolerance*, an obvious interest in the shimmering, which is what I wanted to paint. This is what fascinates me about the Old Masters – for example, the way Velázquez painted the drapery in the portrait of the Infanta. The Infanta's clothes are actually a far more essential component of the painting than the person herself, and that was also the case here.

<u>GB</u> That's a "liturgical robe".

<u>LT</u> It came from the same exhibition as the candlestick. The idea was to turn around bourgeois motifs. Belgium is a very Catholic country, where there are small altars on almost all mantelpieces, which is where *Intolerance* came from. And here, that's simply a shadow – a small child. The interesting thing is that this exhibition with the shadow was a completely different one but was installed at the same time, almost immediately after the *Diagnostic View*.

<u>HDW</u> Were these works made at the same time?

<u>LT</u> No, I never work on two paintings at the same time. I need to concentrate intensely. First of all, as a painter, that's the pleasure that I derive from painting. It's also important for the intensity of the image. I can't achieve that by going back and forth between one painting and another one, especially not if it's a series.

<u>GB</u> And painting wet on wet means that the process doesn't last particularly long – maybe a day or two.

<u>LT</u> Each one of the pictures presented in this exhibition took one day to paint. Each one of them!

GB The big ones too? That must be a very full day.

LT The big ones too. It's a long day, yes.

GB There must be moments when it fails, when it doesn't work.

LT That happens often, but then I either paint over or start again from scratch. I used to paint over because I didn't have money to buy new canvases. Now I just throw them away. There's a kind of uncertainty about the painting – is it good or not? I hold on to the painting for a month or two months, look at it again and, if it doesn't hold up after two months, then I throw it out. Early on I painted over a large number of works and destroyed them, and in some cases that's a pity because in retrospect there were actually paintings I shouldn't have destroyed. At the time I had this incredible self-censorship because I was thirty-two years old when I had my first exhibition and entered the gallery circuit. I had spent quite a lot of time making work in isolation, which means that you really test and examine it. Then you also make mistakes, because of course you're alone in the process.

HDW But should an artist be, or remain, the arbiter of his or her entire oeuvre?

LT I think it's wise. There are far too many lousy works by a number of artists, for example, as we have seen with Cézanne – I wouldn't like to experience that. For me there's a benchmark standard that a painting adheres to or not – if it lags behind, then it has to go.

GB A test phase that lasts for some time? Do they stay in your studio or do you put them in domestic spaces?

LT In the studio.

GB In my experience something changes when a painting moves from the context in which it was produced to a domestic context.

LT Yes, sometimes the results can be terrible, although there have also been good instances – such as with Bernhard Hahnloser, who bought a pretty abstract painting during my exhibition at the Kunsthalle in Bern and hung it between an Odilon Redon and a Matisse. In his home it became really appealing because of the environment. If you see a painting in a collector's home, hanging on its own on the wall, above the couch or some other piece of furniture, it becomes decorative. I don't mind if it's in a room in an institution like this, where it's completely neutralized.

GB The couch is where it becomes a serious matter for art! It has to assert itself.

LT With the *Der diagnostische Blick* series, for example, one collector returned the second *Diagnostic View*, which is now in the collection of the museum in Krefeld, and said: "I can't live with it." This is something that has happened often. He said: "I think the painting's really great, but I just can't look at it. It's too confrontational."

GB We've arrived at a point that's ultimately very important – how paintings like these intervene in daily life, in social processes, how they have a reciprocal effect on the society from which they emerge.

HDW It's a process, isn't it?

GB Yes. What I constantly sense is that the effect is subcutaneous. At first there's nothing, nothing at all, and then it begins slowly and changes perception and behaviour over time, just a little, like a homoeopathic dosage.

LT Well, I can certainly say that I couldn't stand that. For one thing, I don't have a single painting of my own at home – we have paintings by other people, but not by me because I see my own mistakes, and they are always present. It's also strange to see my paintings in other people's homes, and if I'm invited to a meal, I always sit with my back to the painting. For me, the painting remains a foreign body, a real interference.

HDW That brings us to another important question – what does the notion of an oeuvre mean to you? For example, you paint in groups and series of pictures, correct?

LT Not always. Sometimes there is an initial theme, such as with *Mwana Kitoko* [2000], which was almost journalistic. Or in *Der diagnostische Blick*, of which there are only two or three paintings in this exhibition, but it makes more sense when you see the whole series together. I've always wanted to see an exhibition of my work in the way that someone else would look at it. It's an impossible wish but it would be great to look at my own work just for once with complete detachment. That's the challenge. I think most people experience the paintings from a certain distance and the works speak for themselves. For example, there is a man from Honolulu that never liked my work. He saw my exhibition at the Tate Modern and he still didn't like it. About a month later, he began dreaming about the paintings, they came back to him, and then he was really enthusiastic about them – it was a kind of conversion! Pictures can work over time. When I look at *Antichambre*, the complexity of it wasn't clear to me at the time, it's only now that I see it. At the same time, I know that I couldn't produce that painting again. In painting it's impossible to go back. I could produce a technically exact copy, but it would be a forgery.

HDW But that wouldn't make sense, would it?

LT It goes back to what we discussed earlier, when I said that one of the paintings was a fake El Greco, and you saw immediately that there was something wrong with it.

GB Do you keep any of your own works? There are many reasons for maintaining control over your own work, and I'm wondering if you hold on to paintings because you haven't finished with the issues addressed in them?

LT There's nothing like Richter's *Atlas* – nothing of that kind. I do keep all the visual source material, but not systematically. I'm always looking for images and I draw constantly – I keep all that. I've never kept my own paintings though. As I said, I find it annoying and I don't fetishize my own work. When a painting's really finished, then it's finished. It's interesting to exhibit it, to make use of it in a museum context, but by then I've already separated myself from it and am working on a new painting. Before, I would be happy for a week or two because I had created something that, in my opinion, was new. Now when I paint a new picture the happiness lasts for two days! The innocence is gone – I've trained myself, have acquired knowledge and skill, and I know exactly what I'm doing.

GB But you also reach greater heights.

LT Yes, you grow as a painter. I confront myself with new challenges, with regard to the format, or the complexity of the visualization, but now it works impeccably – very different from the earlier days of wasting time. I think that at a certain point, when you've accomplished your goals with regard to business and lifestyle, as a painter you should take a step back and go deeper… perhaps take a step in another direction.

HDW Do you mean that routine actually makes the magic disappear?

LT No, but there are pressures and expectations that reach inhuman levels the better known you become. When I finish an exhibition and am able to withdraw for a while, just to work – these are the happiest moments and when I feel best. Of course the beginning is always torture, but when more than half the painting is complete and it starts to look right, then you really understand what a painter can do, and what the viewer doesn't see.

HDW So, there is a fear of starting?

LT Yes, it's like stage fright.

GB Do you hope that viewers will engage with your work? For example, is what we're doing now interesting to you?

LT Yes, I find the discussion stimulating. When we speak about my paintings, it is more difficult for me because I've done it so often. What interests me most is that we've abandoned the art-historical and referential material and moved on to examining what has an impact and what works – that's very important, especially in the long run. When children respond to the paintings, their responses can be surprisingly astute and completely intentional. For example, I worked on a project in Ghent with children, and when they saw one of the doll portraits, they just smiled – the work instantly "clicked" with them.

GB In art history and art criticism, there is rarely an attempt to understand the specific kind of intelligence that informs painting.

LT The Frankfurt School, specifically people like Ulrich Loock, tried to penetrate the skin of painting and to generate an entire discourse around it, but it's being done less and less in art criticism now because art criticism is self-generating. Curators are not artists, but they almost shape the artists as if they were. A de-visualizing is also taking place.

GB It's challenging to oppose this development, since there are increasingly more and more images, and the ability to engage with them is becoming more rare.

LT Plus it's becoming uniform. Attention spans are also limited – if you measure the time that people physically spend in front of a painting, it's usually between fifteen and twenty seconds. Or they're really fascinated, but usually they look quickly.

GB I teach a seminar with my students in a museum in front of original works of art, and we spend two hours in front of one painting. I tell them what we know about the painting in the first five minutes. They are not allowed to regurgitate any art-historical knowledge or refer to it later

– the knowledge exists, but we get it over and done with. We then take a ten-minute break, they go back to look at the painting and I ask them what they've seen. Although this lasts for two hours, they accept it, and eventually it even becomes very popular. Slowly, this leads to an ability to uncover things.

LT Rubens belongs to a category that incorporates the public in paintings, as we see from their scale. I think it's clear that no painter before him had painted on such huge surfaces. He was actually a kind of Cecil B. DeMille of his day, utilizing a preconceived image from the beginning, organized concentrically in the Baroque period and taking place from a distance. This is what Rubens and his workshop did, and gradually this concept became the most important aspect. The effects were placed at the service of an ideology. After all, the churches were basically empty and he simply filled them up again.

HDW What about Paolo Veronese?

GB He too, and Titian with his *Assunta* [*The Assumption of the Virgin*] from 1518 in the Santa Maria Gloriosa dei Frari church in Venice. That's a painting that competes with a huge church and succeeds in focusing the space. But I think it was very rare before him.

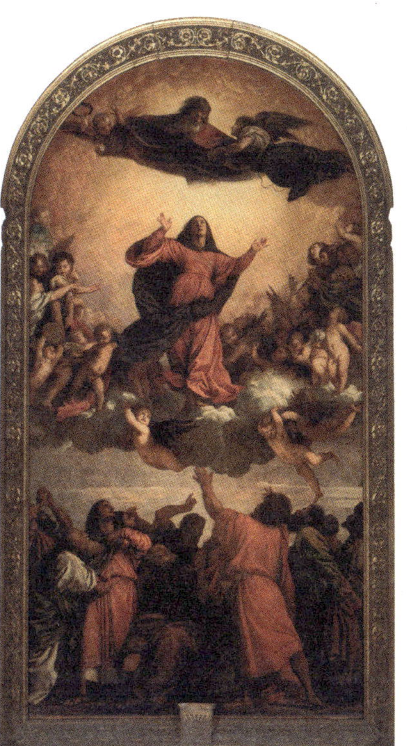

LT Later the notion of the spectator and the public continues through to Géricault, with his *Raft of the Medusa* [1818–19]. This too is a huge painting and a failed masterpiece, in which a Renaissance-type figure looks back and the action is actually farther off. Although he was a great painter, this is not a strong work. I find that the studies for this so-called failed masterpiece are actually more interesting.

HDW His preparations for the work were extensive…

51 TITIAN, *The Assumption of the Virgin, c.* 1515–18
Oil on panel, 690 × 360 cm
Basilica di Santa Maria Gloriosa dei Frari, Venice

LT And that's why the painting failed.

HDW I believe he even had the raft reconstructed in his workshop. We know of many masterpieces that have failed due to the time and enormous effort taken. For example, I don't think Picasso's *Guernica* [1937] is a masterpiece.

LT It's always left me cold.

HDW There were hundreds of studies and drawings for it, and it's the same with *The Gates of Hell* [*c.* 1880–1917] by Auguste Rodin. He worked on it for twenty years, but I think in the end he failed.

LT In such cases the vastness of ambition leads to failure. I think that the artworks that survive best are those that somehow elude your grasp.

GB Yes, you can sense the muscle and ambition in artworks like that: "*Now I'm going to do something really great.*"

LT I've made attempts at it as well but, like I said, the "spectacular" is never a winner. It's a challenge to see how far I can take it before it bursts, especially with subjects like theme parks, Walt Disney or the Jesuits, which is about an ideology and a kind of non-scepticism towards images. For me, there's *only* scepticism about images, and the transference from a religious idea to one of entertainment is interesting – you can see how they engage with each other. The biggest painting is not necessarily the best painting.

The Basel Sessions

When the foundation for this project was laid during our stay in Budapest, we realized that we had engaged in something that none of the participants could have predicted. After that experience the two principal elements in the project – the artist and his academic partners – were now truly connected by a common mission. Not only were both parties strengthened by the fact that their intellectual and affectional systems had not rejected each other – the insight produced by the combination of those two worlds could reveal many hidden aspects that would have never been discovered otherwise. Having accepted an invitation by Gottfried Boehm, the whole group met again in Basel in April 2008 for the second batch of sessions. We had already elected not to enlarge the scope of our discussion with new elements. We would rather build on the foundation laid in Budapest by further exploring the most interesting points already touched on or reconsidering a number of issues that had been abandoned too early. Again, a number of rules had to be established. Our team in Brussels would carefully monitor these sessions and isolate twenty topics of particular interest that emerged during the Budapest talks. From his side, Gottfried Boehm would put together a small portable library containing illustrations of all the artworks we had discussed in Budapest so that pictures of them would be made available when needed. Finally, we would stick to the same basic rules we had established for the first sessions. We met on a sunny spring afternoon on the roof terrace of the historic university building of Basel, where Friedrich Nietzsche once had an office, and that is now used by the Eikones research group founded by Gottfried Boehm. From the very start, the Basel debates became proof that the work done in Budapest was a reliable and solid foundation. From now on the focus of our reflections would become clear: nothing would withhold us from making an in-depth investigation into the nature of an image. While the afternoon session was guided by the special points of interest we had pre-selected, the conversation the following morning reached an unprecedented degree of innovation and preciseness. The different perspectives between artist and theoreticians were still clearly marked; however, their newly-forged alliance had allowed them to come closer in assessing one of the most mysterious products of human civilization: the nature of the image as an artwork.

University of Basel

Gottfried Boehm (GB) | Hans M. De Wolf (HDW) | Luc Tuymans (LT)

HDW Our earlier discussion in the Szépművészeti Múzeum in Budapest covered a number of different topics, such as content, technique and the painting process.

LT We also talked about the concept of dilettantism and how a painting relates to its pictorial content. In my opinion, this relationship gives rise to a certain kind of unease and mistrust of images. The mistrust is actually the feedback response, which in turn relates to the relationship between knowledge and the practice of painting. Knowledge is a mental state whereas painting expresses itself in a purely physical form. However, you can be intelligent with your head and you can also be intelligent with your hands. It's an interesting challenge to think about both together because the concept of time comes to play an important role. There's a big difference between painted time and actual time, which always leads to a "belatedness" or a delay that comes into play due to the dissociation between the hands and the head.

HDW Do you see dilettantism as a form of liberation rather than as something amateurish or undeveloped?

LT Yes, it involves an ambiguity that didn't exist earlier. As an example, in 15th- and 16th-century early Netherlandish painting, all knowledge of the world was subject to strict religious dogma. I believe that this is the reason why we find neither the fragmentation – which we observed in El

Greco – nor a decentralization of the image to the same degree among the Flemish Primitives.

<u>HDW</u> And which we don't find in Courbet either?

<u>LT</u> Exactly. Courbet returns to a centralized positioning of the image, but this decision is linked to his status and to a completely different reality. It has to do with a particular type of aggression. It involves the idea of pathos but in relation to the material of reality – the reality that is actually made manifest in the image.

<u>GB</u> Perhaps we can address the issue of dilettantism in the work of El Greco in order to arrive at a clearer understanding of this concept. If I understand correctly, El Greco's dilettantism is apparent in the way that he distinguishes between what a figure is, what it should be, and how it appears. He makes a strict distinction between the two. In his paintings we see figures that are too tall and too big, which depart from the canon of knowledge and serve to activate an unrestrained kind of painting. "Unrestrained" here means dilettantish, not justified in terms of the figure. Now let us reconsider what El Greco's reasons for this were. One reason could be that the content caused him to despair and say, "I can't capture all of this", and the other reason could be that he was attempting to devise a means of conveying increased vitality. Because El Greco's paintings are incredibly dynamic and "expressive", which is also the source of their modernity, they are an intensification of the visible. It could be argued that this intensification represents an attempt to capture the visible world more fully using the means of dilettantism. And that's the difference between resigning oneself to something and becoming totally involved in it. Does this make sense?

<u>LT</u> I think it does. Once again, pathos shines through, and this should be taken into consideration because there is a certain rational process undertaken when he deconstructs an image. I'm certain that the reasons for this relate to the spiritual realm – this is made, I think, clear in the paintings. Dreaming through distortion is El Greco's way of disorientating himself, which is another way of describing dilettantism, or of losing himself. This is where dreaming meets ecstasy. I used to see this ecstatic aspect as a mannerism because I was unable to grasp its intensity from reproductions in books. Now I understand it in the physical terms of format and scale, through the temperature radiated by the paintings, and through the compositions, which are so utterly different from previous ones. His work is

radically arranged and has, as you mentioned earlier, this dynamism. But in the end it isn't painting – like the Baroque of Rubens – that produces animation. Going back to our earlier discussion about the verticality of the image, it still seeks to twist upwards and there is a point where it disappears. This disappearing–appearing, the visible 'making invisible', leads to deconstruction in comparison with dilettantism because it retains a certain rationale. That's why I find El Greco very important, also with respect to modernity, because he basically opened the door to not-seeing, to abolishing visibility, and to abolishing the image, which he accomplishes in a variety of ways.

GB But the central phenomenon of the dilettantism we're discussing is a shift in the relationship between figuration and expression.

LT Yes, it was van Eyck who was the first to shift the image away from mimesis and to intensify its sense of reality to the point where he began to make a break with the Middle Ages, even while remaining within the ideological limits of the time. In the oeuvre of van Dyck there is an incredible decisiveness and distinct ambition, and van Eyck was very conscious of this changed image quality. This is where I see a first form of abstraction.

HDW I'm thinking of something that the German composer Helmut Lachenmann once told me about music. In earlier times music came into being only for dancing. Music was *made*; it was something you *did*. This continued up until the point when someone sat down, listened and tried to understand the system in the music itself. Isn't this a type of growing awareness, comparable to what van Eyck did when he addressed the image in a way that had never been done before?

LT No, he tried to "de-spiritualize" the image, which was precisely the opposite of El Greco. He made it profane via a considerable degree of awareness and an almost clinical approach to painting – something that no one else had done before. This intensified sense of reality remains a constant presence there, and this relates to the question of how images date, which is what I mean by dilettantism and fragmentation. The question of how an image dates or ages can also be posed in relation to pathos – not only in terms of technique or visual language, but in relation to content and to the simultaneous interaction of two pictorial planes, one that you see and one that you sense. In this respect, El Greco is very interesting because what you intuitively sense in his images is of utmost importance, which is what makes him modern. He was among the first to depict a visionary narrative that didn't exist before.

GB This also brings up the question of time and the fact that we now register two different temporalities. On the one hand, there is the possibility of tracing time in the movement of a figure. It moves, and this motion encapsulates an experience of time. This is the time captured in a motif or in a figure, but the essential difference with El Greco is that he establishes a new temporal dimension on the level of dynamism and freed painterly elements. And while it responds to the figures and to the motif, it also displays a logic of its own that is directly tied to the image.

LT And to gravity – it vanishes, flies, hovers, sinks down.

GB It shoots out of the image…

LT And it falls through. What you see is all so imperfect that it must have been a deliberate decision. It's inconceivable that it simply emerged from the figure intuitively, just like that. El Greco thought about it, and these were entirely new thoughts about the form, the abstract quality of the image, the prism-like plane, how the light acts within the painting and

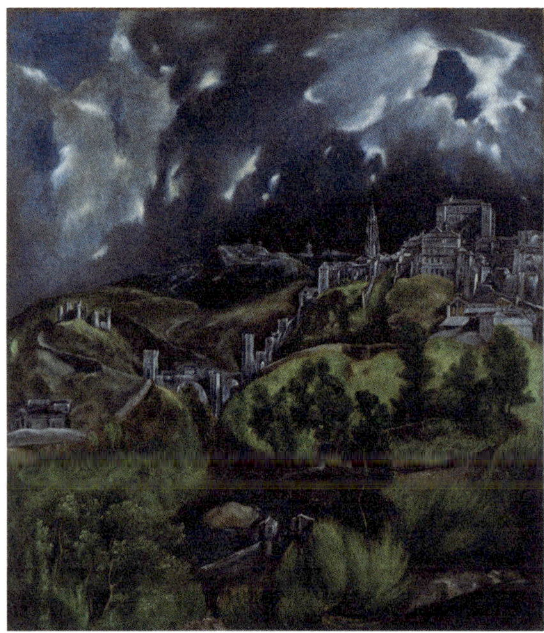

52 El Greco, *View of Toledo*, c. 1599–1600
Oil on canvas, 121.3 × 108.6 cm
The Metropolitan Museum of Art, New York, INV. 29.100.6

is directed back at the viewer. He was also the first to paint a landscape without people. In his *View of Toledo* a bolt of lightning cuts through the sky, and again, something is being broken up. One could say that El Greco was among the first artists to paint ruptures.

GB This is also related to the issue of creativity. At least it could be argued that El Greco experimented with this shift in order to recover the possibility of painting a picture, and that for him it was no longer clear or certain what an image is. With this painting, he embarked on a search for the image and reached a transitory kind of conclusion. This also entailed bidding farewell, in a sense, to definitive formulations.

HDW In Budapest we discussed the fact that these images are incomplete.

LT The point is that they're not painted with completion in mind. This is the main difference between Rubens and El Greco. For Rubens, completion involves looking back to classical antiquity, the Renaissance and Greek sculpture. There is a sense of fossilization and subversion of immutable myths. He was an idiosyncratic painter who wanted to make painting come to life again in the Baroque. At the same time, we find foolish ideas in his paintings – much more than in El Greco's. I've always wondered what Rubens would have thought of El Greco. When we discuss appearances or the form that something takes on, we could use a theological term and speak of "revelation". I see Rubens' work as more didactic than El Greco's, which tended to acquire a life of its own on an individual level and led to his problems with the Inquisition.

HDW Can we talk more about the Inquisition, which is always mentioned in relation to El Greco? How important was it for his creative process? Did he feel a need to oppose the institutionalized hostility towards images? Is it something that forced him to define his intentions with greater precision?

LT His conflict with the Inquisition might have caused his images to become more intense, but I certainly don't think it had an influence on their content or ideological position. It's extremely difficult to achieve his level of pictorial content and form without adopting a particular pictorial ideology.

GB At the same time there were aspects of Counter-Reformation theological precepts that didn't pose a problem for El Greco. For example, the saints in his paintings are intercessors in the here-and-now, which was a role devised for them by the Counter-Reformation. The very notion that transcendental mysteries can have a physical presence is the message of Counter-Reformation theology, and I don't think he disputed this. One must also recognize that he was a successful painter, increasingly so over time. He reached an audience who saw a certain kind of piety in his paintings, which explains why there are twelve versions of some pictures. He painted them over and over again because there was a demand for them, and they sold. I think it was this particular shift that the Inquisition disapproved of, not the content itself.

LT But I am certain that this also didn't fit in with the times.

HDW In Budapest we also criticized Zurbarán because he produced commissioned works and because his art is devoid of spiritual content.

LT The question with Zurbarán is not whether he was a good painter. With him you get yet another stylization of the world. Stylization implies a kind of "abnormality", and yet ultimately it's about normality. Reality appears static and petrified, so that the standpoint becomes extremely inflexible. The simplification achieves a different kind of pietistic quality. This is of course not true of all Zurbarán's paintings, we were talking mainly about *Saint Andrew*, where we found that some things were not really consistent or thought through. It is probably not one of his best paintings.

GB It's also interesting that El Greco was more successful in the religious circles in Toledo than with King Philip II of Spain, although it was his dream to be a court painter in Madrid. He painted the *Theban Legion* [*The Martyrdom of Saint Maurice*] as an example of his art – a magnificent painting that can be seen in the Escorial – but Philip wasn't convinced. Philip had cultivated tastes as a collector – he owned works by Titian, Velázquez, Pieter Bruegel the Elder and Hieronymus Bosch… but not by El Greco.

LT I believe that exotic appeal played a certain role in King Philip's collection, but it might also have been paranoia. There's an old anecdote, which may or may not be true, that Bruegel's engravings disclosed important bits of information, such as army positions, and that this was their main purpose. There's also the theory that Bruegel's work displays a certain underlying humanity, and while Philip had an aversion to him, he was also fascinated by Bruegel. With Bosch, I believe this was very different and we probably completely misunderstand his work today as well. We read his paintings as exotic because we've forgotten about sixty-five per cent

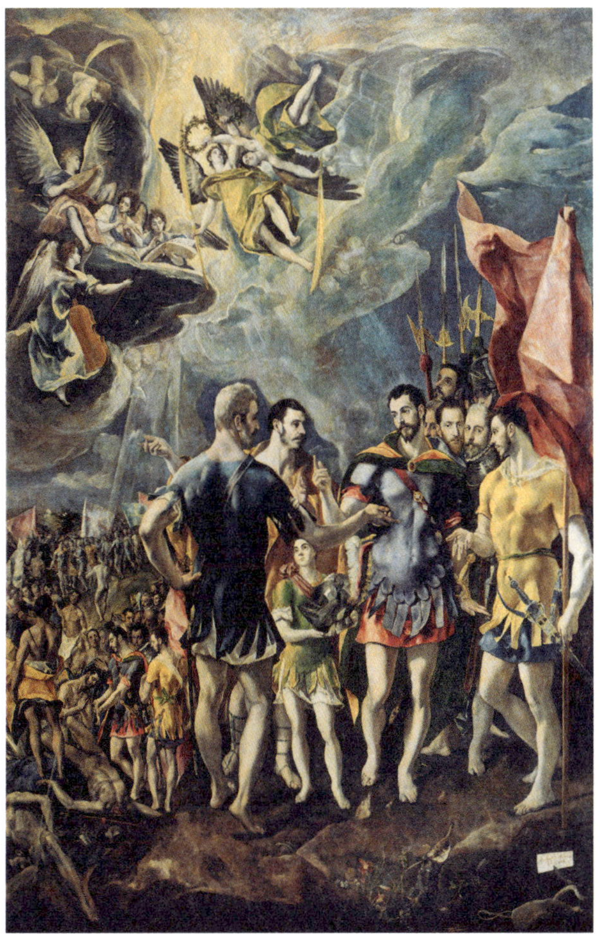

53 El Greco, *The Martyrdom of Saint Maurice*,
c. 1580–82
Oil on canvas, 445 × 294 cm
Monastery of San Lorenzo de El Escorial, Madrid,
INV. 10014707

of the iconography so cannot decipher their iconographical meaning. As a result, we've re-christened them as Surrealist art, although it has absolutely nothing to do with that. Everything in these paintings used to be explicable. But I do think that Philip's fascination with Flemish painting was spurred on by its difference to the works of Zurbarán, El Greco and other Spanish painters whose works have this sense of darkness and are very serious. When you come across these paintings in a collection like the Städel Museum in Frankfurt am Main, you can see their great darkness from far away in contrast to the simplification of the Flemish paintings. Philip probably preferred the playfulness of Bruegel, and perhaps what he may have understood as frivolity.

 Could it be that Bruegel was conveying a new kind of humanity?

LT It has been claimed, but whether it's really the case is another matter. The figures in his paintings are small and subordinate to the landscape. He had patrons and travelled to Italy, but was unimpressed by the Renaissance. Only the landscape, specifically the Alps, had an impact on him – a landscape that doesn't exist in our country. He adopted this landscape and "miniaturized" all the people. He first painted them naked and didn't dress them until later additional layers were applied. For him, people weren't the centre of the world. It was a very defined attitude, quite different from that of the Renaissance. With Bruegel there is an almost journalistic anachronism, where language is incorporated into the image, and this language concerns religion. With El Greco, there's a sense of silence and awe. And with Bosch, the storytelling and narration are finer, and at the same time the narrative is handled like a story, or rather a series of stories.

GB Patinir is another painter who figured prominently in Philip's collection and is interesting because he distanced himself from direct interaction with figures and events, and wasn't concerned with the plausibility of their movements. His works are like a panoramic bird's-eye overview, which is fascinating because Patinir is on the verge of discovering a new notion of landscape – what's referred to in German as the "Weltlandschaft" [world landscape]. This totality of nature is evoked via his use of a curved horizon, which is not dominated by figures or sacred events. With El Greco, there is still a confrontational stance.

LT This could actually be a reason why King Philip was drawn more to the Flemish landscapes. These were landscapes that never really existed – almost all of them were assembled from separate elements.

GB Added to that, El Greco's paintings have a very specific temperature. There is always a sort of "cold heat" that leaves viewers little room, and perhaps this exposure to it was unpleasant?

LT Even today, there is a degree of ugliness to be discovered in El Greco's paintings – like in his very fine portrait of the cardinal Niño de Guevara. He's painted quite violently and harshly, in scarlet red, and has the sharpness of glass and an aggressiveness. That might have been another reason why El Greco wasn't popular at the Spanish court. The King was well known for his paranoia, which is why he had the Escorial built in the middle of nowhere – a self-contained architecture that turns in on itself

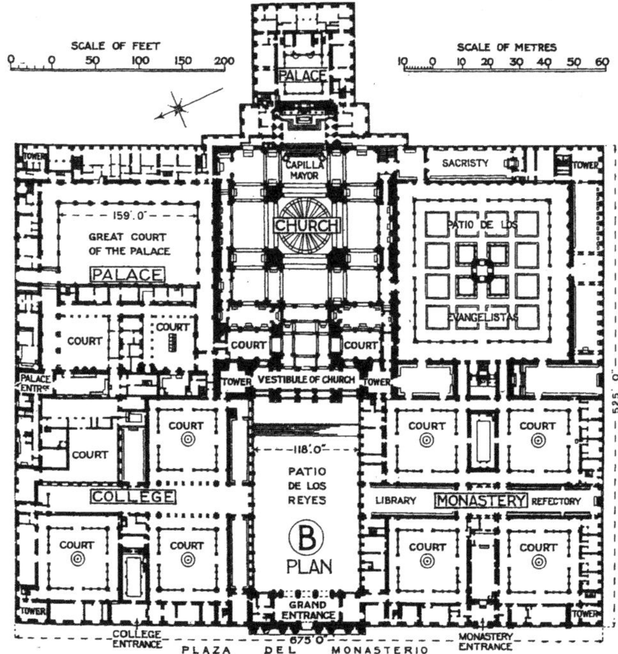

54 Floor plan of El Escorial, Madrid,
designed by Juan Bautista de Toledo in 1563

and completely encloses a person's body. The outside is kept completely separate from the inside and nothing, aside from maybe some light, is let in from the outside world. So this kind of painting was probably the last thing he wanted to see.

GB The Escorial as a self-contained structure fuses the idea of state and church through the floor plan of an imperial palace and monastery – it is about governance and religion at the same time.

LT I first understood this in purely visual terms based on its architectural layout. The entrance gate leads you first to the private area of the King's, then the Queen's, quarters. The third room you see is the King's bedroom with a small glazed window, and then the official area, where the banquets took place and guests were officially received via their own entrance. Then there is Philip's walkway, which is completely covered because he was always afraid of being murdered, so it's not actually set outside, but indoors with a view on to the outside. When you come to the other wing you see the same symmetry in the Queen's bedroom, which also has a small glazed window. Through a very big corridor you arrive at the basilica where you see the staircase opposite the sacristy, and behind the sacristy two glittering windows. That's where I became aware of this idea of a global power on which the sun never sets. You encounter it all at once – power, faith, paranoia, and the closeness of God – all concentrated in a single structure. There's also an anecdote that King Philip II had his favourite monkeys (whom Bruegel painted in chains for the port of Antwerp) burnt for fun. The juxtaposition of fetish, power and paranoia was developed into a system that unfolded from the inside out. This makes you understand why Velázquez's creativity was destroyed when he carried out various commissions at the Spanish court.

HDW How relevant is fetishism to current painting practice?

LT I think the act of fetishizing happens on its own. A fetish is an object that has pornographic significance and, at the same time, is something that you make use of, so to speak, and don't rediscover. It's about an attitude towards an object.

GB Can we clarify "fetishism" in relation to painting? Could it be said that fetishism is concerned with the fact that images, in some way, practise illusionism? In other words, fetishism comes into play when an image denies that it is an image and turns itself into a thing, an object or content – a naked body or a still life, for example. Is that the point of fetishism?

LT I think that, above all, you arrive at a fetish when the image is no longer part of an understatement. You can't compare it to kitsch, but it's about surrendering to a particular naturalism and bypassing reality. Not in the sense that it realizes a trauma, but that it becomes reified. At the same time, this "reification" makes the image reassuring so then reality actually turns into an object of utility. It doesn't remain new or interesting for long. It's no longer a mirroring, just an imitation of the object, and the experience of this imitation harbours the fetishizing. And here is when it separates once more into an abstraction of the object.

HDW Could it be said that the degree of fetishism contained in a painting is related to the amount of control that the painter wishes to maintain over the work?

LT I think it's comparable to compulsive collectors who collect only a particular kind of spoon or stamp, for example. It involves quantity. Everyone collects something and the collection always has to be complete, so the aim is to possess all of an object. That's a kind of fetishism and here it's exhibited very strongly. In a way, it's not so much a case of administering something, but of holding on to and grasping it.

GB A very nice example of this type of fetishism is the Barnes Collection in Philadelphia. Barnes's second passion is installed among the paintings from the collection – door and cupboard fittings, locks and hinges. The only possible way to present these objects and this compulsiveness is together with the paintings – that's a modern "collector's paranoia".

LT I agree. Fetishizing exists in Bruegel in the same way – perhaps more intensely than in El Greco because everything can be captured in more concrete terms. This must have been very important to Philip because of the reassuring effect that this idea that everything can be captured has. It also includes the bird's-eye landscapes and panoramas that take on an interesting significance in this context.

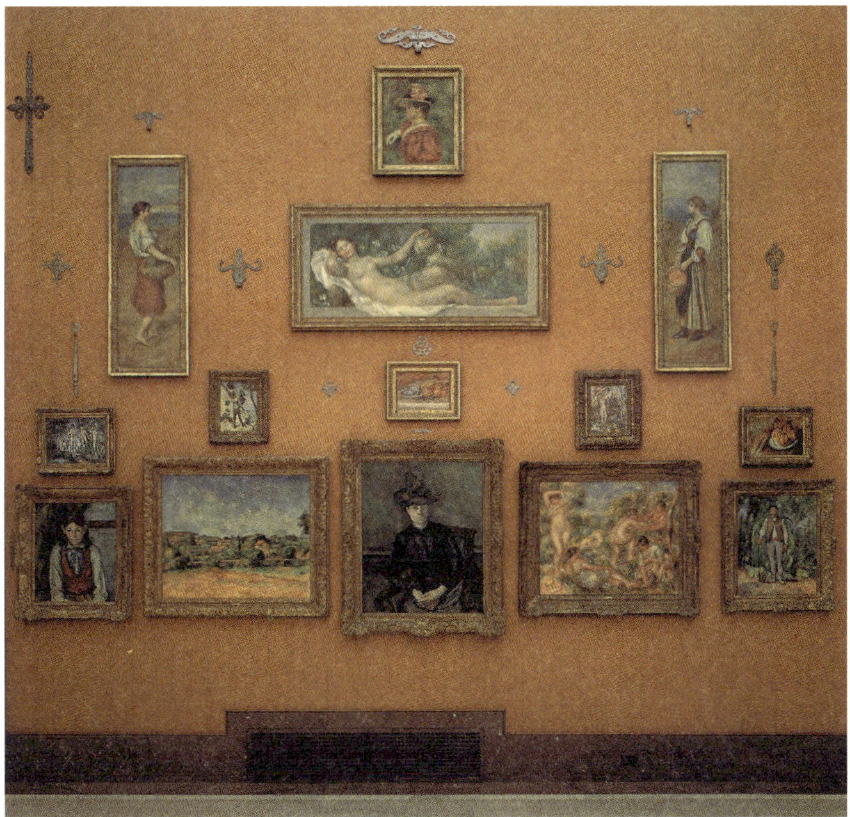

55 Main room of The Barnes Foundation, Philadelphia

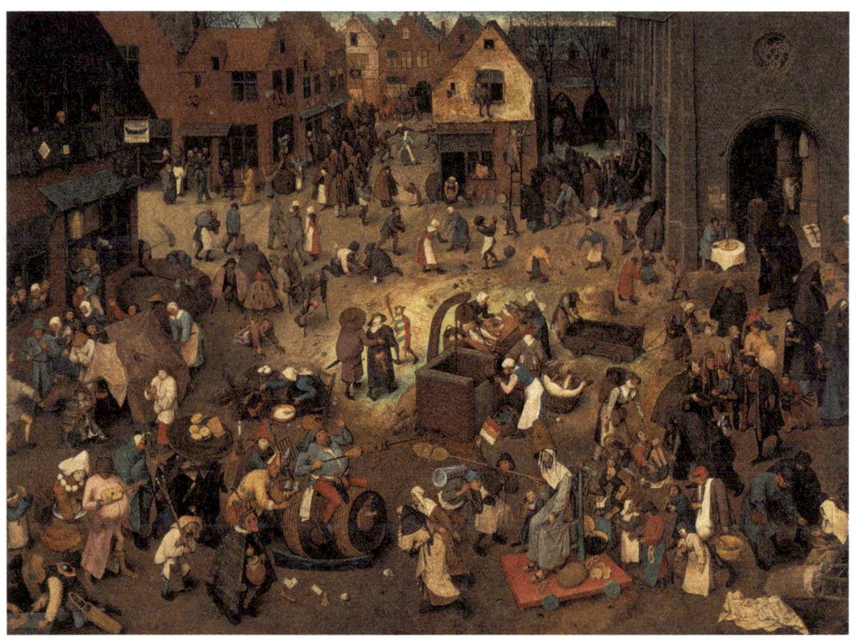

<u>56</u> Pieter Bruegel, *The Battle between Carnival and Lent*, 1559
Oil on panel, 118 × 164.5 cm
Kunsthistorisches Museum, Vienna, Gemäldegalerie, inv. 1016

GB Later, Foucault's notion of surveillance addressed this same issue.

LT Yes, and at the same time the idea of a voyeuristic approach to the object is born. A voyeurism that persists right down to the last detail and perceives the slightest change in the object that is to be collected. The collecting aspect is an important feature of this approach.

GB In order to define this more clearly, also in relation to Velázquez, could it be said that a painter wanting to avoid fetishism can do so through imprecision? Imprecision automatically guarantees that the conditions of representation remain part of the representation of the object. If I blur something when I paint it, then this is a fact. This is well demonstrated in Velázquez's work, which very often has, or retains, this aspect of imprecision.

LT This started when Velázquez increased the pace of his painting following Rubens' six-month stay at the Spanish court. However, the speed with which he applies paint never becomes fetishized, as for example in the paintings by Frans Hals. Velázquez applied the paint to the canvas in "doses", and as a counterpart to the objects, which are almost fixed. So

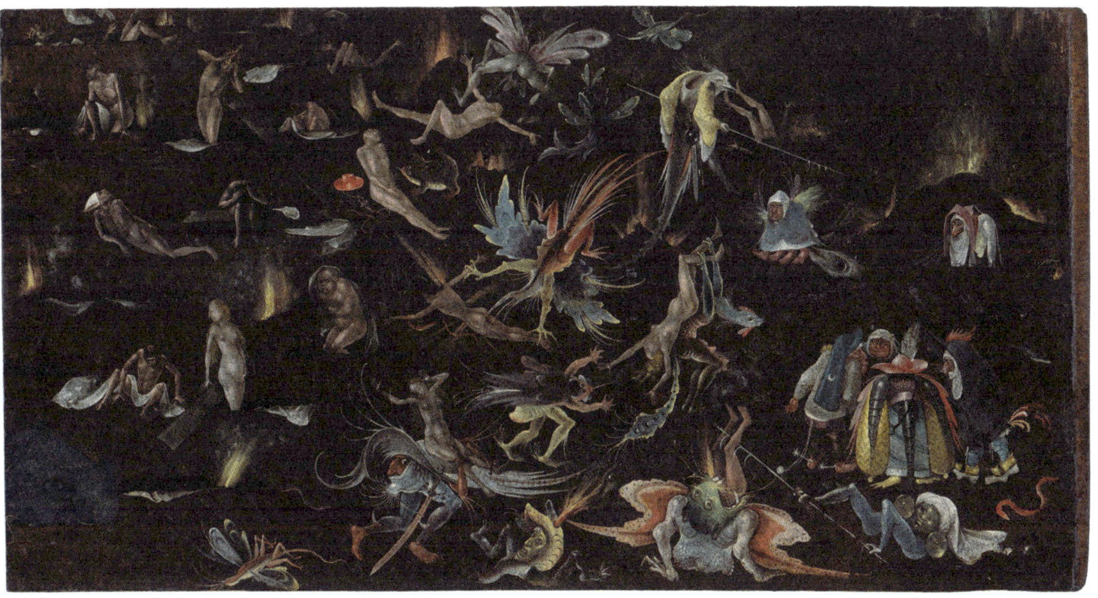

57 HIERONYMUS BOSCH (WORKSHOP OR FOLLOWER OF), *Fragment of a Last Judgement*, *c.* 1515–20
Oil on panel, 59.5 × 112.9 cm
Bayerische Staatsgemäldesammlungen, Alte Pinakothek, Munich, INV. 5752

you get an explosive precision and sharp focus, which, simultaneously, is intensified by the imprecision. He accomplished that entirely through his brushstroke. He played on this lack of clarity and was one of the first to do so with incredible consistency and rationale. Firstly, he dispenses with modeling through this kind of brushstroke, while his painted line can be both a contour and a shade at the same time. It's a line that isn't painted, but only implied – a kind of invisibility. Exactness, speed and the idea of timing and precision all originate with Velázquez.

HDW This is very interesting because, as we mentioned in Budapest, your knowledge is derived from practice. You always make new connections, for example here you align speed with simplification.

LT A certain kind of "fetishizing" can be found in Clyfford Still's painting too. When you see one of his paintings reproduced in a book, it looks accidental, but it's a fairly premeditated "accident". When I see the paintings in real life, they're not convincing because the "accident" is so incredibly stylized and transformed into art that it doesn't really hold up in that format.

Of course there is a lot of talk about Clyfford Still's resistance, how he did not want to belong to Abstract Expressionism, and how he remained this separate figure. However, to me, someone like Barnett Newman is much more honest. Or an early painting by Andy Warhol, which is painted in a kind of *dégoût*, is more efficient because the fluency is subverted by the material. And it becomes a style, which of course is deadly. By that I mean that if a personal touch is developed into a style, then it loses all intensity. The act itself is fetishized and obstructs the image.

HDW The moment that style enters is also the moment at which the risk implied in painting disappears, isn't it?

GB Exactly.

LT Each time you begin a painting, even though you know exactly how to start, there's a risk and anxiety. This is what I always experience, especially in the initial stage. When I've done the drawing and start painting, it's like I don't know what to do…

HDW And that's necessary?

LT It's a necessity. I introduce a certain system, which has naturally increased over the years. Experience plays a part, but first of all you need to get lost. And then, somehow, the picture always comes together – that is, if it's successful. For me, it's always a minor miracle when this happens. And then the pleasure in painting begins.

GB That means that creativity is connected with not knowing. If you know what a picture should look like, then the picture is possible, but perhaps not interesting.

LT Not necessarily. I think that each picture is a challenge that you impose on yourself. The final result will always look different. However you structure it, during the process of painting, many details that you've seen in your mind's eye become clear as well as the problems associated with these details. Decisions are very important and, when it comes to the physical act of painting, pretty much momentary – that's the imprecise precision of the thing. This is what constantly amazes me and that's why it's always a pleasure to paint – otherwise it would be deadly boring and I would be producing some kind of illustration.

hdw Is that also the reason why this moment cannot be grasped in theoretical terms?

lt Yes, theory is concerned with categorization and today there are no more "-isms". A good example of this was a panel to which I was invited at the Hayward Gallery in 2007 in connection with the exhibition *The Painting of Modern Life* – a title derived from Baudelaire. I was the only artist among academics. As part of the panel, Hal Foster spoke about people he knew, like Richard Artschwager. It was fine up until the 1970s, but there was hardly any of the really new stuff, except maybe a bit of Johannes Kahrs because the work had something to do with digitized images. And I said: "Listen, first of all you can't make that judgement because your judgement goes back to Walter Benjamin's old discussion about the mechanical reproduction of works of art, and that's just not an issue any more in contemporary art. It's become a mere tool. To reduce all that to a single point is a big denial of understatement. And to go for Johannes Kahrs, whether you like him or not – and I do like him – that's the easy way out. It's purely formal, then, it's about pushing for the idea of analogy and a picture's field of association." For me, the power of painting is something quite different. Foster understands and talks about the background and the referential scope of paintings, but he doesn't talk about what he sees in a painting. These theorists have withdrawn into institutionalized art theory.

gb There is a latent iconoclasm among theorists and art historians. By treating images in "scientific" terms they seek to destroy the reality of the image. They are breaking the image down into component parts that can be mastered, controlled, analysed and made part of a discourse. The image is made comprehensible in terms of abstract notions, whereas what happens in it obviously doesn't take the form of abstract notions, which is the only reason it's interesting. Otherwise I could replace the image with, or translate it into, abstract notions.

lt And then there would be no need to visualize it. The point here is that understatement is important, and that the multi-layered nature of paintings has very little in common with language. It actually has very little to do with language. That's why for me the notion of speechlessness is important in relation to the condition of painting, and why it is very difficult, not to say ridiculous, to speak about paintings. You can talk about everything referentially, but you talk it to death.

GB We're dealing with two very important questions here. First, what is an adequate way to talk about images? And second, how does the form of knowledge differ from the form of doing, of painting? Taking the first issue, I think that an adequate way of talking about images is to avoid saying what they are, and instead to say how they work. If I describe the "close reading" conditions within which an image works, then I don't take possession of it by means of an abstract notion. Instead, I give viewers a clue as to how they should look at it. For me, that is the form of knowledge that's meaningful for art-historical practice. Of course, there are certain facts one ought to know and in which there is no harm – for example, some biographical details about King Philip II of Spain. However, the heart of our activity when addressing images should be to determine the way in which the image works, and to draw attention to the role of the eye as the highest form of approach.

HDW I agree. I ought to say that I did research on Marcel Duchamp for five years, went through all his notes and called them a "diary of a traveller". There really are things that one can find out, discover or decode. But that should not be the end of it. It's like visiting a country. You take with you a particular accumulation of experiences that you can verbalize and there is nothing wrong with that. But those experiences are not identical to the country. In fact, someone else could have different experiences, perhaps even in the same places, and could make the same discoveries, but the ultimate goal is experience, an enrichment of some kind.

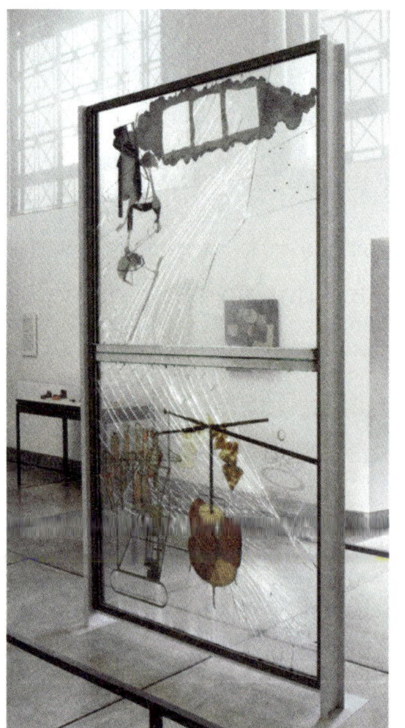

LT What was your experience with Duchamp?

HDW My experience with Duchamp was very complex. In 1911–12 he started out on a radical project that he never finished. When I was asked to write an article on Duchamp's early work, I replied that this doesn't apply to him because he can't be divided up into periods. His project really began in 1915 with *The Large Glass* and was ongoing up until his death, or in fact even after his death, in 1969 when *Étant donnés* was made public. In the end, I said

<u>58</u> MARCEL DUCHAMP, *The Bride Stripped Bare by Her Bachelors, Even (The Large Glass)*, 1915–23
Oil, varnish, lead foil, lead wire and dust on two glass panels, 277.5 × 177.8 × 8.6 cm
Philadelphia Museum of Art, Philadelphia, INV. 1952-98-1

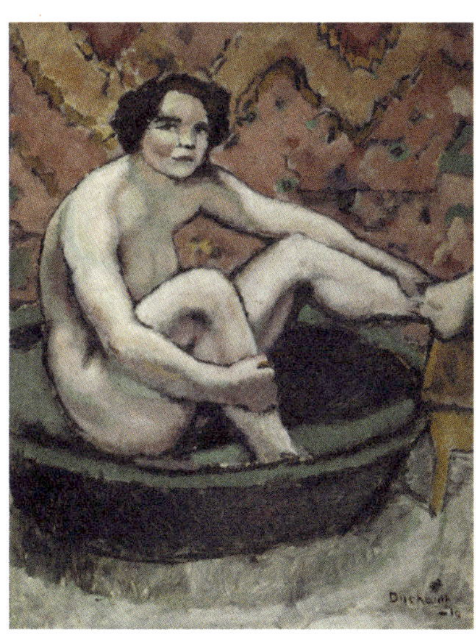

59 MARCEL DUCHAMP, *Nude Seated in a Bathtub*, 1910
Oil on canvas, 92.1 × 73.1 cm
The Art Institute of Chicago, Chicago, INV. 1974.227

that if you observe his work and the oil paintings that preceded *The Large Glass*, such as *Nude Seated in a Bathtub*, you can already find there the idea of voyeurism and all that stuff about violence, bachelors and the bride.

LT And the luxury. I think that Duchamp is part of the *haute bourgeoisie* as Peter Schjeldahl, a New York-based Vietnam veteran and art critic, once wrote – something that no European would be allowed to say about Duchamp. He is an artist I value greatly because he addressed the whole idea of aesthetic content, I think due to his own voyeurism and sexual drive. The content is extremely pornographic. And pornography is understood here not so much in the sense of the Marquis de Sade, that you ought to find a hole into which you disappear, because coming from the *haute bourgeoisie* it's very close to the aristocracy – but that it has a lot to do with play. Play that doesn't exclude reality or the idea of designating and touching things. For me, there's a medieval aspect to Duchamp. I don't really perceive him as avant-garde, but as a medieval master in the modern age. When I stood in front of *The Large Glass* in Philadelphia, it immediately struck me as similar to Hieronymus Bosch. The difference being that with Duchamp the iconography is interpreted psychologically, whereas with Bosch it lies in the domain of an independent iconography. The game, the dilettantism, is played out to the end, and the charlatan emerges. This is combined with voyeurism and is, for me, an obviously strategic move. That's why Schjeldahl made me smile when he said: "[Duchamp] is an artist from the *haute bourgeoisie*, from the upper class, who started with a game and ended with a game." This is true, and clearly describes the theoretical misunderstanding we're experiencing now because the idea of metaphysics has been eliminated. The designation of things … The minute we start to talk about fetishizing, that's when we arrive at its endpoint. Duchamp is the biggest fetishist I can think of in the whole of art history, but he did it very cleverly and without actually doing very much. He also did it at just the right time – he looked very closely at history, saw the opportunity, and grasped it. Not like Picasso, who did so with variety and quantity, but by way of reduction, taken to its natural conclusion with the *Boîte-en-valise*, that little suitcase with the portable artworks. That was a very European last ploy, which had incredible consequences after the war. I think that has to do with him sensing that Europe's power waned, in the field of culture as well. Before the First World War, which America joined very late, it wasn't a world or military power. But following it, and certainly after World War II, America became a world power.

<u>HDW</u> It's actually very clear that the relationship with America was extremely important to him.

<u>LT</u> Yes, because, like Bruno Bettelheim, he played the psychoanalytical card. This angle was later used by theorists to explain Mike Kelley's work, which is wrong because it's severely limiting to view his art through this lens only. It's also too severe a limitation for Duchamp, although he did make use of it. Like Bettelheim he was accepted into American society, in which psychoanalysis was accepted as a science much earlier than in Europe. This was a complete misunderstanding that Duchamp exploited as a myth that he himself played out in public.

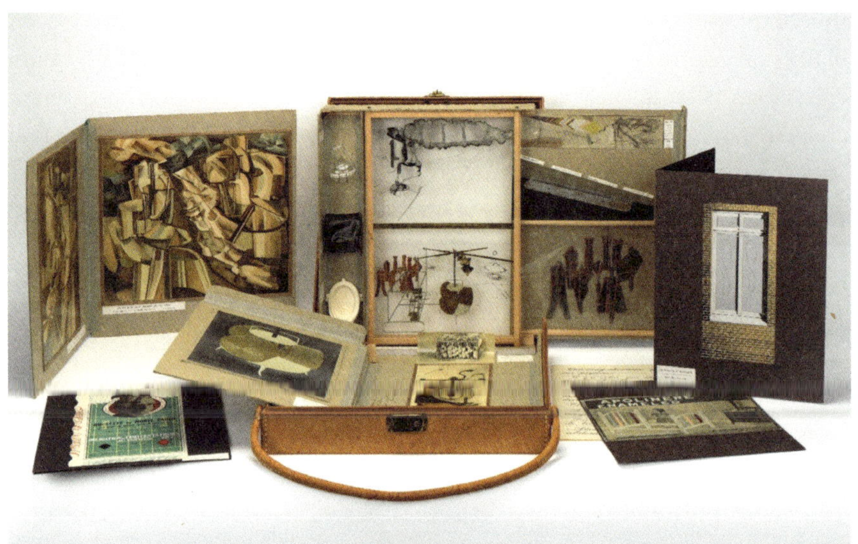

<u>60</u> MARCEL DUCHAMP, *Boîte-en-valise*, 1935–41
Leather valise containing miniature replicas, photographs, colour reproductions of works by Duchamp, and one "original drawing" on large glass, collotype on celluloid, 40.7 × 38.1 × 10.2 cm
The Museum of Modern Art, New York, INV. 67.1943.A–RRR

HDW I understand what you mean, but there's another level here. Many people think he was a chess-player, a strategist, someone who planned everything very precisely. That's true up to a point, but by the end of 1911, there's a clear break and a departure in his oeuvre that has to do with the male and female principle, and the fact that they will never understand each other. It makes no difference if it's a romantic love story or the rape of a girl in a village in the south of France – no communion is possible. He enlarged on this concept right up to the end. Everything Duchamp did can be derived from it – ready-mades, *rotoreliefs*, and everything you have mentioned. In addition, there is a social level. How should a clever artist behave in order to survive and to be able to carry through this project to completion, in the most radical fashion and without compromise? That's the story of Duchamp, who's always absent, but then always there again. Who does the exhibition for the Surrealists but disappears on the evening of the opening. Now that's fetishism. In my experience the two are inseparable, you can't understand one without the other.

LT It's clearly an obsessive approach to his own oeuvre. Like I said, it mainly has to do with his origins. He was very educated. And an educated man has a certain kind of perversion within himself, because that's the only thing that remains. In that sense for me it's logical. There's an encyclopaedic process that becomes a psychological one via the body, and then there's mutilation, another fascinating theme in Duchamp's work, above all in the *Étant donnés*. There is the idea of nearness and farness through the keyhole and, at the same time, this voyeurism.

GB To summarize, it can be said that Duchamp is an author who registers a rift in the world. The world has two parts that can never be altered, and this produces voyeurism. Actually, without making too much of a point out of it, it's the condition of impotence, isn't it? However, I still have a couple of questions. Why does this have to be lived in the form of an artistic existence? Why wouldn't it be better to breed sheep in Australia? I mean, if I register a condition of impotence, why must it be celebrated for an entire lifetime? And, finally, why was it so infectious? Duchamp is the most important academy of the twentieth century.

LT Because it corresponded to a certain kind of bourgeois mentality – the *ur*-bourgeois mentality, the misunderstanding of the avant-garde. It's also the misunderstanding of luxury. Luxurious surroundings give you time to think something up, but at the same time produce boredom. Boredom results in a certain kind of perception of reality, which intensifies it and, above all, embraces objects and fetishes. Which leads me back to the fetish, because it was infectious, bold and a kind of insult. It was perceived as a statement that addresses the spectator physically. That carries on right up to Jeff Koons, but strangely enough, it has little to do with Warhol. I think Warhol was more closely related to another great voyeur, Salvador Dalí. It was also a provocation. If you compare Russian Constructivism with what happened in the West, Russian Constructivism believed in change and the provocation was aimed at change. Provocation in this context was not aimed at change but at a circle of initiated.

HDW I think one perspective that was important to many artists of that era, around 1910–12, was that if an artistic project was not all-encompassing, then it wasn't worthwhile. Stéphane Mallarmé worked out something extremely radical and avant-garde – the huge, all-encompassing oeuvre. That's a goal that Duchamp clearly had, as did Courbet.

LT Sure, but given the rudeness of *L'Origine du Monde*, Courbet is perhaps even bolder than Duchamp. When I saw the Courbet exhibition in Paris in 2007 at the Musée d'Orsay, I was amazed at the open aggression of those paintings. Not how they're painted, but what they signify. There is genuine aggression in both the landscapes and the portraits. For the first time, spectators' very reality was attacked. With Duchamp it's different because he's almost never there. Courbet is always present. That's probably the main difference between the two even though their point of departure is quite similar. In both cases there is a relationship with reality that each has embraced individually, and a particular status, which is enacted with certain knowledge. No doubt about it. It's very French.

HDW The relationship between Courbet and Duchamp fascinates me because I don't think that any other painter got on Duchamp's nerves as much as Courbet. I've seen the original documents of interviews with Duchamp. The French journalist and critic Alain Jouffroy interviewed Duchamp and

61 GUSTAVE COURBET, *L'Origine du Monde*, 1866
Oil on canvas, 46.3 × 55.4 cm
Musée d'Orsay, Paris, INV. RF 1995 10

Duchamp edited the entire piece because he had such a flawless command of language. He was a talented editor – he didn't change the content, but he improved the text. There are only two passages in these interviews that Duchamp crossed out and both are passages in which he discusses Courbet.

LT What did he write?

HDW That he finds Courbet a dreadful artist. For him, Courbet represents the point where everything went wrong because earlier painting had always been a matter for specialists and connoisseurs, people who had acquired an in-depth knowledge of art over a long period of time. For Duchamp, Courbet is the point at which art is opened up to everyone and is no longer intellectually demanding. What actually interests me about Courbet are the high points when he does these paradigmatically important things like *The Artist's Studio*, which is exactly what Duchamp did a century later in *Boîte-en-valise*. He assembled his work and presented the oeuvre as an oeuvre. Both Courbet and Duchamp have a similar approach to the oeuvre, controlling it vis-à-vis the spectator, with the artist as a demigod at the centre of the painting. With Courbet, the artist is presented in the act of painting in his studio. In other words, the painter is painting what the

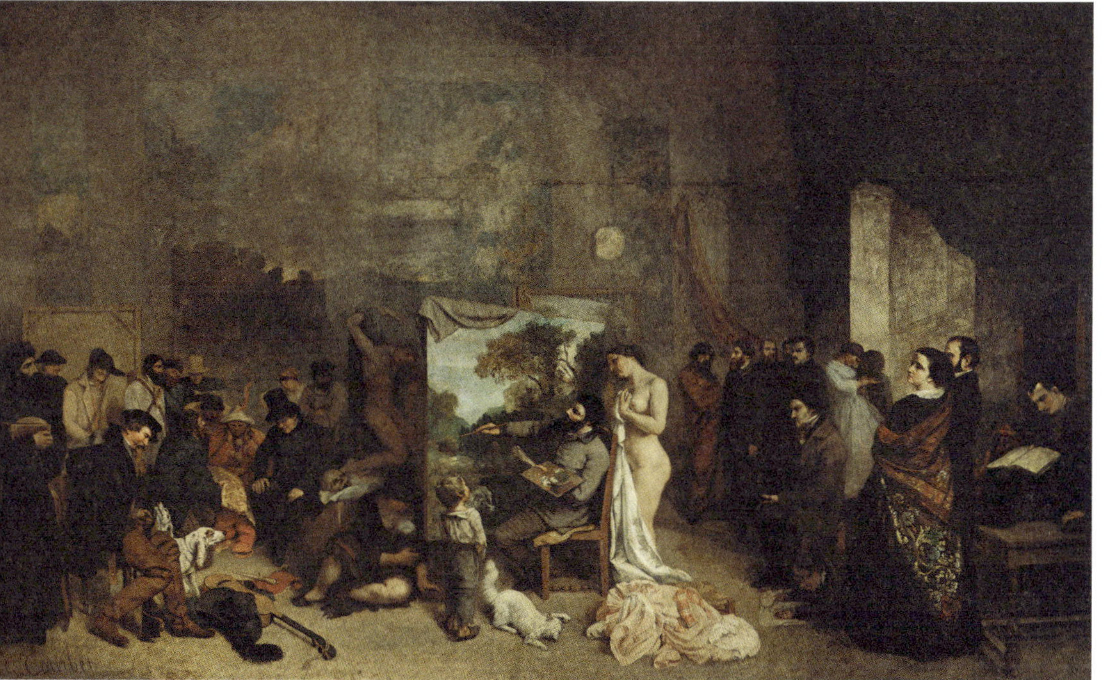

62 GUSTAVE COURBET, *The Artist's Studio, a Real Allegory Summing up Seven Years of My Artistic and Moral Life, c.* 1854–55
Oil on canvas, 361 × 598 cm
Musée d'Orsay, Paris, INV. RF 2257

painter paints. And the spectator is looking at spectators looking at the painter. It's a circular narrative. Duchamp's things are circular too. This is how they're similar, but also where they part company completely.

LT It's certainly interesting that Duchamp made that remark about art for the initiated and about the proletariat's erosion of the intellect. This sensitivity to position and context was born with Courbet and has carried on, via artists like Duchamp, to the present. The biggest difference between contemporary and historical art is that now the artist controls the discourse around his or her work and how it is contextualized, and this is expected. The artist being part of the painting, being in the work, basically constitutes what contemporary art is. Also with the renewed validity of documents, it's always a referential world that comes into play. What fascinates me is that we now find our bearings in an almost virtual realm, and that's the reason for my series on the Jesuits in which the idea of education opens up a spiritual level and an ambiguity between power, faith and fools (but that's only an ephemeral understanding). This continues into the series in which everything is completely bereft of content, like Disney World, in a place where you're deprived of your imagination, where everything is instrumentalized and accommodated. The idea of quality no longer plays a part, instead the hits produced by a search engine determine what's important or not. Voyeurism has become exponential, and you become part of your own system, completely interactive and pornographic right to the end. You become your own pornographer. Duchamp fits in with this perfectly, while Courbet was the starting-point.

Now, if we return to the relationship between painting and knowledge, we talked about the idea of delay and about the various kinds of intelligence that should be kept separate. What I say about my paintings I only say because *they* don't say anything, they're completely silent.

GB There's an interesting issue here – we're accustomed to equate knowledge with what can be expressed in terms of language. But there's an important kind of knowledge that will never become language, and if we didn't have this knowledge we wouldn't be able to live. This is our motor functions, which determine the way we look at each other, at objects, how we use our hands, but which we are not or rarely aware of. We point when we gesticulate, yet I'm not conscious of making these gestures, unless I'm an actor perhaps, and a bad one at that. So there's a whole dimension of knowledge that's not linguistic in nature. I would like to make a special emphasis on this point because otherwise we leave knowledge in the hands of language, and knowledge is too important for that.

LT We've touched upon this before – if it were possible to reformulate everything in terms of verbal notions, then there would be scarcely any need to visualize it. However, the need to visualize will always exist, simply because we must have something to look at. Cognition is already there, already functioning, and via memory (even if inadequately, as a fragment) we experience something. This experience isn't merely an analogy or association, but also has to do with recall, and the idea of "approaching" an image in a physical way without actually grasping it.

HDW Is that connected with the fact that our education system revolves around cognitive intelligence?

GB Yes. That's the European tradition, of course – the reduction of *logos* to linguistic articulation. But, if you look more closely, in the manner of discursive individuals who rely on linguistic predications, we can look at how they monitor cognition through questions like "What does my proposition do correctly?" They then invoke evidential conviction, and have done so ever since Descartes – "What I say is evident." Under certain conditions it is evident, and because it's evident the proposition is correct. What's happening here? I invoke something I perceive intellectually as justification for something I say in linguistic terms. This means that if you want to put forward an argument, if you want to engage in a discourse, if you want to know something, you must make use of supporting elements that are apparent, are evident. The very category of "evidence" emphasizes this clearly. On the other hand – and we've actually been talking about this throughout our conversation without using the term – there is an evidence generated by images. There is the fascination that arises from the statement, "I see it like this and only like this, and I see it like this only here, and it can be experienced like this only in this place." This presents powerful optical evidence – that's what the image accomplishes. Conversely, images harbour an element of assurance, of acquisitive potential and, ultimately, of knowledge. It's just a completely different kind of knowledge based on non-verbal notions, on something seen.

HDW The sculptor Adolf von Hildebrand [1847–1921] had a wonderful theory that the image stores within itself certain impressions that we don't understand and that assert themselves as reality. Therefore, reality is not comprised of our surroundings, but is an act of understanding through the realization of an image.

GB I think it's important that images are capable of generating meanings and significance, and that they don't depend on reproducing pre-existing meanings. If images are powerful enough, then they generate meanings on their own.

LT Yes, and they evince painterly ambiguity and complexity because an image, especially if it's a painting, is so intricate that you can't remember it in its entirety. It can assert itself physically, can be measured, but that won't explain it. It is different when you go back to language, for example to reading fiction – then the image element suddenly increases – and is different in relation to reading history. So this concept exists in language too, which is why we have poetry.

GB And metaphors.

LT Metaphors and imagery. This concept has always existed, not just for mythological reasons, but in relation to catharsis. It's a discharge that takes place in an instant, during the act of looking. Or, as Rilke says in the *Duino Elegies*, when the spectator continues to see things that way. It's the idea that something else exists apart from language. Or a different kind of language and that's the image. However, the image can't be replaced by language, and language can't replace the image. This is an old understanding that goes back to various dialectics, from Catholicism to Calvinism, where it was fully developed. There it gains a crude ideological basis because it has to do with pleasure or non-pleasure, which involves the matter of guilt and invites complicity when looking at images. One becomes an accomplice when looking at images, because one realizes the images while looking at them – a complex and deeply physical point. The viewer has become a key to the image, but the anonymity of the viewer vis-à-vis the prominence of the image-maker – the artist, painter, photographer or whoever – is permissible. The spectator is, as with Rilke, in the dark.

GB Can I return to this point from another angle? The viewer as accomplice or perpetrator, the author as the born perpetrator, the producer. What role does the body – of the painter or photographer, of the person who produces something in the primary sense – actually play here? I find that interesting because it needs to be explained that there's another way of dealing with the world besides through knowledge or the contrast to knowledge.

Making is interesting because it brings into play a possibility that cannot be replaced by any other activity. Kant, who's certainly not known for having spoken on behalf of painters, made a fantastic formulation with, "I can understand a line only if I draw it." There, in an instance, you recognize that, ultimately, in drawing, in doing, in a bodily action, something is brought to light here and nowhere else. Let's examine this a bit. What actually happens when you're standing in front of the canvas, with something in mind and in your sight, when you know something, and you're painting? What actually happens there and then?

LT Well, when you make the first mark, it's either successful or unsuccessful, and you sense this. Kant was right – first of all you have to make the mark. It's important how much concentration goes into the mark, and the balance between how much intensity is needed to make it and how much you exclude your own person. You become a mediator – it's a means of conveyance and no more. When I'm painting I'm connected to the image. When I look at the speed with which the paint is mixed, it's never in a state of frenzy. I know exactly what I'm doing, but the manner and pace with which I paint can only be explained by the fact that I partly exclude myself. You have to empty yourself to make way for painting, otherwise it's not possible. When the gesture dominates – and this may be a bit of a problem with Clyfford Still – if it's exploited systematically, becomes stylized and cultivated, then you're left with nothing because you don't leave enough space to just experience painting. It's already become completely solidified. My personal experience is that I lose all sense of time, and no longer notice whether it's cold or warm. Everything disappears and I'm left with only the pure concentration on painting, on the act of painting, the dedication to making an image.

HDW How do you decide when a painting is done? Does it coincide with the point at which all this stops? Are there different phases?

LT It varies from artist to artist. My attention span is short, that's why I work at great speed, but with great concentration. The painting is finished when it discloses itself to me in a convincing manner. And when that happens I lose all interest in it. I haven't got a single painting of mine at home and would find it unbearable because, in my opinion, a really good painting is never finished. It's the viewer's role to finish a painting. You sense the possibility not only of leaving things out, but also of not painting. This brings me to an important point, because for me Picasso was always a very good technician. He's not a painter who moves me – he's completely cerebral, a great technician and academician. He could do almost anything, but there's nothing moving about it. But, he knew very well when to stop.

HDW And he always worked at great speed.

LT Yes, but he also painted a lot of rubbish.

GB The painting discloses itself – I think that's the crucial formulation. It reaches a conclusion and is then able to communicate, although not in words.

LT It communicates and then it's finished. We've talked about revelation, but it's also actually about how you as the "image-producer" reach a point at which the image becomes alien. That's why I've never believed in those tormented painters who equate images with their own bodies, who crawl into the painting and then kill themselves.

HDW Because, in the way you've described it, the image is independent.

LT Yes. I think you need a certain distance not only to look at paintings, but to paint them too.

HDW Are you talking about Edvard Munch's figures?

LT No. Munch was a great and very powerful painter with an almost stubborn way of painting. He's one of the few painters whose gestures, in the best

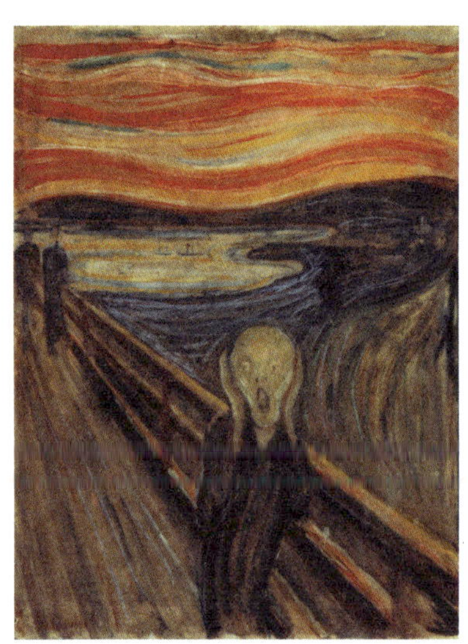

of his works, are impeccable. But he's also one of the few who went through this depression, yet painted a picture like *The Scream*, which is so to the point that it took its place in the age, whoosh!, instantaneously. This is why the exhibition in the Architektenhaus in Berlin in 2007 [*Edvard Munch: Behind the Scream*] was incredibly important – it offered a shock. With the *Frieze of Life* [1902] he was the first who actually viewed the whole thing as a *Gesamtkunstwerk*, gave it visual form and

63 EDVARD MUNCH, *The Scream*, 1893
Oil, tempera, pastel and crayon on cardboard, 91 × 73.5 cm
Nasjonalmuseet, Oslo, INV. NG.M.00939

exhibited it that way. Film was also important for Munch, as a way of comprehending images and the whole course of life in cinematographic terms.

HDW Let's return to Édouard Manet and his relationship to the bourgeois.

LT I think that, compared with Duchamp, the term "bourgeois" in connection with Manet is an exaggeration although it probably also stems from the *haute bourgeoisie*. His approach has more to do with flesh. There are carnivorous and cannibalistic aspects, and in fact he really did adopt a position like Velázquez, but in his own time, with the knowledge of his time and with a very specific, thoroughly worked-out scepticism. You can see it in the paintings, which are sometimes even better painted than Velázquez's. They have a greater depth and a hardening of contrasts. Manet also painted from photographs, which is evident. But he did something that others hadn't done before, and that's an intensification of contrasts without lapsing into kitsch like the Spaniards did. He partially cut the light from his paintings, so that *Olympia* is actually a whore and the black woman who enters the painting doesn't so much add a touch of the exotic as becomes part of the décor. Fleshiness is reduced to a minimum in this painting, yet it's incredibly physical. It has a brutality that we can already see in Caravaggio, but here it moves into infinity. It's also the first thing that you see. This is what

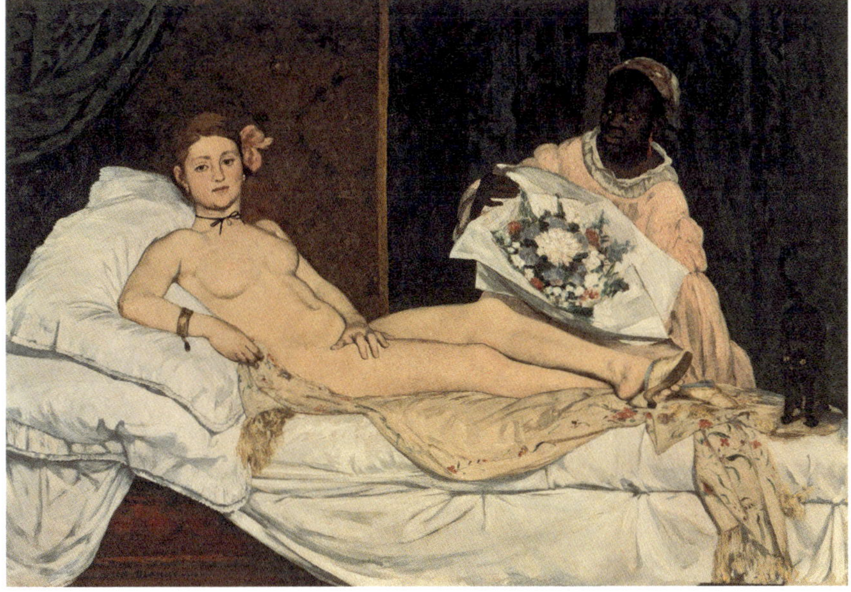

64 Édouard Manet, *Olympia*, 1863
Oil on canvas, 130.5 × 191 cm
Musée d'Orsay, Paris, inv. rf 644

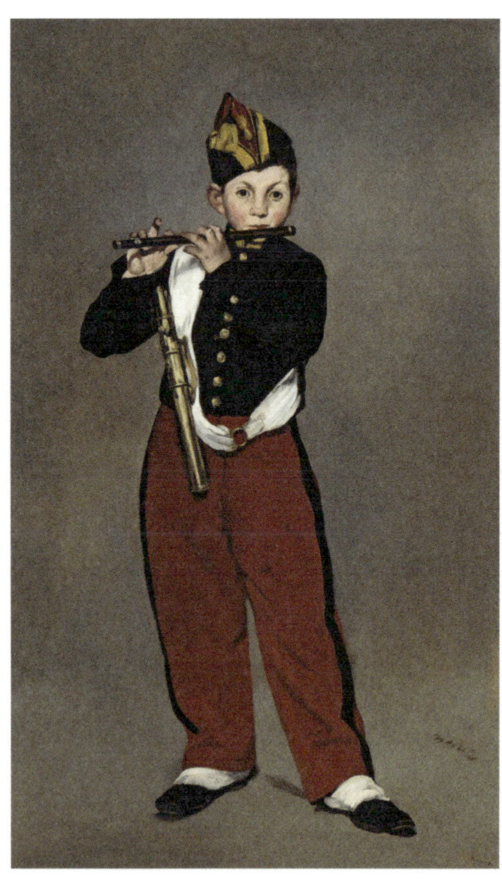

65 ÉDOUARD MANET, *The Fifer*, 1866
Oil on canvas, 160.5 × 97 cm
Musée d'Orsay, Paris, INV. RF 1992

66 ÉDOUARD MANET, *The Dead Toreador*, c. 1864
Oil on canvas, 75.9 × 153.3 cm
National Gallery of Art, Washington D.C., INV. 1942.9.40

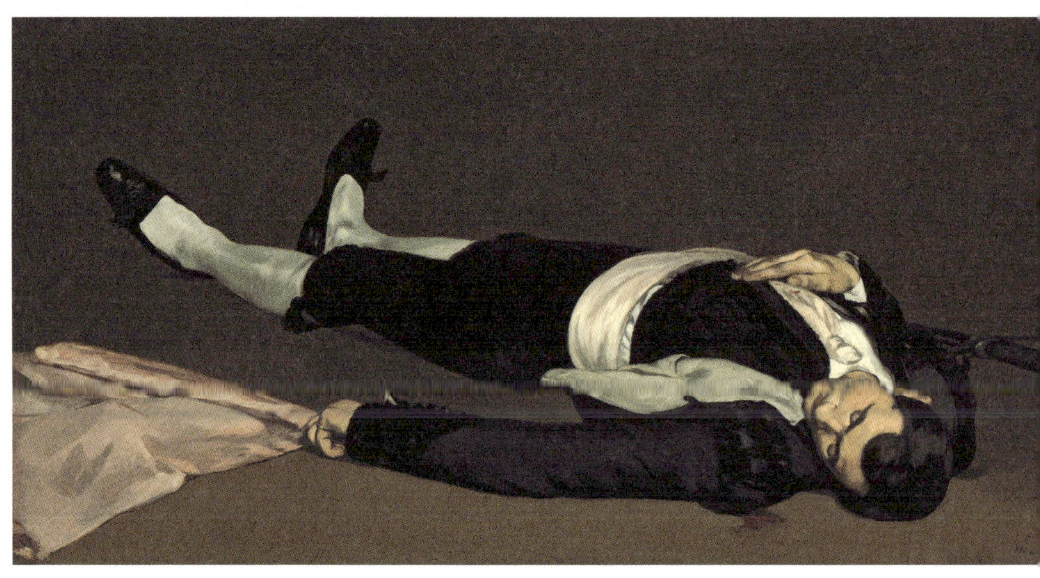

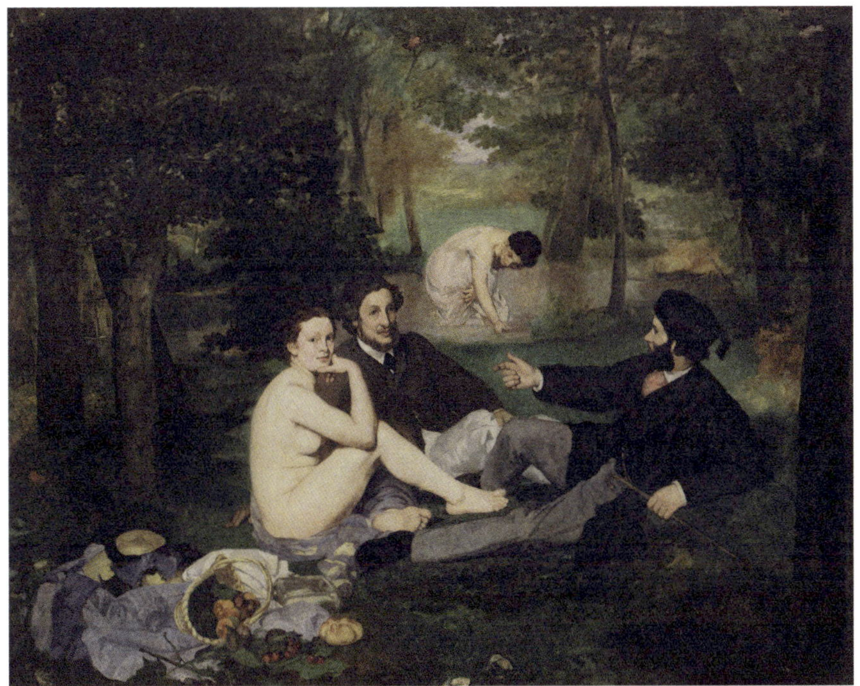

<u>67</u> Édouard Manet, *Le Déjeuner sur l'Herbe*, 1863
Oil on canvas, 207 × 265 cm
Musée d'Orsay, Paris, inv. rf 1668

has always fascinated me in Manet – a harshness and starkness, which Courbet also had, and that doesn't appear again in French painting after him. He invokes the great classic artists, but at the same time adopts an approach of eliminating the background by isolating the figures, like in *Le Joueur de fifre* [The Fifer], and by introducing violence, like in *The Dead Toreador*. He has this physicality that I find incredibly powerful.

GB Doesn't it interact with a counterweight that we might term as a "plane"? When I look at *Olympia*, the white robes or parts of the background, it's to a large extent plane that I see.

LT Of course he was also the first to disorientate the image in that way, almost through collage, so that *Le Déjeuner sur l'Herbe* was a shocking painting because it was bereft of depth. The area around the naked woman, is that foreground or background? It's not clear at all. Everything becomes décor but at the same time it isn't. It's basically an assembled painting.

What's the relationship between all these people in the painting? And what about the woman active in the background, the only one who looks out of the painting, or the two men who, almost separate from this woman, are somehow entangled in a kind of relationship? There are completely separate narratives that have absolutely nothing to do with each other. It all exists side by side. I think the word "separateness" is important for Manet – he separated something. The lighting appears first in his work, a lighting that comes close to over-exposure. That sparked an incredible scandal because the idea of beautifying, of aestheticizing, suddenly was no longer there. Pleasure was eliminated – it was plain flesh. Materiality was taken to the utmost brutality. I believe that was Manet's desire. Later, with the move to Impressionism, he actually asserted himself a little less and, in my opinion, became a little too frivolous.

HDW I would like to compare him with paintings by the German Romantic painter Caspar David Friedrich, who is one generation older. There's a total, all-encompassing engagement with the notion of nature in Friedrich's work that is completely missing in Manet. Manet's people are Parisians, plucked from very complicated social relationships and plonked down in this landscape. They have no relationship with nature.

GB The background setting could almost be wallpaper, couldn't it?

LT Yes, I believe Manet is a city painter. He comes from an urban environment and has nothing to do with nature. In *Le Déjeuner sur l'Herbe* the image becomes another form of deconstruction, as with El Greco, but involving an actual reality that is brutally thrown back at us.

GB This term "separateness" makes a lot of sense to me and also explains why the moment depicted in the painting can't be established. What is it made up of – a woman looks out, she is in a different time from the man pointing at her or the second man, and the woman at the back is in yet another time. None of them share the same time.

LT I reckon it was painted in various stages. If you look at *The Execution of Maximilian* [1867–69] – there was a great exhibition at MOMA that showed the series of five compositions depicting the execution together with other works and documents that showed their development – Manet painted the picture anew many times. He only had written or graphic accounts of the execution of Emperor Maximilian of Mexico to refer to. It must be

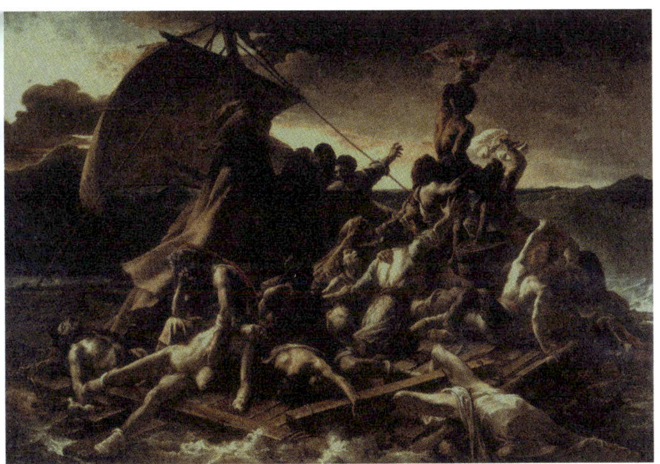

68 Théodore Géricault, *The Raft of the Medusa*, 1818–19
Oil on canvas, 491 × 716 cm
Musée du Louvre, Paris, inv. 4884

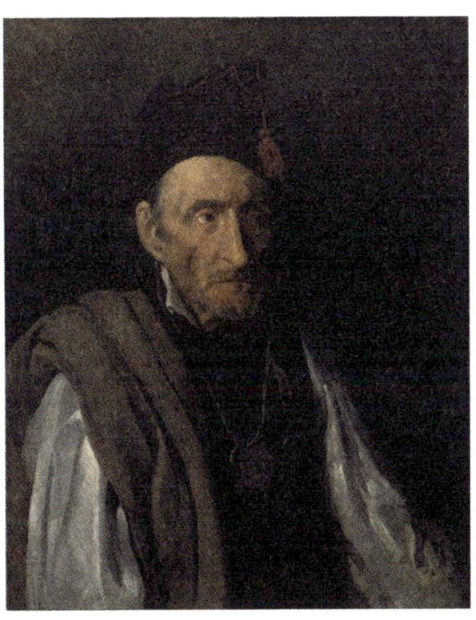

69 Théodore Géricault, *A Man Suffering from Delusions of Military Rank*, c. 1819–22
Oil on canvas, 81 × 65 cm
Oskar Reinhart Collection 'Am Römerholz' Winterthur, inv 1924.7

understood as a sequel to Théodore Géricault's *The Raft of the Medusa*, the unsuccessful masterpiece in which a figure derived from classical antiquity also looks out of the picture at the viewer. Here we have social content as well as a reference to a current event. Géricault made all these preliminary studies, which are actually better than the final painting, of body parts from the morgue. He had the idea of "doing research" and incorporating it into the painting by collaging. But when you compare these paintings with the madman he painted, it's a completely different world.

HDW For *The Execution of Maximilian,* Manet brought a squad of French infantry into his studio to pose for the picture, and had them do a drill for an entire afternoon, so he could understand how it worked.

LT But Manet also made use of documents and transformed them into something else. With him, reality becomes meta-reality. *The Fifer* is also interesting because it's a painting that has become completely silent. Everything is excluded and it is almost shadowless. The figure has a little shadow, but it's very small.

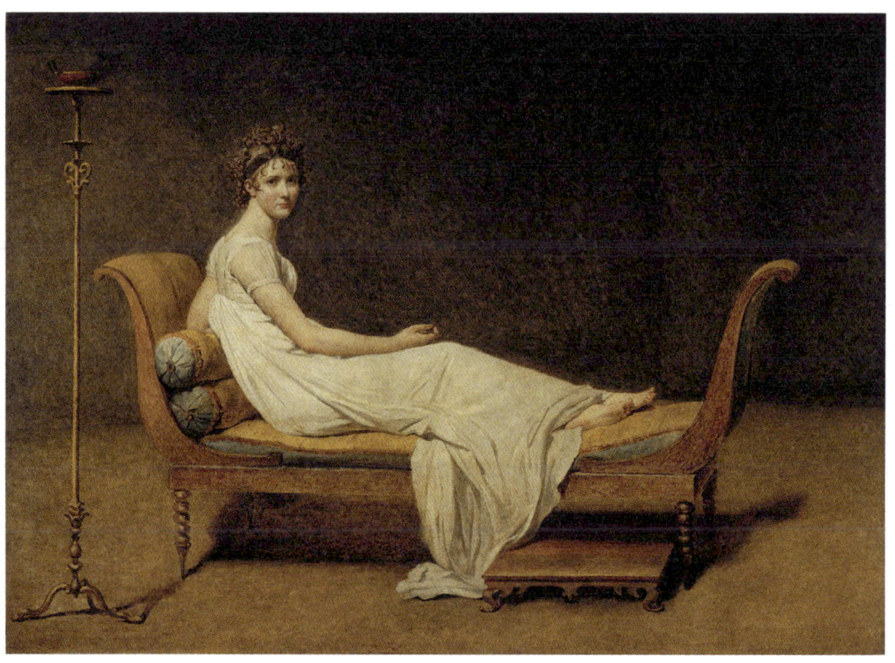

<u>70</u> Jacques-Louis David, *Madame Récamier*, 1800
Oil on canvas, 174 × 244 cm
Musée du Louvre, Paris, inv. 3708

<u>GB</u> There's something of that in Jacques-Louis David's *Madame Récamier*. The candlestick standing on the left has a small shadow that almost dissolves.

<u>LT</u> But *The Execution of Maximilian* later became an iconic image that was reproduced everywhere as a postcard motif. There is a play with the youth, the uniform, war, and the relative sizes, the trousers – it always intrigued me how their shape develops. As well as the pose, which appears in the painting almost like a cut-out, as something independent.

<u>HDW</u> Again, it goes back to the question of how painting and knowledge relate to each other. I'm almost certain he had a youth in the studio and looked very closely and studied or photographed him.

<u>LT</u> And then looked at that. I think the idea of dressing-up is important too, although not in a Toulouse-Lautrec kind of way. The masquerade is carried out in a travesty of dress-up where he made use of everything he wanted to use, but in an impeccable manner. This corresponds to necessity

and is why it's not reproduced in any other way. That's quite different again from Velázquez, where the posed quality differs, but in terms of painting perhaps close to each other in their stance, because it was a very individual stance, aimed at independence and a certain consensus that they knew who they were. And it's a little bit different with Duchamp.

HDW That's true. But wasn't there significantly more pressure on painters in bourgeois Paris than on Velázquez?

LT Manet sold very few paintings and basically painted for himself. He was well known through scandals, but I doubt he was a popular artist. Because he had money he was able to survive and it probably sharpened his stance. Not being popular almost became a subject.

HDW He did have friends. Baudelaire, for example, who defended him.

LT Yes, but a circle of friends is not an audience. In my life that's actually almost inconceivable, because many people who have nothing to do with art actually like my work or at least have heard about it. In fact, people come up to me every day to say they admire my work. In a way, it's the complete opposite. It's mainstream success. It's strange – I would have never thought it could happen.

GB This was a different time though. Manet provoked the wider Salon public with paintings like *Olympia* but it wasn't the public who commissioned the paintings. Who were his clients? Fellow artists?

HDW You can understand what it must have been like when you see what was on view at these Salons. In comparison *Olympia* looks almost like an advertising image, doesn't it?

GB Like a poster.

LT Something eye-catching, yes.

HDW It's understandable why it was shocking – it has no sense of depth. Interestingly, Manet could have said, "I don't care, I know exactly why I'm doing it." But that wasn't the case. He was convinced of the quality of his work, and was distraught because the reviews were always hostile.

LT I also think that he saw himself as a classical painter in terms of his skill and creativity. He developed a particular anachronism, which he must have been aware of and which contributed to the temporality of his paintings.

Ultimately, the aggression towards his paintings, the scandals and the aversion to them made him realize that he was on a path to somewhere. This gave him the confidence to dress himself up as a great master, in the same way that he dressed up people. I think he always saw himself as a great master in a small world. The relationship between Manet and Goya is also interesting to note. Both Manet's *Olympia* and Goya's two paintings *La maja desnuda* and *La maja vestida* [1798–1805], in which the *maja* is portrayed first dressed and then naked, testify to a certain commitment to art. It is an intervention in reality. There is a need for presence, which Goya had too – almost infinitely. They were also united by the theme of violence.

HDW When Manet was carried to his grave his coffin was followed by two people carrying his civic honours on little cushions. This recognition by bourgeois society was important to him.

GB Yes, and not just to him. There's an incredible story about Cézanne meeting Rodin, who had been honoured with the *Légion d'honneur*, and Cézanne went down on his knees, kissed his hand and said: "A master with the *Légion d'honneur*." Cézanne was obsessed with getting it. He never received the *Légion*, but for him the distinction it bestowed was the dream of his bourgeois existence. That has now vanished. If we think of the bourgeoisie today – what is it?

LT Everyone is now a bourgeois. I don't think it's something you can escape. The significance it had then, however, has changed in relation to its meaning today. Different kinds of bourgeois mentality exist, and there's also the *nouveau riche*. The bourgeoisie tends to be in the middle, not at the top. I think it's lost some of its significance.

GB But how is this? Is bourgeois mentality connected with the incredible success of modernism within the public at large? A certain kind of modernism is amazingly popular with hundreds of thousands of people interested in this art. It's surprising that the very same art that set itself against the bourgeoisie, good taste and the academy, is now embraced by the public in such a monumental way. Perhaps this has to be understood in light of what the bourgeoisie is today.

LT It has to do with the way something is presented. People suddenly started visiting exhibitions of artists like Mark Rothko because of the publicity. Another important aspect is history, and the way that artworks were promoted and elevated by the post-war victors. It's also related to the concept of modernity, of the birth of a completely new world dedicated to progress.

<u>HDW</u> But the bourgeoisie also attached great value to education, at least in retrospect.

<u>LT</u> That's no longer the priority though. Education has become unnecessary, and has been taken over by consumerism. I think it's more complicated than we imagine because the bourgeoisie has disappeared from sight. It has crept away, scared off. The United States, after two Bush administrations, has seen paranoia take over, coupled with the complete infantilization of society and the demonization of intellectual life. While the United States is still a world power, there is a fear of everything outside itself. It's a narcissistic business – they're focused entirely on themselves. The story of Narcissus gazing at his face in the water probably best describes the bourgeoisie.

<u>HDW</u> Can we return to Kandinsky?

<u>LT</u> Sure. First of all – and I think Alexander Rodchenko could have told you this, or Ivan Kliun, or any of the good Russian Constructivists, such as Kazimir Malevich – every work by Kandinsky exudes opportunism. Early paintings by Piet Mondrian are very well painted, precisely because they are village landscapes. Early paintings by Malevich have a certain density, a mass, this *matière* [matter], which, in my opinion, was not right from the start. Klee doesn't appeal to me either, he's too modest and has this musical, lyrical trait, which may be significant in art-historical terms, but to me is one of the biggest misunderstandings. Not a single painting from the Blaue Reiter group would make me stop in my tracks – especially Chagall, whom I find to be Jewish kitsch.

<u>HDW</u> Because it has no substance?

<u>LT</u> Because it has no intensity. Van Gogh was the son of a preacher, and if you look at many of his paintings, you can see how he tried to achieve something akin to faith with his art. This doesn't work. Mondrian was annoyed that Rudolf Steiner didn't visit his studio – Mondrian was part of the anthroposophical society, and mysticism had an enormous impact in the nineteenth century, especially on the beginnings of modernism. This was a huge misunderstanding, right up to Rothko.

<u>HDW</u> The Bauhaus became very important after the Second World War. It put its formal stamp on the whole of European society, but without any substance.

<u>LT</u> Yes, the Bauhaus was a blueprint to organize art, which went back to the Arts and Crafts movement in England, already a reduction of art. The same is true for Darmstadt, where Henry van de Velde [1863–1957] worked. The belief in a total work of art, in which all forms of art are meant to look like "Art for Architecture", is naïve and, ultimately, unsuccessful. This kind of total learned utopia is – again, in my opinion – one of the biggest mistakes. Even today, some curators still cling to this utopian ideal, especially in the field of architecture and city-themed exhibitions, such as *Cities on the Move*,[1] which glorify urban development, globalization and, ultimately, the destruction of the process of visualization.

<u>HDW</u> I would like to return to the Courbet painting we were discussing earlier, *The Wrestlers*. Gottfried Boehm commented: "The painting communicates nothing." I would like to follow that with the question – why and how do images communicate? This painting in particular is interesting because it's about nothing at all.

<u>GB</u> I found that Courbet painting so strange because it leaves no room for interpretation or engagement. It shoves these unpleasant bodies in my face and I don't want to look at them. This is the reason why, in my opinion, it's not a strong painting – it falls short of what an image can do.

<u>LT</u> The scale is also wrong and the bodies are positioned awkwardly, so you don't know whether you're above them, below them or on the same level. The two wrestlers are almost floating in the space, which is too heavily painted. Courbet probably worked far too long on the painting and wasn't able to come to grips with it. It's an unsuccessful painting in every respect – with regard to its content and handling. Basically, it's a Salon painting that only re-presents, whereas I think it's interesting when a painting denies re-presentation even though it could be a re-presentation. Abstracted images always have more of a motif-like character than figuration. Figuration is much more abstract for me, more difficult to grasp,

---

1 "Cities on the Move: Contemporary Asian Art at the turn of the 21st century", was curated by Hou Hanru and Hans Ulrich Obrist. The exhibition opened at the Wiener Secession in Vienna in November 1997 and travelled to venues in Austria, France, the United States, Denmark, Britain, Thailand and Finland.

not because it relates to reality, but the opposite. It is, and always has been, unrelated to this reality.

HDW Like we did earlier in Budapest, let's now discuss Luc's work in relation to the image – its characteristics, format, how it works, its relation to space and memory. I would like to begin with a discussion about the way that images can define space and tell purely spatial stories. How does perception work in a particular space? The way in which artworks are hung has a direct influence on the space.

LT First of all, I never hang a painting in the middle of the wall because it should adopt a position in opposition to the space in which it's exhibited. On the other hand, some of my paintings form a space within a space, which sets up an area of conflict about how to define the painting. They're shown unframed so they can expand into space. And, by leaving quite a lot of space around them whenever possible, gaps in between arise that allow for a freedom of movement, since the paintings themselves are already immobilized. The format controls everything. In Budapest that was clear because it was like a reverse movement – you only saw the painting at the end of the exhibition, when you approached it from the other side. And focus is altered with distance, so that a small painting can appear monumental. Incidentally, the three exhibitions in Budapest, Munich and Warsaw turned out to be completely different from one another, but one of the consistencies has been that a very tiny work, such as the *Die Zeit* paintings, can take on a monumental scale. It still registers from a distance of 30–40 metres, although monumentality is not only measured in square metres or dimensions, but in how the works encroach and present themselves within the space. Monumentality has to do with the format only in its precision and in the way in which you use the format pragmatically. A small format should be conceived in terms of distance, and a large format the other way around.

HDW Don't you think that monumentality asserts itself as an essential aspect only in the effect that the painting has on the spectator?

GB In addition, by what means can small formats become monumental? Does it have to do with presence? And what does the term "monumentality" signify in this case?

LT I think it has to do with the fragmentation of the image, which is something that comes from film. A close-up represents reality in the sense

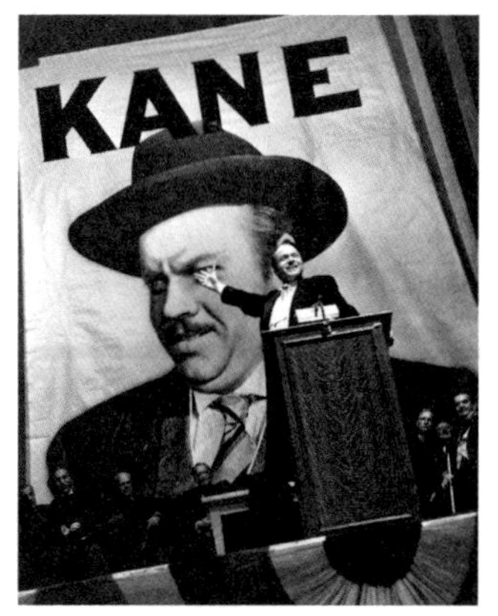

71 Film still from Orson Welles, *Citizen Kane*, 1941

that you can see much more than with the naked eye. This was a huge shock for perception, and has increased with the ability to edit and crop an image.

HDW I remember when I first saw *Citizen Kane*, on a very small screen. There's an image of Kane giving a speech in front of a huge photo of himself – the monumentality of that image was amazing, although I was only looking at a very small picture.

LT Yes, but in this case the person is doubled. By standing very close to his own huge image, he is the only one who moves. In that sense, the surroundings are linked with one another, and of course it's a monumental construction because of the doubling and mirroring. For me – and probably for most painters – it's important to have a mirror in the studio, irrespective of its size, because it allows you to "check" a painting from a distance and creates a stage in between you looking at the painting, and others looking at it. You can also turn it upside-down so you can spread the whole thing out at a distance. In this way the painting is formulated from afar and is almost a simulation that's incorporated during the painting process.

GB We can also find monumentality in small-format works by the Old Masters. One example that comes to mind is Andrea Mantegna's *Death of the Virgin* in the Prado. The dimensions are only 54 × 42 cm and yet it's unbelievably monumental, which I think has more to do with the subject and the way in which the architecture in the painting leads to the reclining Mary, and opens up a window behind her. Everything fits together and is tightly interlocked, without any open spaces. Arriving at monumentality in this way is a tremendously interesting insight, also in terms of pictorial theory.

HDW The word "monument" suggests that something should be remembered, doesn't it?

LT Yes, it has various connotations. It also has to do with an interest in decay and ruin, which leads us back to the Baroque, but which also came back at a later age. For example, Albert Speer was asked to predict how and

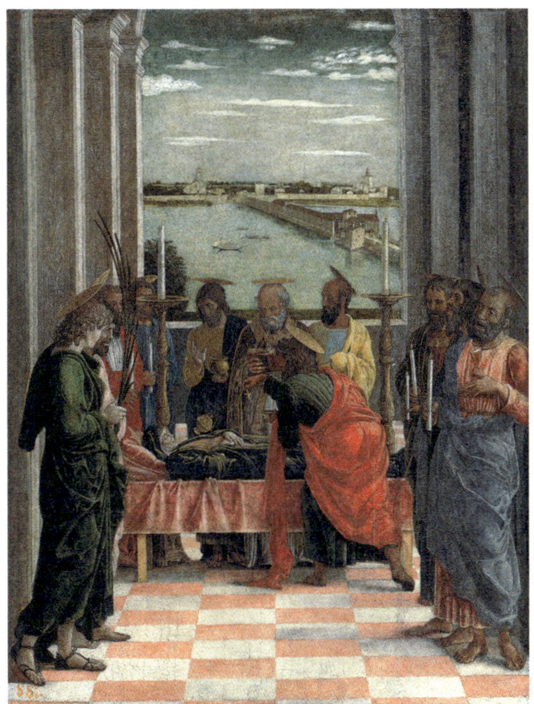

<u>72</u> ANDREA MANTEGNA, *The Death of the Virgin, c.* 1462
Mixed technique on panel, 54.5 × 42 cm
Museo Nacional del Prado, Madrid, INV. P000248

in what way buildings would decay in one thousand years.[2] To speak about images in terms of personal melancholy is another kind of monumentality, one that creates a cognitive image that plays with the viewer's expectations. This premonition can be either bad or good – although usually bad and is therefore more exciting. It recounts a pleasure in terror, something that has been inherited from film and the cinema – a crowd event that takes place in the dark, where people are anonymous, which is projected and not broadcast like television. Fragmentation of the image close-up makes it fragile, but at the same the fragment is presented as complete and acquires a new monumentality. Film practice has shown that distance not only through mirroring or through projection, but also through editing, especially the detail. Enlargement has a huge impact on the significance of a picture and

2 Hitler asked his chief architect to factor thousands of years of decay into his buildings. For baroque Christendom, the ruin was linked to Judgement Day. The mixture of decay and apotheosis made the antique ruin something honourable.

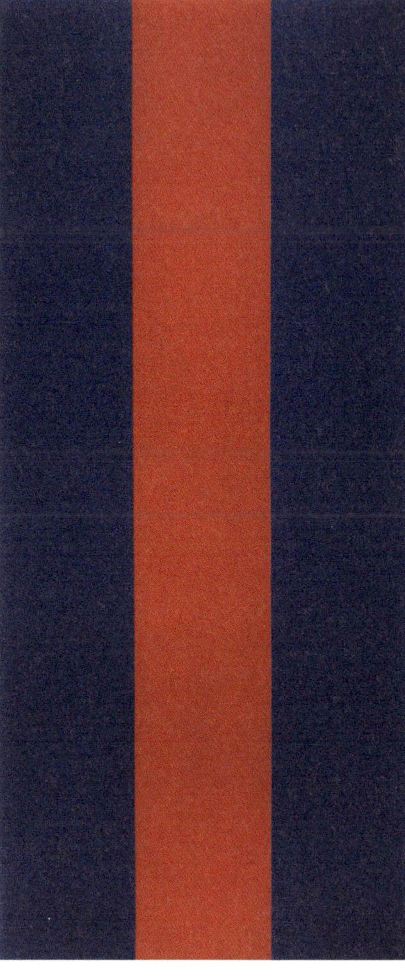

73 ELLSWORTH KELLY, *Two Panels:*
Yellow with Large Blue, 1970
Oil on canvas, 261.6 × 276.9 cm
The Museum of Contemporary Art, Los Angeles, INV. 85.58A-B

74 BARNETT NEWMAN, *Voice of Fire*, 1967
Acrylic paint on canvas, 543.6 × 243.8 cm
National Gallery of Canada, Ottawa, INV. 30502

its lasting effect. As a result, people don't register the format of pictures, but they remember them as images, which leads to my rather unusual way of using colour, whereby the hues have a tonality rather than a clear colour, generating a sculptural effect. With Ellsworth Kelly, you tend to perceive the sculptural, whereas with Barnett Newman, you get this monumentality that connects with modernism and positions itself architecturally in space – not in opposition but in tandem with space. Abstract pictures tend to acquire an emotive character and your engagement is a one-to-one relationship, with an understatement that is only hinted at in formal terms in its immediacy. There is an openness. By contrast, my pictures tend to produce a closed quality where you're meant to discover things, and images are produced in the brain, recalled from memory, and then later contemplated over and over again.

HDW Is this why you hung the big painting at the end of the exhibition and the tiny painting in the beginning?

LT Yes, if you look at the big painting carefully from very close up, you can see that it was painted at great speed.

HDW Its subject is very simple compared to the small paintings, which are more complex. Opposite from it, if I remember correctly, were *The Cry* and *Swimming Pool*?

LT Yes, the exhibition was arranged along an axis because the building is constructed like a church, with a stuccoed apse at one end. You might as well stick a big wall in it, but that wouldn't make sense because just as paintings shouldn't be hung in the centre of the wall, they shouldn't be placed in relation to the architecture and engage in a questioning that doesn't generate anything. At the same time, it shouldn't feel like a harmonious given either – a self-evident quality should be allowed to emerge instead. A certain vibrancy is achieved if this self-evidence relates both to the space and to the paintings, otherwise you get nothing. The exhibition in Budapest was the clearest of the three in that it produced the greatest aesthetic effect. In Munich, the paintings remained in the foreground and the exhibition became much more political, while in Warsaw there was a dreadful compression which created a claustrophobic effect. The difference in the architecture of the spaces – the classical buildings of Budapest and Warsaw, and the dominant 1930s architecture of Munich – also had an effect on the paintings.

HDW Why did the paintings work so well in Munich?

LT Because that building is quite painterly, whereas the other buildings are "real" architecture from a certain period. The Haus der Kunst was based on symmetry and the idea behind it was less architectural *per se* than about an *idea* of architecture. The 1930s was a period that used classical forms to build an image of itself architecturally, but ones akin to pastiche and inflated to an almost unbearable scale. The architecture was built quickly with already deteriorating materials, hence the buildings are in a constant

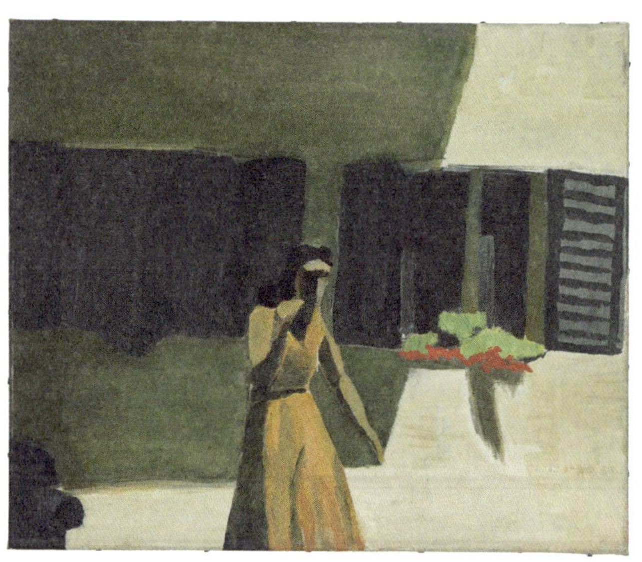

Private collection, Belgium

<u>76</u> Luc Tuymans, *Swimming Pool*, 1998
Oil on canvas, 98 × 68 cm
Linda Pace Foundation, San Antonio

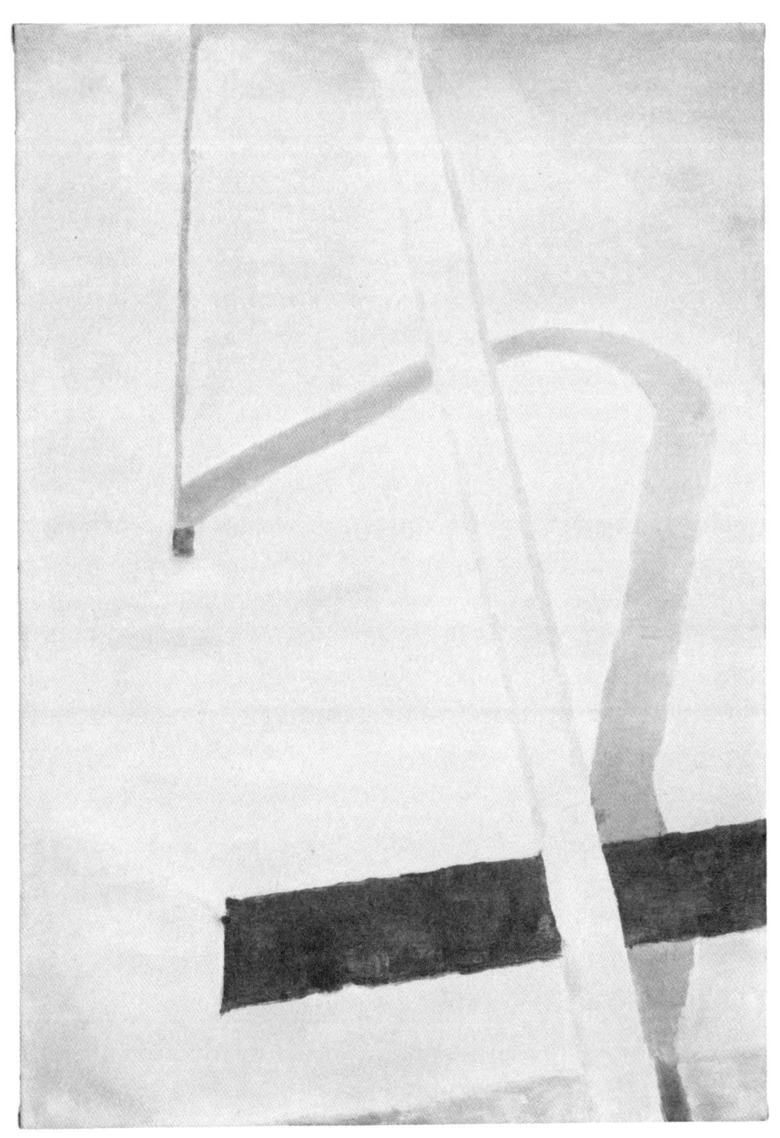

state of restoration. You sense this decay and it's an "unearthly", unreal environment.

HDW Can we return to this relationship between a painting and architecture? I always feel that architects don't know what a museum should be or how to design an exhibition space.

LT I reckon that people like Karl Friedrich Schinkel, who was one of the inventors of the modern museum, did have an idea of what a museum should be. Early Neoclassical buildings offer the best architecture for museums in my opinion. For example, the Pergamon Museum in Berlin is a museum of museums. More recent museum architecture sets itself up in opposition to the arts and starts to compete with it, such as the Solomon R. Guggenheim Museum by Frank Lloyd Wright in New York. It is designed like a multi-storey car park where the floor is a slanting spiral. This makes it difficult to show art and it always goes wrong. The new building for The Museum of Modern Art in New York, designed by Japanese architect Yoshio Taniguchi in 2002–04, isn't that great either. Of course there are also exceptional recent museum architects, like Renzo Piano, but it's become a difficult task because museums are now built to promote current developments. Formerly, works by living artists weren't accepted into museum collections – it used to take eighty years for a work to enter a collection – now it happens right away which creates a problem of how to design surroundings for images without having any time to think about them, when time is reduced to a one-to-one scale.

HDW To see your work exhibited in different venues has made the role of architecture very clear – it adds to the exhibition and helps to tell a different story each time.

LT A touring exhibition should make sense – not that the spectator needs to follow it – but there needs to be some consistency while allowing for different possibilities and layers of meaning. My exhibitions are rarely arranged chronologically, and my survey exhibitions are never traditional retrospectives. There are always fresh pockets of meaning that emerge from the juxtaposition of various works within the context of the space.

GB Have you ever created a square painting?

LT Yes, but not many. Most of my oeuvre is vertical – very few paintings are horizontal or have a panoramic layout.

GB *Dusk*, for example.

LT Yes, and *Alice in Wonderland* from 2007.

HDW Some paintings from the Walt Disney series are enormous.

LT I found the curators' response to these paintings interesting. At first they were perplexed because the paintings seemed overly abstract, which was not my intention. At the same time their scale and subject-matter positioned them among American art. The subject is understated – it doesn't address Disney directly but heralds a utopian ideal. Various influences are also at play in the work, like Cubism, although that wasn't intentional either.

GB I find that your formats always seem to address the viewers' bodily experience and make use of asymmetry. Our optical assessment of images always differs between what we see on our left and on our right, meaning that the paintings' format affects our perception with characteristics that manifest themselves in terms of our body.

LT I don't project images on to the canvas, so when I start a large painting such as *Rome* or *Alice in Wonderland* [both 2007], I begin by applying the colour of the ground, the most luminous colour, on a canvas attached to the wall with nails. At the outset nothing is fixed and size is only roughly determined. After I apply the ground colour, I draw the outline of the whole painting in pencil in the wet paint. So its size is established physically by the drawing and is mapped out as I draw. I draw in loops, so I'm drawing and measuring until the area finally determines the size of the painting. I've been doing this for years, always drawing on pieces of canvas that I can change later – although by now I usually predetermine a specific scale in my head. Then I wipe away the pencil a bit and begin to paint.

HDW Once the format has been established?

LT The drawing maps out the entire image, so it is a completely different way of working than with a projected image. At first there is the "appropriation" of the image, to make it physically visible, to understand it, and to find the size. The precision increases, unlike with a projection, because there will always be errors. For example, if I painted you, your head might become more elongated, whether I want it to or not, through the act of physical translation. Even if I work against it, it will always happen. This is unavoidable, I think, and points to the fact that there are limits to painting, in terms of monumentality and format, which is why no two formats are exactly alike. Gerhard Richter works on four or five formats simultaneously that are all pre-established. It is unlikely that he paints them as separate images.

GB In your painting process, is there a possibility that your pictures might end up with an irregular shape? Not necessarily a shaped canvas, but a format that doesn't agree with the conventional pictorial field?

LT Yes, for example *Gas Chamber* is not rectangular because part of the stretcher is at an angle. That was deliberate because it's about the painting documenting itself, the idea of documents and their reassessment over time. It also plays with warmth and spatial elements that destroy or flatten space. It's not about shame or a specific form, although they bear significance.

HDW What happens when a painter chooses the wrong format? For example, in Budapest you felt that El Greco's *The Annunciation* had the wrong format. Has that happened to you too?

LT Of course. I think it happens to everyone. Distance reveals this, and if it's really bad, I either paint over it or cut the painting down. You can see how Manet probably cut down his paintings or foregrounded certain parts.

HDW I would like to move on and talk about how your paintings relate to additional information that we might have or want to have, but don't. Am I correct in thinking that this information is inseparable from the work?

LT I don't think so. I provided background information because people seemed to really want it when I first showed my paintings. Earlier we discussed this urge for contextualization, which is now becoming part of contemporary art. It's almost like a sociological experiment – an artist's statement reveals what they mean to society. In 1964 Bertrand Russell said that we haven't just become democratic in external forms, but that we've also interiorized democracy. I don't want my paintings to appear as if they come from a mysterious place, and I struggle against the myth of the artist – especially of painters – who stands silently and mysteriously in the corner. The old adage about paintings speaking for themselves isn't relevant because the world is no longer like that. For this reason I thought it would be more interesting to provide some background information, and most journalists welcomed this because they had absolutely no idea what to write so this gave them a place to start. Now people think it's arrogant if I don't offer information and almost won't look at the paintings without it, which I think is unfair. An example is when *The Diagnostic View* series was first shown in 1990, the response was very divided. Then a journalist asked what it was about, and I explained everything, including the way that I applied the paint horizontally for the first time, producing a grid. I told him that I had intentionally averted the gaze of those portrayed to eliminate any empathy between spectator and subject, stripping away the psychology of the portrait. When I told him, very pragmatically, how it was painted he asked me to explain further so I finally said: "No, you should see that for yourself – it's visible." In this sense, it's a mistake on my part to guide the public to see the things I've pointed out. As the picture-maker, it's important for me to know the themes I'm engaging with, what the painting is about and it gives me a pointer as to how to paint a picture. It's certainly not for the painting to confirm that because paintings themselves must be silent and they must allow enough room for the spectator to construct his or her own vision. To provide information begins to take on a self-sufficient referential position where the painting can no longer defend itself.

GB That touches on a point we were discussing earlier about "creativity". Background information, as you've just described it, does not allow the painting to do anything other than confirm that same information. Since a painting is always certainly more than the sum of this information, viewers are engaged in a tightrope walk. I think it's always best if we first encounter a work without any prior knowledge so that we can look undisturbed at what is on the canvas and what it does. Even if you don't understand what's being referred to or recognize who is portrayed, you can still see what's being shown and how, which are both important if you really want to take painting seriously. Afterwards, additional information allows us to relate it back to the way in which a specific painter makes something visible under specific conditions. This has nothing to do with the painting speaking for itself or speaking autonomously, but it's organized in such a way that it should, and can, be taken literally. In other words, if you don't want to end up with simplistic iconography, information is intertwined with the act of presentation in painting itself.

LT To me it's pretty clear that the first thing you do when you visit an exhibition is to look at the pictures. The first step is purely visual while the second step is to think about potential meanings. The problem is that people are no longer left simply to look. All three curators of my exhibitions in Budapest, Munich and Warsaw asked me for descriptions including specific information about each work's subject-matter to be inserted in gallery handouts and distributed by gallery attendants to visitors at the exhibition entrance before they even have a chance to look. We owe this didactic approach to Friedrich Schiller[3] and to his ideas about educating the bourgeoisie through art in *On the Aesthetic Education of Man*. The notion of art's function as an educational and civilizing entity brought a huge number of people into museums, although it underestimates the majority of the public's intelligence. And people, like paintings or circumstances, should never be under- or over-estimated. They should be left alone. Today that is no longer permitted because of a new system of subsidies and funds that are accompanied by a whole new set of responsibilities. This is a global phenomenon.

GB This then leads to reducing the image to an illustration of information.

LT In the worst cases, yes. Surprisingly, many people find my paintings beautiful – even mainstream audiences that come across my work by accident and do not usually move in cultural circles.

HDW When I installed Marcel Duchamp's readymades for the 2004 exhibition *Friedrich Christian Flick Collection im Hamburger Bahnhof* in Berlin, I wanted to impress the idea that they were never conceived of as sculptures so I showed the *Bottle Rack* with an engine that made it rotate and a light that cast a strong shadow. Although that wasn't my aim, the result looked beautiful so people criticized me for aestheticizing the readymades.

LT This brings us back to teaching people about a "product" and the mistrust of images. It's not for the sake of mistrusting but more about getting people to think. This whole movement, especially within theory, has turned against itself because, from the outset, contextualization is required. And when context is provided, that is also bad. It's infuriating – whatever you do is wrong. What basic standpoint can you adopt? It always surprises me that painters are expected to have a position within such a long tradition. They are immersed in the complex history of painting, while also being part of its social business, if not at the centre, then at the periphery. Painters are always asked what they think about their paintings, whereas a media artist

3 J. C. Friedrich von Schiller (1759–1805) was a German poet, philosopher, historian and playwright. In his pivotal work, *On the Aesthetic Education of Man in a Series of Letters* first published in 1794, he gives the philosophic basis for his doctrine of art, and indicates clearly and persuasively his view of the place of beauty in human life.

is confronted with that question less often. Not that it bothers me – I'm just noting that painting has nothing to do with temporality because it exists outside time.

HDW That brings us back to the relationship between images and memory. How can an image capture an utterly abstract notion of memory in a way that language cannot? It's a question about the inherent intelligence of images. Let's return to the painting of your uncle, *G. Dam*. That picture is an attempt to capture something that's impossible to capture.

LT *G. Dam* was my first painting that attempted to deal with memory, and of course it was deficient. I never knew my uncle in person, only family myths about him. The portrait is based on an oil painting that shows my uncle in a three-quarter view. Strangely enough, it had survived when my grandparents' house burned down during the war and all other existing photos of this uncle were destroyed. It's an idiomatic image because it probably doesn't have anything to do with him – but this is how we remember things, and what memory does. Earlier, I spoke about how images are authentic fakes, in that no image can ever be an original because it is always based on other images. I painted this portrait based on an image, but turned my uncle's face to a frontal view. The photographer August Sander[4] was an influence both for his frontal portraits as well as for the way he preferred an adopted, as opposed to a "natural", pose. For him, a "fake" staged pose actually represented truth. He combined this with a pragmatic, archival approach that attempted to capture everything. There is a sharpness to his images that allows for a sense of infinity. The figures appear like statues, either against a white or a completely neutral background. I find that the pictures have a neutrality and timeless quality, although most of them try to capture the particular period and specific trade of the subjects. Sander rigorously stuck to this concept.

HDW But the image the baker has of himself is even less real than the photo composed by Sander.

LT But Sander's composition is based on the iconic idea of a baker. It's reduced to his occupation, which he's not actually performing because he's busy looking at a lime tree.

---

4 August Sander (1876–1964) was a German portrait and documentary photographer, and has been described as the most important German portrait photographer of the early twentieth century. Sander's first book *Face of our Time* (*Antlitz der Zeit*) was published in 1929.

GB The people in his photos are paused in their activity. I think that's why they appear so timeless.

LT "Pose" and "pause" are the two key words. Almost all the occupations – bricklayer, mason, and so on – involve particular kinds of movement that seem to have been arrested in a flash. I find that Sander's group images do that less although they're also composed.

GB "Pose" and "pause" are two helpful terms to understand the issue of context and image. It's important to realize that what had originally informed painting and had created a space for memory, now appears in a new context and under different conditions generated by the image and its author. In Sander's case this can be described in terms of pose/pause, but with Luc it has to do with indefiniteness, among other elements. This means that the information is still legible in an entirely different context, but it appears under different visual conditions, acquires a different status and a different kind of presence from the one it had in its original context. We're dealing with a process of transformation. That's why people shouldn't look for written explanations of your intentions, which is ultimately what gallery brochures are about. If this shortcut is permitted, then no reasonable reception of the work can take place. People simply focus on the information, believing they understand, so they no longer engage with or experience the actual images.

LT I think that the repeated question of whether or not I'm a political artist is a critique of art. No artist can be political. You can never give a work of art a political charge from the outset. Of course, life has to do with politics, and at a certain point a work of art can acquire political significance – but that's a different story. It can never be the other way around. When an artist writes "Art = Politics" on a gallery wall, that's not everything that it's about. People want to know what something is, and name it. The idea of naming is a logical conclusion to Duchamp who started naming by designating his objects as works of art. In his case it was a different game though, because the naming was confusing. Now everything needs a catch-phrase.

GB With modernism, there is always the possibility of "Untitled". Donald Judd is one of many artists who didn't use titles. This prevents the title from generating a literary interpretation or from introducing a narrative. Apart from this, it's a phenomenon that signals, "I resist naming", where the artist states that it can't be said what the work is. This reluctance to rely too heavily on linguistically predefined contexts is justified.

LT Yes, but on the other hand "Untitled" has become institutionalized and is now almost a title itself. It's based on the premise that a work speaks for itself, which is why I started to title all my works. Occasionally, my titles are purely descriptive, but usually they relate to a different, unpainted image. The meaning of a word or a sentence evokes its own picture, which doesn't exist. I find that the use of titles as a counterpart is even more interesting because it's conceptually subversive.

HDW Duchamp once said that it's like adding a mental colour to a picture.

LT Since we are discussing the relationship between text and image, a good example is *Our New Quarters*, which I painted from a reproduction of a postcard from Theresienstadt [Terezín]. I chose a non-colour that's similar to military green and darkened it a bit, which gives the space a kind of *sfumato* at the edge. I then, very quickly and graphically, painted the building and the tree. Suddenly I had the idea to take some white and yellow paint and write its title, "Our New Quarters", on the painting itself. It looks like a subtitle, gives the painting a strikingly bold element and, at the same time, incorporates an almost documentary element. The title actually becomes the destruction of the painting but from within.

HDW Why did you decide to paint over the text in your picture?

LT That has to do with the genesis of a painting. The first painting, from 1988, I primed and then intuitively had an idea related to de Chirico's midday light, *pittura metafisica*, so I wrote on it in Flemish "niets in zicht" [nothing in sight]. I immediately started working on the second painting, which was an enlargement of the first painting's urban scene. Then came the third painting with spinach tablets and the fourth, in which I integrated a photograph and reincorporated it into a painterly context. I then painted over the words in the first painting because they didn't make sense any more – I didn't know back then that I would make a group of four paintings. This is why I titled the group *Die Zeit* [Time], because it was the result of an experience of time.

HDW I'd like to explore in further detail what we began to discuss in Budapest, which is the difference between the common perception of an image as something fixed, as a fact, and how viewers, as Gottfried Boehm described, actually engage in a searching movement when they look at images.

GB I think that observation has two closely linked sides to it. There's the simple fact that, as human beings, we are seeing, understanding and orientating in constant motion, even when we move our eyes, which we do all the time. This motor activity determines how we perceive, and even whether we perceive. Restricting this – even for half a minute – is virtually impossible and would require extraordinary effort. This demonstrates how our entire physical apparatus is determined by movement. The same thing happens when we first approach an image, as images determine our perception of phenomena in the world.

But there is another side of the image when it offers certain information under the prevailing conditions of painting. We previously cited the de-familiarization of photos. As viewers, we are faced with various facts presented under the conditions of a single whole, and of a format, large or small. These facts and the format, the single entity, constitute a relationship that, although not physically or perceptually rigid, hangs on a wall and is fixed once and for all. On the contrary, we must continually relate all of the interacting elements to one another. The image doesn't emerge until we've accomplished this ordering. Before that, it is strictly a physical phenomenon, and only when we accept its potential for movement does it become an experience that contains a potential for meaning.

The image depends on movement in order to realize itself, otherwise it would simply be a physical "fact" on the wall. In that respect it's constitutive – that's why temporality is the category most central to the image, especially to the stationary image. Temporality is the mode of ordering, is what offers our gaze the possibility of accomplishing this ordering.

LT That's why each painting, as with Manet's black shadows, also has its own "bursting" point. Although the physical painting is immobile, it always has a weakness. That weakness is the point where the armour cracks, the point where you enter the painting – which is usually the first point you see. This final point is an important part of a painting's immobility, because when a painting hangs immobile on the wall, you need this clear point of reference. If this point is lacking – and it can be placed anywhere in the composition – then the painting lacks a point of entry. I find that many images, especially paintings, have a specific point where the picture is actually oriented from, the central point of its orchestration.

GB With regard to photography, Roland Barthes makes the distinction between *studium* and *punctum*. By *punctum* Barthes means a slight deviation, which in photography very often results from elements of chance – a slight deviation that causes the image to function. Barthes's *studium* is what registers everything, every fact of the image. But if I register an image as "fact" then, frankly, I haven't even begun to experience it as an image. For this you need the *punctum*, which is the aspect that Luc is referring to – asymmetry, shifts and marks.

LT Advertising does this by producing the appearance of an image, but never any kind of relevant image. There's something terribly empty and didactic about this mediated model, which is related to publicity, the need to be seen and is only concerned with the job of selling. It's fascinating the way that the same things are shown over and over again. You see Selma Hayek, for example, with a bottle of Campari, turning towards the viewer, almost life-size and tangible. What does it mean? At first we're simply struck by this very beautiful woman, then we see the bottle of Campari. But we don't just see it once, we see it a hundred times around town. Again, this is not an image, it's the deployment of an idea of an image, which is manipulative and meaningless.

GB It's like a sermon. "Do this, if you please."

LT Despite the fact that the mainstream is often perceived as inferior, with its prefabricated forms, we should not underestimate its significance as a working system especially when you see the visual power and impact that advertising has in our society. Unfortunately most of it lacks any intelligence whatsoever. I suppose some intelligent advertising does exist, although it's more likely to be clever rather than intelligent.

HDW I'd like to return to this notion of premonition.

GB I find "premonition" and "intuition" to be very useful terms, and I think they can certainly be given considerable prominence, even though they sound rather imprecise. When you "intuit" or "sense" something, there is often a negative connotation that suggests that you don't fully understand it. We need to look at what intuiting actually involves. First, I think it can be said that intuition becomes important when I know nothing and can't say anything, in which case I must rely on intuition. If I enter an unknown territory and feel exposed or threatened, I ask, "How can I process this? What does it mean?" in order to find a path using my sense of intuition. These powers are very important because they permit me to get my bearings in unfamiliar conditions.

HDW It also uses this kind of intelligence that we spoke about earlier, doesn't it?

GB Exactly. And the question is, why is intuition intelligent and how can it be intelligent? I think the power of intuition can create trial relationships, experimentally, testing, between specific individual facts and the overall situation or surroundings in which I find myself. Ultimately, intuition is an orientating sense. It links – this is the intelligent thing about it – the individual entity with other individual entities, and with the context in which I'm moving – the image. It does this in a flash. And I don't need to think about it at all – it's just there, it opens itself up. Having an intuitive sense of images is the be-all and end-all of it. If you haven't got it, then you're really on a lower plane than that offered to you by the image.

HDW Premonition also has an element of recognition.

LT I find this idea of orientation very interesting, as though we are in the dark. Baruch de Spinoza once pointed out that intuition should be considered a category of intelligence, as well as a process of orientation. The two go hand in hand because they're elemental. Although intuition is purely physical, it can take place in an instant inside your head driven by a necessity to behave within certain limits, whether it's looking at a painting or reacting to a situation. It's important that we take a position directly, because we also can feel threatened, completely and physically. Not just this idea of an evaluating system; it goes further than that. We don't really have time to evaluate, or to size things up – we can only rely on this particular instinct, and we must decide immediately, at a stroke.

GB Perhaps it's helpful, at least in German, to introduce the word *spüren*. For example, if one enters a room where people are sitting, in a flash we've read the situation, we know what the mood is and whether the group has been quarrelling. We sense it immediately, we can "take their temperature" and intuitively determine the tone of almost any gathering.

HDW Right, although as a society, we haven't yet managed to incorporate this within our rational system of thought.

GB But we'll manage to do so right now by examining the relationship between simultaneity and succession, which is what determines our orientation with images. Intuition is the articulation of this relationship.

LT Because we are speaking about intuition – or *spüren* – we must also consider the idea of astonishment. We also discussed the "pause" in August Sander's portraits, in the lives that he is depicting, and the pose. With painting, there is a moment where we are astonished by it. For a few seconds, you really don't know where you are, you're somewhat struck – it's a real bang! This is the moment when viewers are immobilized, they stop moving, and it's very brief – usually lasting for five seconds at most. That's the point of impact, not only where viewing begins, but where the effect takes place. There are various means of measuring intuition, though to attempt to assimilate them into an empirically measurable system would be complete madness. It would also be futile because the moment one focuses on it in this way, one is robbed of the possibility of it occurring. It's like when people ask me, "Why do you still paint?"

GB They specifically ask you, "Still?"

LT Yes, "still". It is a question that no artist has ever asked me, only critics, art historians and theorists. Stan Douglas, John Baldessari or Mike Kelley have never asked me this question. Why not? Because it's a totally idiotic question! This whole idea that painting – or any other form – could possibly be dead or alive is a ridiculous, pointless non-discourse.

HDW But I'd like to return to this "lightning-like" moment in which something really becomes recognizable. What comes after that?

LT After that comes the process that Mr Boehm was referring to, when movement enters into the equation. The painting is looked at – scanned. Then the painting is, perhaps, enjoyed. And then it's consumed. For example, the viewer asks how it's painted, how it looks, how it's constructed. And lastly, and perhaps, most problematically, they ask what it means.

HDW But that flash might not contain the full truth of all this, right?

GB Sure. It can also involve disappointment. One experiences something spontaneous, even visceral, and perhaps it never returns. But as a rule, if you've experienced this kind of intensity from seeing, it can actually become an acute level of awareness, since we're able to draw on the experience in many ways, such as a form of reflection. We could say that one gains experience with these occurrences. If we trace *spüren* back etymologically to ancient Greek, then it's a sense of smell and its connection with game, hunting and the hunter. Interestingly, the Greek word for intuition is the same as the word for reason – *nous, nueín*. In other words, for the Greeks the capacity to sense and to intuit, to scent, that subtlest of senses, is associated with the notion of reason, which I find very apt. Reason is not simply rationality without a connection to our senses.

LT Yes, though if we speak about the Enlightenment, then we come across some rather problematic issues. The "dislocation" of time and abstraction isn't necessarily a bad thing because it allows the virtual to enter, as well as utopian thought. But it developed separately. Actually, the idea of imagining and measuring the territory of knowledge and making something your own is a luxury. It's astonishing to see how deeply we've sunk when you read Greek philosophy now, for example Simonides' idea of the art of memory. When you read how people formulated things at that time, you understand that we have lost quite a lot.

HDW The Greek language is unique in my opinion. It registers experiences at such a high conceptual level and links experience and knowledge linguistically.

GB Yes, it formulates terminology directly from experience.

HDW I believe we've strayed from that path.

GB Considering astonishment – this was from a Greek motive for embarking on philosophy. It has to pass the caesura that Luc described. You have to be detached for a moment from conventional behaviour, and perhaps be alarmed, and then we can set about thinking.

HDW Let's return to the idea of indefiniteness as an important determining element of images. We've discussed how the visible has a genesis that emerged from the image, how it's somehow impermanent and it oscillates. One never knows exactly how difficult it is, and this difficulty changes constantly. How does that look from the point of view of creating the paintings?

LT The first thing to say about this is that the formal indefiniteness I have is, in fact, very sharply focused because it's painted. There is no modality,

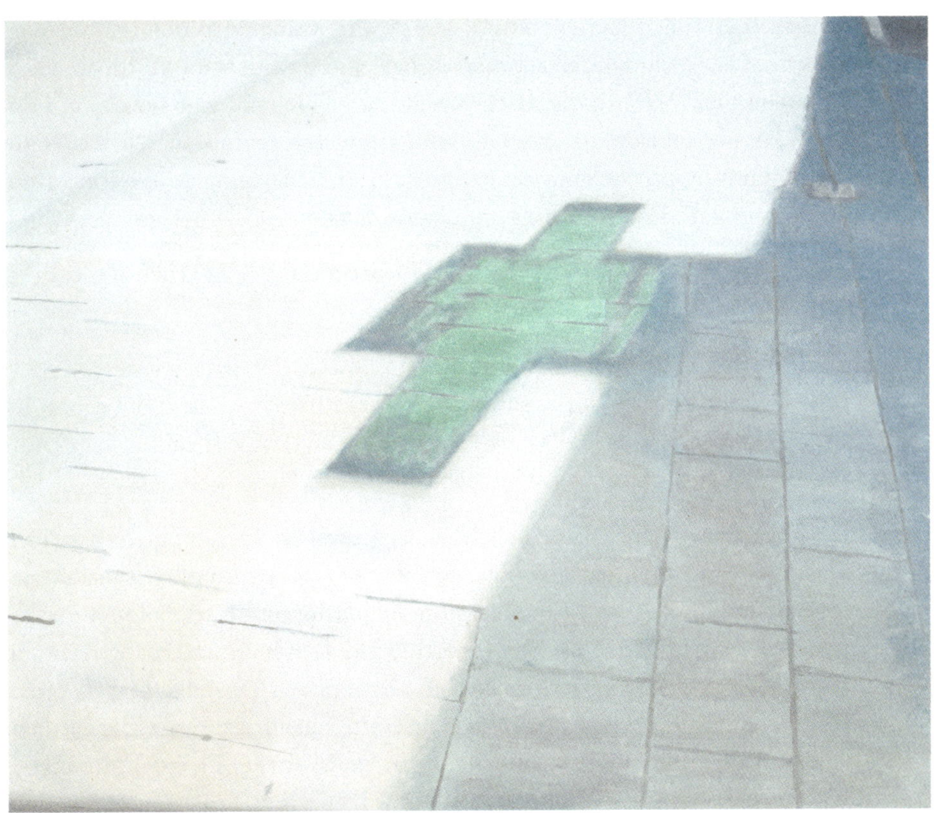

<u>77</u> Luc Tuymans, *Apotheek* [Pharmacy], 2003
Oil on canvas, 157.5 × 190 cm
Private collection. Courtesy Hauser & Wirth

this idea of reduction, of retraction. First of all, you can see it in the work. If you compare *Time* with later works like *Pharmacy* or *Plant*, you'll see that I now permit myself far more elaboration than I used to. In my earlier paintings, I used a lot of colour and strong gestural components. After my forays into film, and to acquire some distance, I stopped painting like that. You can also see that, initially, there was a tendency to emphasize graphic elements, as with *Our New Quarters* and *Time*. The sharpness and contrasts that came about later were related to the idea of abstracting – of distancing in a different way, and also to the change in format. You can clearly see that the indefiniteness is painted – it's present as an object of painting, which makes it very difficult to approach the paintings. I am always astonished when the unstretched canvases are on the wall, before the paintings are mounted on the stretcher bars. When they're reshaped as objects by being stretched, it's as though a second skin has appeared in front of the painting – a screen that inserts itself. That's when the whole reality of the object happens. For this reason, painting a mural is much less stressful – I'm able to begin painting pretty freely on the wall. With a picture that I've conceived as an oil painting, there's always a certain tension.

HDW Does this have something to do with the fact that when the canvas is placed on the wall it is also an interface?

LT Probably. One intends to produce an object. But with regard to indefiniteness and the idea of separating the painting, there is also a phase in which the painting actually discloses itself analytically. It can be very complex, this increase in focus, which is vaguely perceived.

HDW I'd like to open up this whole idea a bit by including the issue of "objectivity", a claim made by photography. We could also relate this double idea of indefiniteness and oscillation to photography from the viewer's point of view. Gerhard Richter took this indefiniteness and made it into a painting system. The series that perhaps interests us most, his *October* cycle [*October 18, 1977*], involves images taken from a historical magazine context and projected into another historical context by means of indefiniteness. I realize there are a lot of issues here, but I think they're all related to each other. Luc, you mentioned that the *October* series was painted in black?

LT Yes. Richter painted various pictures in black, white and shades of grey. But what particularly fascinates me about the *October* series is that a specific painterly precision appears here, which is lacking in some of the other works, and the formats and sequencing work very well. The first painting is as if it were from an album of family photographs – that's how it starts. This idea of intensification is very interesting. From a totally trivial idea we see the anxiety of the bourgeoisie, and that's the theme.

HDW The first time these paintings were shown in the Haus Lange and Haus Esters Krefeld, a lot of politicians attended the opening, yet nothing happened. It was almost completely silent. I find it to be one of Richter's most important series of paintings to date.

LT That's interesting because I find something theatrical about it at the same time in the way it progresses.

hdw Right, but these images already existed. We've seen them *ad nauseam* in the press, in *Der Spiegel* for example.

lt Yes, but by being taken up again, the images, the changes in format and, as I said, the indefiniteness that's been added to them, acquire a completely different temporality. It's almost reconfigured as an iconic work. And to do that is, I find, very intelligent. It's a whole era that's been captured, an important moment in time, not just for Richter, but also for Rainer Werner Fassbinder and for the entire post-war generation. He avoids moralizing, but he also isn't taking the position of a spectator. There is a certain sense of pain in these paintings that you don't sense as much in other Richter paintings. This is why they have a completely different emotional value and carries on in this way, right up until the figure who has hanged herself. Here Richter is no longer Richter fighting photography – there is much more to it than that. It relates to content, facts and levels of meaning. It is about Germany. It's a terrible shame that the paintings are no longer in Germany but, incomprehensibly, in New York where they're only occasionally shown.

hdw All of them?

lt All of them, which is a shame. For this reason I donated *Our New Quarters* to the mmk in Frankfurt am Main, because the paintings are now in the place where they make most sense.

gb Regarding indefiniteness in relation to Richter, I think it sets in motion an indicative activity, something that is easily overlooked. Indefiniteness is the moment when something in the image presents itself to me, rather than just already being there. It is the moment of showing, a deictic aspect, which is why it's used so much in this crucial moment, by Luc among others. It is used when it's a matter of letting the image come into its own, bringing external aspects – documentation, information and so on – under the aegis of the image, which then acquires powerful potential. There are also other strategies, such as collage, but they don't operate with indefiniteness – a very powerful deictic practice. When I looked at Luc's paintings closely in Budapest, my gaze was confronted with it directly, each time in a new and different way, and I learned a lot about that.

lt For me, perhaps less so for Gerhard Richter, it's important that the sense of depth in a painting isn't an illusion but a fact, meaning that it's more than a relationship between foreground and background. You can develop the depth in a painting through tonality. In this respect, my approach

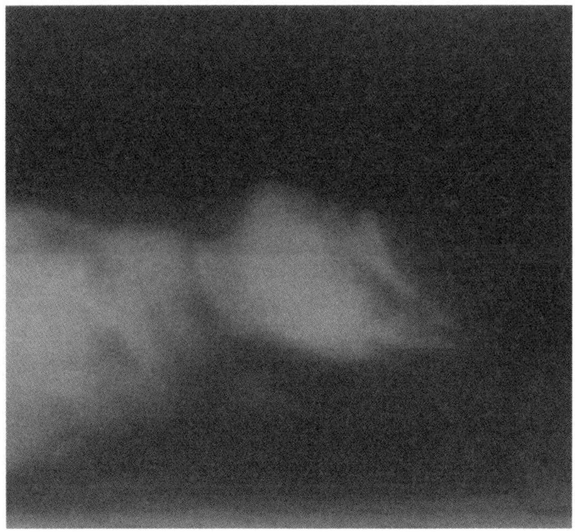

<u>78</u> Gerhard Richter, *Dead (October 18, 1977)*, 1988
Oil on canvas, 35 × 40 cm
The Museum of Modern Art, New York, INV. 169.1995.A-O

differs from Richter, who emphasizes the flatness of the image. This isn't the case in all of his paintings, but his photographic approach derives from magazines, especially mainstream publications, which is how his working system developed. It's symptomatic of his generation – there was a boom in the 1960s and '70s with the widespread proliferation of television and broadcast materials. These existed before but not on the same scale. Above all, a resistance to photography's singular position as evidence, or "truth", emerged. It's an interesting conflict that Richter engaged with, one that no longer takes place in my generation because we view photography as a tool or a mode via which we arrive at completely different images.

<u>HDW</u> It's interesting that the problem of photography had already been addressed a century earlier by Manet, and yet Richter still hadn't worked it out completely.

<u>LT</u> Well, the situations are not comparable. Richter actually incorporates the photographic process and creates something almost static, and, of course, he combines this with abstraction. I've never considered Richter to be an abstract painter, even though his gestural approach suggests he could be considered as one, but as an image-maker, he's not like Ad Reinhardt, Barnett Newman or Ellsworth Kelly. Richter sticks with figuration in his own awareness, as he applies paint very carefully with so-called "chance".

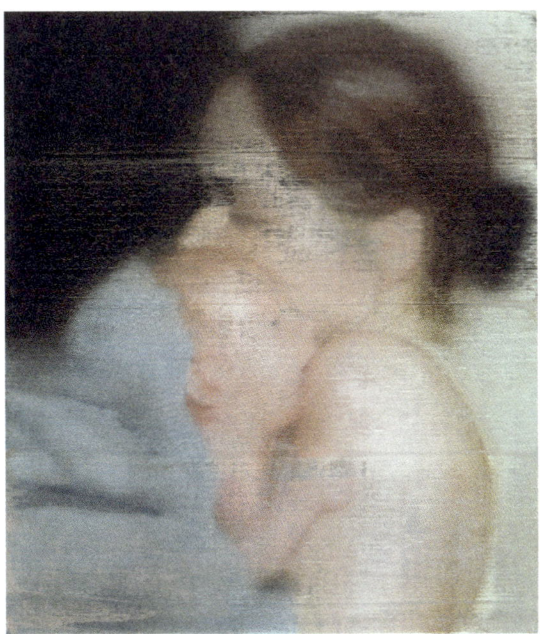

79 GERHARD RICHTER, *S. with Child*, 1995
Oil on canvas, 40.9 × 36.4 cm
Hamburger Kunsthalle, Hamburg, INV. HK-5536

Perhaps the tragic dilemma with some artists is the attempt to be simultaneously complete while withholding. This discretion and reserve is coupled with a tremendous desire to overwhelm, which can lead to a misunderstanding of formats and of how to engage with your own oeuvre. You don't have to constantly document and corroborate it *ad nauseam*. For example, I find the series *S. with Child* [series of 8 paintings, 1995] with Richter's wife and child to be problematic. The focus is removed and we enter a private realm in a way that's creepy. I mean, why should I want to see that? I'm not questioning Richter's significance, but I wonder how his work will be perceived in twenty or thirty years without the aspect of process or groupings? Or should the work be kept together? You shouldn't show the *48 Portraits* or the *October* as separate paintings. In 1989 I didn't know his work well, I had only seen a few abstract paintings. By chance, before I left for Cologne to take part in a group exhibition, *Wahrheit und Dichtung* [*Truth and Poetry* – a reversal of Goethe's *Dichtung und Wahrheit*], I saw an hourlong documentary about Richter, and I thought it was great because it was so unpretentious and full of integrity. I wrote him a letter straight away. At that point, I had already painted *Time*, so his work had no influence on my painting then or now.

HDW So you're saying that there is a sense of indefiniteness with Richter's painting?

LT With Richter there's a tactility to the painted surface. It's a systematic indefiniteness, applied as repetition, model, technique and style to the painting and fed back into reality as a trace. My question is whether this trace could actually measure up to reality. And that's why Richter's indefiniteness is a systematic indefiniteness, unlike mine, which is painted. I value Richter's approach, his choice of imagery, the way in which he stays consistent until the end … and his occasional reserve.

HDW I would like to return to discussing painting's relationship to photography and Luc's series *Time*. In the portrait of Reinhard Heydrich, the final painting in the series, part of a photograph is glued to the cardboard and is then obscured within the painting.

LT The photograph of Heydrich was cut from the Nazi propaganda magazine, *Signal*. It had already been published and disseminated, and while the paper was very good, it had yellowed with age. In that sense, the photograph had already been subjected to a major alteration. I had this intuitive idea about time as I was adding a specific anachronism to the painting. For the first time, a document became part of a painting's history, as well as its genesis. The first painting was formed intuitively and chromatically, with the addition of a green tinge to the black and white. To reiterate, I never use pure black, only van Dyck brown mixed with emerald green to produce a very dark so-called black – the result is a green tinge and a "cold warmth" that operates in way that's hard to characterize. Mixed with white, it also produces a green tinge, and in Budapest the colour of the floor almost mirrored the grey in the painting. Returning to the painting of Heydrich, the image was stronger when I made the work in 1988 – it has faded even more since and there's paint on the photo

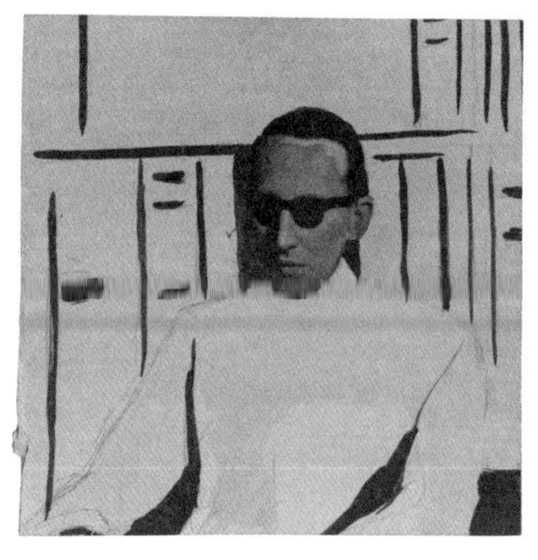

<u>80</u> LUC TUYMANS, detail from: *Die Zeit* [Time], 1988

because the reproduction was glued to the cardboard with paint. While the subject of the Holocaust represents just a small part of our respective oeuvres, I must agree with Richter that if you paint something in shades of grey, every common subject acquires a historical character and becomes material.

HDW This radically addresses the connection between painting and photography.

LT Yes, by incorporating photography with the painted-on sunglasses, darkening his hair and placing the figure in front of a bookcase – in the actual photo Heydrich appears in protective clothing – he acquires a painterly context. That was the intended point – to mask the figure within a painted environment, which leads back to the authentic fake and the appropriation and integration of all of the elements again. In *Time* there is also a shift in the chromatic quality and the temperature of the colour. The next in the series, *Cif*, is the first painting I made about advertising – it depicts a kitchen cleaning product, from which I removed the price and completely altered the colour, darkening it to preserve only the emblematic nature of the image. It is also a painting that made me uncertain, and initially I wanted to paint over it. But after some time, I realized the importance of conjuring up the colour, the quality of light and the cooling effect.

HDW *Time* is also a series that, in my opinion, has an interesting connection with film because of its seriality. For example, the Odessa steps scene from Sergei Eisenstein's 1925 film *Battleship Potemkin* is very well known, and you could show that scene in four paintings, in a sequence. Is the cinematic term "sequence" appropriate here?

LT Sure, although this term is fully charged with cinematic significance. The scene of the steps in Odessa was purely pragmatic. At the time, nitrate film was scarce in the Soviet Union, which is why Eisenstein filmed it with about twenty cameras in very short takes. The use of so many cameras produces the montage effect. They were trying to waste as little film as possible so it was basically a shortcut.

HDW But via these same means, do your paintings acquire greater meaning or a different significance?

LT They acquire a variety of meanings but, more interestingly, they invade space in an almost sculptural way. The space in between the paintings changes with each installation, which, in turn, changes the paintings themselves. For example, the closer you hang them, the smaller they appear.

GB Yes, unlike in film, the sequence we're dealing with here – of the static image – is legible in two directions. In film it passes by and then disappears. So, in addition to the sequential aspect, there's something here that can be called rhythm. Rhythm means more than the clear presentation of a temporal sequence – it's not one-after-the-other. In that sense I find the comparison with film enlightening, but the paintings maintain a quality of their own. Four paintings in this arrangement are much more autonomous and carry their own logic.

HDW Right, but their order is fixed?

LT Yes, but, as we've previously mentioned, you can also view them backwards.

HDW But that doesn't change the order.

LT Yes, but returning to Mr Boehm's comments and to what I mean when I describe the paintings as "sculptural", is that they are perceived individually, but the gaps between them prevent establishing a real narrative. In film there's automatically a narrative, no matter what. Even when the film doesn't actually tell a story, there is a beginning, middle and an end. The series, on the other hand, is like the hands of a clock moving forward, an image that gave me the idea for *Time*.

HDW Painting is traditionally very direct, in that the painter stands in front of the canvas and engages with the history of painting. In your work, Luc, there are technical intermediaries, such as Polaroids and handmade maquettes that are photographed. This generates new visual material, which in turn leads to the final result. How does this work? Are they just technical aids?

LT Yes, it's similar to a sketch. In a Polaroid, the work is at furthest remove from the imaginative power of photographs, because a Polaroid is not the same as a photo – there is a physicality that goes beyond the simple "reproduction" quality of photographs. It's a unique print that develops much like a painting – but in reverse – from the brightest to the darkest part that appears at the end, when the developing process has finished. There's also an element of chance as the process cannot be fully controlled, especially with the old camera that I use. It's important that this process allows room for errors, which then create further possibilities.

HDW And which also can't be controlled.

LT Which are uncontrollable. I started using Polaroids for my *Heimat* exhibition in 1995.

HDW You also use empty slides. Can you explain the process?

LT The empty slide projections are my Rothkos. It's an empty field, which relates to our earlier discussions of emptying the painting.

HDW Why is the urge to empty the painting so important?

GB To create room to manoeuvre – it's related to our debate about indefiniteness.

LT Yes, and at the same time there's nothing. The paintings give shape to endpoints and show only light, and this particular light is perhaps comparable with Edward Hopper's *Sun in an Empty Room* [1963]. In one exhibition they were shown with the monkey paintings [*Exhibit #3*], which are Rococo-like in comparison with these pretty badly painted pictures. But essentially it's about a deficit in painting, rather than a loss or removal.

GB What I also find interesting about the issue we're discussing now is the artistic decision to bring the world into play via visual products, and not via a direct experience of objects or a reality that has not already been represented. I think that is a decision with unpredictable consequences that influences everything, and is the basis of what we're discussing now – what is real to me as an author, as an artist. Cézanne sat down in front of the Montagne Sainte-Victoire and stared at it. To him, that was the epitome of generating reality. Well, if visual products belong in the context of civilization, then this whole context is determined differently. It's obvious that that's how it is, of course, but I think it's worth taking note of it.

HDW I'd like to move the discussion in the direction of colour, tonality and shadow – all important components of Luc's painting. Let me start with some pictures that Hans Theys showed me of your studio in which a series of canvases can be seen nailed to the wall. What's interesting is that the *Jesuit* series [2007–09] is fairly muted in colour, yet there are a lot of coloured dots on the wall that constitute a blaze of colour.

<u>LT</u> Well, it's very difficult to get the exact tonality you want. As I mentioned earlier, there's the issue of temperature, as well as of colour itself, and both involve playing with the sense of depth. If you ignore the contrast, you lose that too because it becomes frozen and then very clear, like liquid. It's a difficult and time-consuming process. I mix the colours entirely intuitively – I see the colour and then try to get the components right. I begin and carry on until I have the right tonality. Of course I test it on bare bits of canvas, where I haven't painted yet and where it will eventually disappear. You can't see colour correctly on a palette, or even if it's a bit of canvas. You always have to have the thing upright before you can really get the true impact or the true effect of what you want to do. Even a grey-toned canvas consists of an unbelievable number of colours – there's a lot of violet and cobalt blue, and many shades that are incorporated.

<u>GB</u> Tonality is actually the relative lightness or darkness of a colour independent of the actual colour. Tonal painting occurs when chromatic components are included in such a way that their energy is felt, but they're no longer identifiable as a specific colour.

<u>LT</u> They circle around it, actually. Here we again have this idea of indefiniteness but in relation to colour because it's de-familiarized. You no longer recognize it, but sense a trace of it, like a shadow. I've always found painting shadows particularly challenging because shadow is not an object, rather space – an intermediary space that has darkened and is almost imperceptible in terms of colour. How do you paint a shadow? You can approach it like Manet, who paints it very hard and operates entirely using contrast, but you can also paint it subtly, then it's perhaps more difficult, but very interesting.

<u>HDW</u> Shadow in painting is still an instrument of illusion, isn't it?

<u>LT</u> It's an instrument of illusion, but at the same time it's an instrument of delimitation because it's never really part of the background. It's something that stresses and defines the foreground. And if a shadow is very sharp, like in Velázquez's work, it's almost like an outline. With luck, you can combine the two, like Manet did. If you go a stage further it's much more difficult, because you have to maintain your bearings in a hazy world in which shadow almost leads a life of its own. What's important is that it's a virtual space that you can put your arm into, which would then likewise darken. So illusionism is only one of its many aspects. I also think that

representation and vision have perhaps been oversimplified, it's much more complex than that.

<u>HDW</u> But how does shadow relate to colour?

<u>LT</u> It doesn't relate to colour at all. Shadow is a non-colour, a non-space. It certainly has a temperature but it swallows up every colour so there's a sense of saturation. It's saturated and it's actually saturating – like fat.

<u>HDW</u> Perhaps we should discuss the importance of the ground – the ground as plane, as the point where painting starts? We've already discussed how a painting frees itself from the ground and then disappears into it again. This dynamism of the ground is, in my opinion, one of the most important things about your painting, Luc. Would you say that the ground is the factor in a painting that makes it dynamic?

<u>LT</u> Yes, but you have to make a distinction, so as not to confuse the origins of things with tradition. The ground is more of a deliberate goal that you begin with and that, in terms of the visualization process, you actually tend to encounter, rather than discovering it for yourself. The ground persists through various paintings, not just one – this is something that you realize later, throughout the practice of painting, rather than conceiving it from the outset. Yet neither does the ground repeat itself in paintings, it's always different.

<u>GB</u> There are certainly many more factors that could not be considered if you speak about the ground only as a background plane. I think that what's interesting about the experience or determining factor of images, is that the ground always plays the "inexplicit" part in relation to the explicit. For example, a ground can contain differentiation – it needn't be completely plain. But in relation to what we can focus on it's always the inexplicit or the implicit. This is actually the crux of painting – it's possible to open up this differentiation. The ground is also the source of potential within the image, which can then become more subtly differentiated. But the ground should be taken seriously in its constitutive role as the foundation of imagery also, at such a "logical" level. It forms the basis of the possibility of generating visual imagery. Without this basis there can be no image.

<u>HDW</u> The point of departure?

<u>GB</u> Yes. If you take the implicit seriously, think it through in terms of its potential and ask, "What is this actually?" then it still belongs in the realm

of the unordered. There is something chaotic, something that's somehow present, but hasn't disclosed itself yet. Conceptually you can see how vibrant, important and constitutive this relationship with the ground is. It's the pivotal point, the hub in the nature of the image. For example, when we look around and perceive something, we order space. There's the table, the heating pipe, the window and the wall. They follow each other, and that's how I see it. But there is a curious reversal if you experience these same things in an image. The image orders what it shows in relation to me, and that's connected with the ground. This experience reveals the reversibility of the reversal. The image can't just be seen the way reality is seen – it shows me something and it can only do that in conjunction with the ground so that I can't pass through the image, not even through a painting on glass. I can optically pass through a painting on glass, like Duchamp's *The Large Glass*, but what it shows comes forward and this is eminently important.

Abschied und Gegenstand: An Intermezzo in Brussels

In the spring of 2009, the Brussels-based art centre Wiels organized the first comprehensive overview of Luc Tuymans' work in the Belgian capital. The exhibition became the subject of an evening programme called "Abschied und Gegenstand" (Farewell and Object) that allowed us to present the project to the public in Brussels. The event took place on May 13th. Footage of the Budapest and the Basel conversations was shown in public for the first time, augmented with live comments by Luc and Gottfried. The confrontation with the public in Brussels introduced a new protagonist – the German Language. The decision to adopt German – an idiom in which both Luc and myself are fluent – as the official language of our conversations had never been a point of discussion until then. Suddenly we were forced to switch to English – an unexpected event that made us realize how the preciseness and the expressiveness typical of the German language have considerably contributed to make our dialogue deeper.

The Brussels Sessions

If the conversations in Basel delivered a result in terms of excellence that we could have never anticipated, therefore being proof that the model we had developed as an answer to the Bologna reform was a valid and workable one, we also came to the conclusion that in the Basel talks the two systems of reflection – the artist and the academic – reached a state of perfect cohesion at the same time. A new field of interchange had been mapped, with both parties now feeling very comfortable with the results they had achieved. This was more than just accumulation of knowledge. Experience had played a big role and now the artist and his academic counterpart were so acquainted with one another that they could have gone for more. It then became important to subject this newly-acquired common ground to a kind of "stress-test" abroad. We all know Gottfried Boehm is one of the founding fathers of a tradition in German art history called "Bildwissenschaften" [Image-Science] – a tradition that goes back to Warburg and Panofsky and considers the phenomenon of the IMAGE as the key object of their deliberations. They had partially renounced the traditional approach to art in order to accept the image as a much more complex and multilayered system in itself. We thought that it could become interesting to confront our newly- acquired common ground with another approach of a very different nature. By inviting T.J. Clark to join us for the last couple of sessions in Brussels, we brought in a celebrated art historian known for his understanding of creative processes as part of larger social and economic structures. At the time T.J. had just received the status of professor-emeritus at the University of Berkeley and had moved to London. For the Brussels sessions the language would shift from German to English, and the tone of the discussion would become different, with other accents enriching the debate. The two final conversations took place at the Palais des Beaux-Arts (BOZAR) in Brussels in April 2011 on the occasion of the comprehensive retrospective exhibition Luc had that spring. T.J.'s contribution enriched the project with new fascinating angles that reinforced the understanding between the artist and his academic partners already in place. T.J.'s participation would go on to confirm in the brightest possible way this victory of intelligence over the obscurantism introduced by the Bologna reform.

Gottfried Boehm (GB) | Timothy James "T.J." Clark (TC)

Hans M. De Wolf (HDW) | Luc Tuymans (LT)

HDW T.J. Clark has joined us here in Brussels where we continue our conversation about images and formulate new ways of organizing knowledge that makes sense to both painters and theoreticians. As a painter, Luc deals with pictures every day. As a theoretician, Gottfried Boehm was instrumental in introducing the idea of *Bildwissenschaft*. T.J., as someone who has worked in American academia for a long time, what are your thoughts about the current institutional discourse on this topic?

GB Do you think that art historians are able to make public contributions that are strong enough to convey that these developments in academia are misguided? Do we have valid arguments, and if so, what are they?

TC I am a realist. I think that the forces against us are formidable. Although I do believe that we have strong arguments. When so many different people are talking about a shift towards an image culture, and particularly a screen-image culture, we have the opportunity to consider what this means. What changes can we instigate in the nature of cognition and public discourse, or in the exchange of knowledge? What is the difference between a screen-image, an image on a page, an image in a frame, on a canvas, and so on? Luc, this is one of the underlying subjects of your painting. What does painting have to say in a context where the power of the image is shifting so fundamentally? What new technologies are affecting the notion of image making?

<u>LT</u> Painting is anachronistic, but its power stems from its loaded history. One of the most interesting arguments is that art is not only about quantity or skill, but rather a commitment to continuity and content. Take the example of my friend, the Chinese artist Ai Weiwei. He has reached a level of consistency in his work and he has been able to maintain it for many years. However, when I spent time working in China, I felt this was generally lacking. Discontinuity and a lack of content seem to be becoming a problem in the United States, Europe, and across the West as a whole. With my exhibition here in Brussels, there has been a lot of press coverage, with five or six interviews every day. This forced the politicians to see the show, not because they wanted to, but because there was so much attention surrounding it. And while there is a long-standing belief that art is inaccessible to the mass, and that didactic information is most of the time a patronizing exercise designed to tell you what to think about the work, this is not the case. Artists will always be more important than politicians because art survives with the passage of time while politicians are forgotten. Therefore, I think it's important to use the image as a critical mass and the point from which you can deliberately engage and invite dialogue, especially because there is so much visual oversaturation in our society. I can understand the way a film like Orson Welles' *The Lady from Shanghai* from 1947 has been edited, whereas contemporary soap operas have such seamless editing that it's nearly impossible to spot it. I think you have to be *insolite*, as the French say, and not oversaturate things in order to allow space for reflection.

<u>HDW</u> Are you saying that those two different modes of operating with images are incongruent?

<u>LT</u> No, nothing is incongruent any more. It is not a question of winning the battle – just a question of survival.

<u>HDW</u> I'll pose the question differently. How could a filmmaker try to work along the lines of *The Lady from Shanghai*, which has its own set of aesthetics? Art now exists in an environment in which people already have fixed ideas about images. Should you take that into account or not?

<u>LT</u> *The Lady from Shanghai* is just an example. The film has its flaws, but it also has iconic imagery, such as the final farewell scene in the hall of mirrors. What makes the imagery iconic is the fact that it might just as well have been painted. It relates to how images evolve, how we know them,

and how we deal with them, in different layers. I've always liked this film because it jumps up and down in terms of tone, and ends in a roller-coaster. It is very unlike *Citizen Kane*.

GB We haven't used the term "art" until now. Why not?

TC I think this has to do with how we present our concerns, our perspective on the image world, in a way that makes sense to those who are demanding relevance. I certainly use the term "art" all the time, but if you immediately trot it out, you seem to be conceding that your concerns are limited and traditional, and that they don't involve wider culture. This is a bad initial move, although I actually think that this strange European, early modern-age phenomenon called "art", or high art – the art of the courts, the bourgeoisie and museums – is extraordinarily important. It is part of modernity, so I am not apologetic about it as an objective study, but what was the place of that self-reflective, highly cultivated work of the image? In each case, what was the place or the point of it, in the wider culture of image making? I think it had a point, it had a place, and perhaps part of our argument is that, if art gets completely dissolved into image culture, something very important has been lost – a space for renewal and for criticism.

GB Do you think that our somewhat old-fashioned discussions about art and the image offer a window of opportunity for public discourse?

TC Yes, they do. Although, as you know, I am profoundly bored by the Anglo-American art-historical apologetic apostasis in the face of art. For over two decades in academia, the word "aesthetic" was used with a sneer in order to get cheap sympathy from the academic audience, to ensure they're on your side. Now, the anti-aesthetic movement is completely exhausted in the art world.

LT I have experienced this myself. It has to do with contextualization. Bertrand Russell said in 1964 that we have become democratic in our outward forms and our innermost convictions.[1] This is when an all too apologetic contextualization sets in, surrounding the whole framework, making it more available and comprehensive. At the same time, it backfired by annihilating its own discourse from within. Now, when we talk about the image, it is different from the early twentieth century, when positions were more clearly defined. Although I believe that it is still relevant to take a

1 Bertrand Russell, *Freedom and Organization 1814–1914*, Allen & Unwin, London, 1964.

position with respect to the image, and the most important artists – from El Greco to Velázquez and Manet – have all done so, it is less of a priority nowadays.

<u>HDW</u> We've been discussing how images function and how they should be perceived, but equally important within the context of Luc's work is the notion of commitment. This is something that T.J. has been addressing in his scholarship – relationships and connections with social and ideological violence, and the way in which an artist reacts against, or works with it.

<u>TC</u> Maybe I should comment first on Luc's work in this regard. I don't have an *a priori* commitment to the idea of political or politicized art. I have had a life-long interest in left-wing politics, and therefore I am interested in those moments within the history of modern art where political means have intersected with art, for example, with Jacques-Louis David, Courbet, and the Soviet avant-garde during the Russian Revolution. I have always argued that these moments are exceptional. You can certainly say that all artists are committed if they are serious artists – they make art, which in some way must be engaged with a sense of the times and the purpose of image making at a certain moment. But of course, we mean more than that – "committed" is a tricky term.

<u>HDW</u> When we discussed the connection between a picture and its meaning in Basel, Luc said that there is no such thing as political art.

<u>LT</u> I certainly wasn't so blunt. First of all, likening art to politics is one thing. Every human transaction in relation to art is political, but art cannot be political from the start – that is propaganda. However, art can have a political stance at a certain moment in time, which is why memory is so important when it comes to politics and specific moments. Art must create a meta-image to recall those moments. I was reading about Jean-François Millet's iconic painting *The Sower* in T.J.'s book, *The Absolute Bourgeois: Artists and Politics in France, 1848–1851*, where at a time of dramatic social change, Millet recorded a disappearing peasant presence and simultaneously expressed timelessness through the repetition of commonplace pastoral imagery, but one with a violent turn. This heroic interpretation of a gesture like working the field immediately reminded me of *The Falling Soldier* [*Loyalist Militiaman at the Moment of Death, Cerro Muriano, September 5, 1936*] by Robert Capa, which supposedly depicts the death of a soldier during the Spanish Civil War. It became one of the most iconic

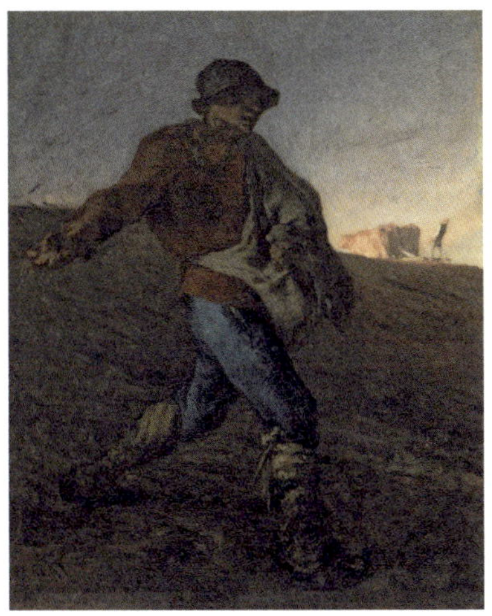
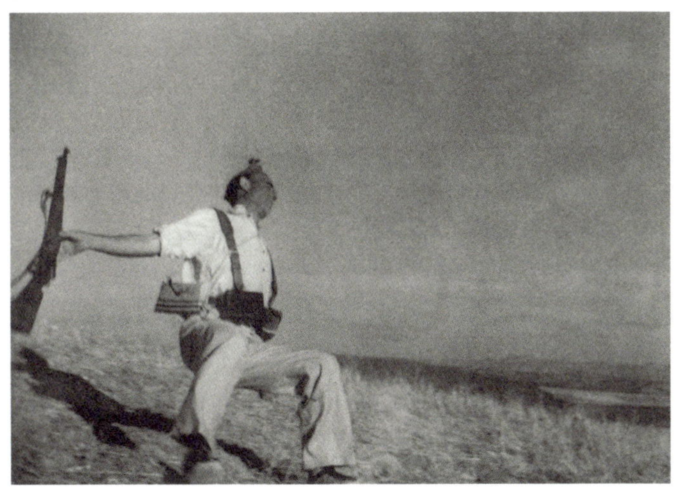

<u>81</u> Jean-François Millet, *The Sower*, 1850
Oil on canvas, 101.6 × 82.6 cm
Museum of Fine Arts, Boston, inv. 17.1485

<u>82</u> Robert Capa, *Loyalist Militiaman at the Moment of Death, Cerro Muriano,
September 5, 1936*, 1936 (printed at a later date)
Gelatin silver print, 24.7 × 34 cm
The Metropolitan Museum of Art, New York, inv. 2005.100.166

images depicting a historical event, but later it was discovered that the photograph had been staged. That is what I mean by remembrance and how we constantly "distrust" imagery.

TC Maybe we can refer to the four panels of *Die Zeit* as an example [see pp. 62–63]? I remember being deeply impressed when I first saw them. I did not understand exactly what was happening in the compositions, but I knew that an intense amount of thinking about images was going on, which I found very engaging and this made me struggle for a cohesive reading. Even if I had not been told that the portrait was of Reinhard Heydrich, I would have known that it involves some kind of twentieth-century horror, and that something appalling is taking place in *Die Zeit*, carefully disguised by bureaucratic faces, anonymous-looking buildings and spaces, which give nothing away. Coming back to our earlier discussion, what is the relationship between the political instigation and the painting itself? I'm not saying that the material transcends the painting, but there is a distance and a difference between the photograph of Heydrich and Heydrich as he appears on that canvas. And what is the relationship of this ominous, yet guarded face to the other three images? Where does it place me in relation to the close-up of the two pills next to it? Am I going back from a close-up to a mid-shot? What kind of discourse am I meant to take from it? I immediately knew there was some kind of reflection on the politics of the twentieth century, and its ability to mask extreme horror in something akin to muteness, or blandness, or routine.

<u>LT</u> Routine is a good word. In terms of a position, from the very beginning I sought to avoid Modernist or Minimalist approaches. Instead I focused on issues related to recent history because the consequences were so immense, and the image building that accompanied these thought processes was, likewise, enormous. I was also intrigued by a different kind of non-representation. What is especially relevant for a group of works like *Die Zeit* is that much of World War II history is remembered in black and white. When George Stevens[2] arrived in Europe and filmed the liberation of Paris in colour, it resulted in a completely different understanding of that history. When I saw his films, everything became much more "in the moment" because of the colour. It's a very different, physical approach. Gerhard Richter has noted that if paintings are built up in shades of grey, or black and white, they immediately create a distance and become part of an archive. The series is titled *Die Zeit* because it is a reflection on the concept of time, but also about a specific idea of time. The Heydrich painting is only partially painted, his face is a cut-out from *Signal* magazine, so there is a link between what figuration is and what abstraction could be, which is where the archive and the document come into play. You begin with an image, you then create *your* image, and finally you detach yourself from the image that you've just made. I was never an abstract painter in the conventional, gestural sense because I've always felt that it was too emotive. Figuration allows me an in-between step. I never saw a difference between figuration and abstraction. Figuration is loaded because you must know what you are going to depict in order to understand how you are going to depict it. There is a clear image in *Die Zeit* and a legible relation to history. But this actually only occurred from the third painting onwards. The first two paintings possessed a certain degree of innocence. They became less innocent with the face of Heydrich. The inner face and the colours of this sort of cityscape are uniform and objective, but it still has an element of *pittura metafisica* – a midday setting with defined shadows.

2 During World War II, Stevens joined the US Army Signal Corps and headed a film unit from 1943 to 1946 under General Eisenhower. His unit shot footage documenting D-Day – including the only Allied European Front colour film of the war – the liberation of Paris, and the meeting of American and Soviet forces at the Elbe River, as well as horrific scenes from the Duben labour camp and the Dachau concentration camp. Stevens also helped prepare the Duben and Dachau footage and other material for presentation during the Nuremberg trials.

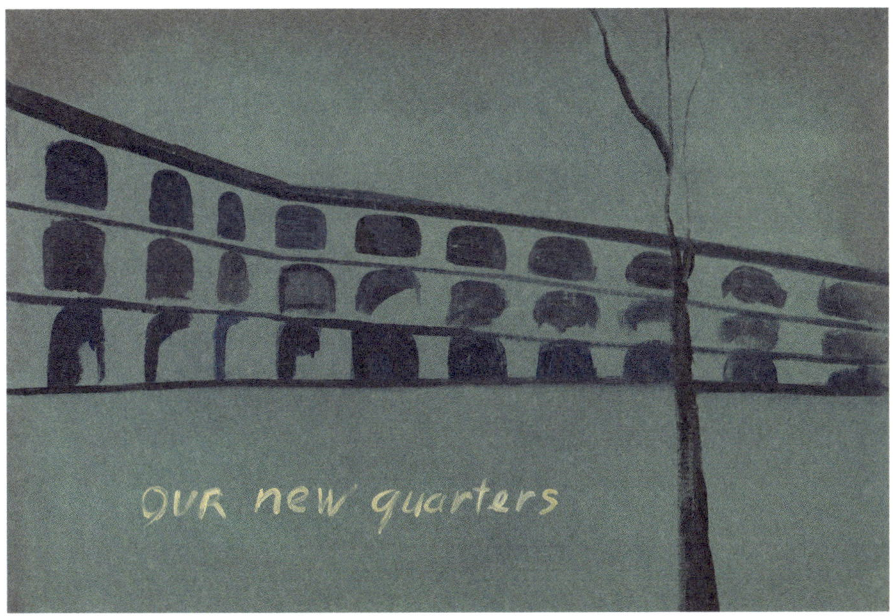

83 Luc Tuymans, *Our New Quarters*, 1986
Oil on canvas, 80.5 × 120 cm
MMK Museum für Moderne Kunst Frankfurt am Main. Schenkung des Künstlers. INV. NR. 1994/62

TC When you refer to "the first two images", do you mean the past or the present tense? *Are* they completely innocent, or *were* they completely innocent? This matters.

LT Actually, they were not completely innocent, because if you look closely at the first image there is a sentence that has been painted over and which reads, "niets in zicht" [nothing in sight]. It was included on the spur of the moment, but the four paintings were all made in one day.

HDW T.J., your description of your personal response to *Die Zeit* confirms what we had concluded in Basel, that pictures are autonomous – particularly these four pictures – and they contain an inherent intelligence. Knowing that their content is derived from a Nazi propaganda magazine is meaningful, but only to a point. There is another, autonomous level to these images, which has something to do with what you referred to as "an experience", and which is also difficult to grasp. And then there are paintings like *Our New Quarters*, in which Luc also uses text, which brings us back to the notion of language and introduces another possibility or level of conveying knowledge.

LT *Our New Quarters* is almost no longer a painting. It is important on a pictorial level, but it is also relevant and vital as a concept. The words, painted in a yellow-white, light up like a subtitle in a documentary film. Here, language actually destroys the imagery, while simultaneously supporting the image. I have combined text and image in this way a few times. However, let's discuss the muteness of imagery.

TC That reminds me of one of my favourite quotations by Nicolas Poussin: "Moi qui fais profession de choses muettes"[3] [I am in the profession of silent things].

GB May I come back to a remark you made a few weeks ago? "I really don't know what is happening", which is the oldest metaphor for art: *Je ne sais quoi.* I suppose we must rethink the relationship between our discussions of images and the wider discussion of art. Or, let me put it more cautiously, some qualities of the inner organization of the image – muteness, reflection, multifocal presentation. I think we have an opportunity to combine these discussions of art and images.

TC Yes, if we think that the art aspect of image making that crystallized in Jan van Eyck, Rogier van der Weyden and many others, emerged at a certain moment in time. In terms of the qualities you've just mentioned, it seems as though a certain craft culture is seizing the opportunities of the image that enables complex, open-ended reflection, an indeterminacy in the statement of proposition. Or a muteness – it is not quite a proposition, but something is being said without being proposed. This seems to be associated with an early modern moment, as I would put it (being an old Marxist), a time of city-states and highly sophisticated court cultures in Burgundy and Northern Italy, predominantly aristocratic and monarchic, but infiltrated by new kinds of rationality and new world-views, giving it an instrumental push. So the big question for me is, why is it so important in this culture that there should be a new fascination with the density, complexity and open-endedness of image making? I have my thoughts, but I would love to hear yours.

GB One answer is the model of compensation. Ours is a culture that resists the development of modern, natural sciences, rationality, language, and the human perspective, which also forms part of this conversation. One could

<hr>

3 From a letter in 1639 addressed to his friend de Noyers.

argue that this central density of the image is a mode of resistance and compensation. This is a very well-known model that could be a possible answer to your question.

TC In other words, an area in which ends, means, rationality and an instrumental attitude to the world – which is what is going to triumph, after all – can already be found in the Burgundian court, subject to distance and resistance. The paradox is that Domitian tells us that a sense of perspective is a tremendous advance in image means and rationality. Two centuries before Descartes, he already saw a model of total comprehension, manipulability and measurability. Van Eyck and his contemporaries were already deeply involved with this model of rationality.

GB This is a paradox because, on the one hand, there is a discourse around the rationalization of the image – in Albrecht Dürer, for example – and at the same time, there is a legitimization of the sensual aspect of the work. Sensuality is as legitimate, and seen as existing on the same level, as concepts. In the new type of image we find in Renaissance- and Burgundian-era works, both aspects are granted equal rights.

TC That is exactly what I unrepentantly celebrate in the high art from Burgundy, which brings us back to the present. Have we entered a reverse situation? Does our social avant-garde believe that it will make up the future social order? Is it perhaps staking everything on the senses, such as affect and appetite – the culture of image consumption?

LT Moreover, it would seem that the pornographic has taken over. Websites and virtual reality now allow us to alter and interact with images, to be within the image, as it is being conceived. Of course, this is not an endless game, and it appears that conformism is rather important these days. This can ascend to astounding heights, not only to legitimize images, but also to constantly manipulate imagery. Pornography is very strange and abstract, and there is a lack of investigation into what the term "vulgar" might mean. Consumption means literally how one consumes imagery, as well as the attitude that goes alongside it. There is a physicality, a weight even, when imagery is accumulated and repeated. A singular image in this society is hard to process – exceedingly so – in that its singularity is actually a threat to the context of imagery itself. This is where silence and power become important aspects of image building, especially with regard to the aristocracy. For example, in a play like *Marat/Sade* by Peter Weiss [1964], the aristocrat's ultimate goal is to disappear. His final request is to be buried in an unmarked grave so that "all traces of my tomb may disappear from the face of the earth, just as I hope all traces of my memory will be erased from the memories of men". It is an authoritarian vision of the world, a soap-opera vision. Today, this no longer exists – only as an image, as an ideal, as something that was once equated with excellence. The word "excellence" is important within the visual. Silence, power and excellence are old-fashioned, but they are still relevant and are in total opposition to the other aspects I've just mentioned.

HDW In the same way as sociology?

LT I think sociology has been abused in the arts. A lot of art from the 1980s that was based on sociological hypotheses is interesting, but it's also ridiculous. Disconnecting the visual from its discourse is not a valid proposal, yet this happens widely. When curators are formed through curatorial programmes, such as the Bard Center for Curatorial Studies in upstate New York [ccs] or De Appel arts centre in Amsterdam, knowledge becomes reduced to a synopsis of Gilles Deleuze or Jacques Derrida. This reductive way of thinking not only obliterates the image, but also obliterates the knowledge surrounding it – again leading to conformity.

HDW Yes, but you also need the discourse.

LT Discourse is important, but it's not disconnected from the visual. I have engaged in many discussions, and some arguments, with these curators about the importance of the visual. After all, I am a visual artist so my position will always be from the perspective of the visual, and not about a particular discourse.

HDW This brings us to the tension between theoretical approaches and image content. How do we manage to maintain that tension? I think we have to do so through a constant reinvention of systems.

GB What we are doing as art historians and critics is a paradox. On the one hand, we use concepts to make distinctions, and on the other, we attempt to describe what is not part of the concept. If we do not consider both aspects together, we have nothing. There is a certain type of art historian that is totally iconoclastic – they destroy what they are discussing by translating it into a language of distinctions, *Begriffen* [terms] and *Konzepten* [concepts]. Would you agree?

TC For the most part, yes, but in all fairness to art historians, it is a paradox of the discipline. We are confronted by a non-verbal world and our job is to translate it into verbal terms, which is actually an ordinary human activity that we spend most of our lives doing. Yet it's also very difficult and mysterious. In everyday life, we have the language of gesture, which points to the fact that our words aren't sufficient. But how do you make that part of an art-historical practice?

LT This is due to the fact that art history is highly hypothetical.

HDW Indeed, probably because we want to share experiences that are difficult to verbalize. In a sense, there is constant repetition. For example, in 1933 a French writer, Henry de Montherland, noted in his diaries that he found Rembrandt terribly inspiring. Then in 1952 he wrote that he couldn't remember why he wrote such a thing back in 1933. It was a mystery and Rembrandt was absolutely not inspiring. I think this is part of the paradigm – you have to begin all over again, partially because art history is not a static thing but always in flux, as Gottfried Boehm has pointed out.

LT I think that discussions about art, its criticism or even its history (which is inherently flawed), can only ever take the form of a conversation.

GB Luc, I would like to come back to a point that you made earlier about your concept of pornography. Could you expand on that, because I think it is quite different from the common understanding of pornography?

LT There are aspects of repetition, obsession and possession – all of which are corporeal and focused on the object. Pornography is no longer about the physical act, but rather the object of desire or lust. This is fascinating because it leads to a tremendous amount of falsification, which takes over to the point of becoming more real than reality. On a social level, we are struggling to understand what these dependencies are. It is a grave thing to admit, but we have become more dependent on objects over time. What people think they need to exist is amazing. As far back as fifteen years ago, I did not have a mobile phone, just a landline. Now if you don't have your mobile phone with you, you feel castrated. Such things seem trite, but they are ultimately pornographic. I think a lot of people do not understand that.

HDW So pornography for you is really a kind of addiction to objects?

LT It is more of a fascination than an addiction. I'm intrigued by what it produces and brings forth. It also creates an exceedingly strange imagery

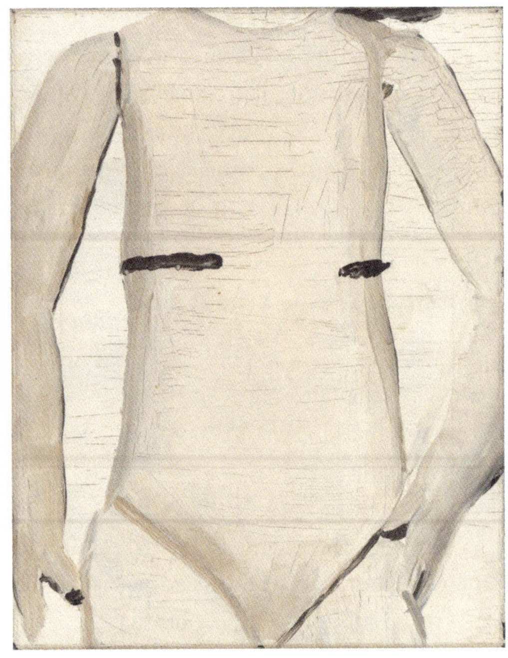

84 Luc Tuymans, *Body*, 1990
Oil on canvas, 48.5 × 38.5 cm
Collectie S.M.A.K., Stedelijk Museum
voor Actuele Kunst Gent

because, when you return it to its own position, it takes place at a trivial moment, rather than at a moment of importance.

HDW But is it empty?

LT Yes, there is a sense of quietude.

HDW Your concept of pornography makes me think of the famous Alfred Jarry quote in *Le Surmâle* [1902] about sexuality being of no importance, because you can do it every time again. Because you can repeat it as much as you want, it has no value.

LT Yes, but we are referring more to images, objects and the visual, rather than the sexual act. My work has been described as asexual, which is exactly why it is, actually, sexual. Sexuality is obviously an underlying theme, made clear in a painting like *Body*. It is not about depicting any act. Rather, it is about everything else. This is the interesting side of pornography – it's a place where a meta-image originates, which is a timeless concept. The aspect that relates to it as a "filthy" concept I find less gripping. Because it is something that is continuously suppressed (although not in the gender-related Freudian sense of repression), it connects, historically, to a lineage of suppressed imagery.

TC I am struggling to understand your notion of the pornographic, but I think I am getting there. It has something to do with an image-life, in which there is a continual offer and presentation of the image and a continual addictive fascination with it, which is delivering both pleasure and a kind of passivity. You are toying with that idea. It links in my mind to other people's description of – dare I say it – the "society of the spectacle", a spectacular burden, a particularly new, recent constellation of a sociality based on an infinitely replaceable image-form. So am I right in thinking that your art increasingly becomes about that? It is an attempt-picture, a state of image fascination and the conditions of its production. To me, this seems increasingly to be your subject.

LT I think the word "condition" is quite interesting. Thus far, we've spoken about an image that is progressive, or new, but we've not yet spoken about the condition of the image. With the condition of the image I do not mean the state it is in, but a larger idea. I play chess, and the way that things have evolved over time is a bit like chess. Earlier on, in the Romantic era, one could still win a game of chess even after making mistakes and sacrificing pieces. The game was open and tactical, and winning was secondary. Now every move you make has to be the right move. It is all about this one move, and that is the condition. Even if you think thirty-five moves ahead, it doesn't help because, logistically, all games have already been played. I think, nowadays, the image has arrived at an end-point in terms of what is real within the context of imagery. This is why I use the word "pornography". It is an adversary of the distinction between what is false or real. This present condition – the ambiguous state of mind and a visual ambiguity – is now here to delve into. It is a difficult kind of research, because all references are intertwined with the imagery. Nevertheless, it also presents a completely blank slate, which is an interesting challenge. Perhaps some people might make paintings that seem to be painted the way that I – or any other artist – might paint them, but that doesn't matter, since it is the intentionality that has the most profound effect upon any image. Without the drive of intention, you merely have surface. It's devoid of meaning.

HDW I am thinking about Duchamp, who once said that drawing comes closest to chess. You know the rules, but every game is different. He thought chess was more interesting than design because in the end it's ephemeral, there is nothing left. And then it always starts all over again. If you look at obsessive chess players, you can see a relation with pornography.

LT However, once you are in the throes of the game, it is the most asexual game there is, although it is extremely visual.

TC So, Luc, what is the difference between the present-day condition of the image, and the condition of the image for a viewer of van Eyck, in a Burgundian setting?

LT That is an interesting question. While we were shooting the documentary film *Goudvis: afstand/timing/precisie* [Goldfish: Distance/Timing/Precision – Canvas, Belgian Television, 2010], I made a point of visiting the National Gallery in London after public closing hours specifically to see *The Arnolfini Portrait* by Jan van Eyck, which is one of my favourite paintings. As an image-maker, van Eyck, and especially that one painting, is important to me because it opens up to the world. Velázquez must have seen it because we find a similar depiction of the mirror in his *Las Meninas*, as well as the position of the artist, who inscribes himself with his name in the image above the mirror, thus opening it up to the outside world. Van Eyck's realism is unforgiving. He discarded any sense of sentimentality. He is the first artist to detach the world from the image, and the first to cut loose from the mimetic imagery of Christianity and its pervasive dogma. I therefore cannot think of anything more powerful. This image must have seemed very modern at the time – perfection coexists with total imperfection.

TC I hear you say that the difference has something to do with the fact that a van Eyck painting has distance built into it, and a level of reflection on its own difference from the real – it is a model of the real. It offers a view and some form of comprehension.

LT Yes, but it does so by miscomprehending, by not giving it away.

TC So am I right in intuiting what you mean by pornographic negativity, which has something to do with a collapse of that distance, in that you are always already inside the image?

LT Yes, that is really important, especially the words "condition" and "collapse".

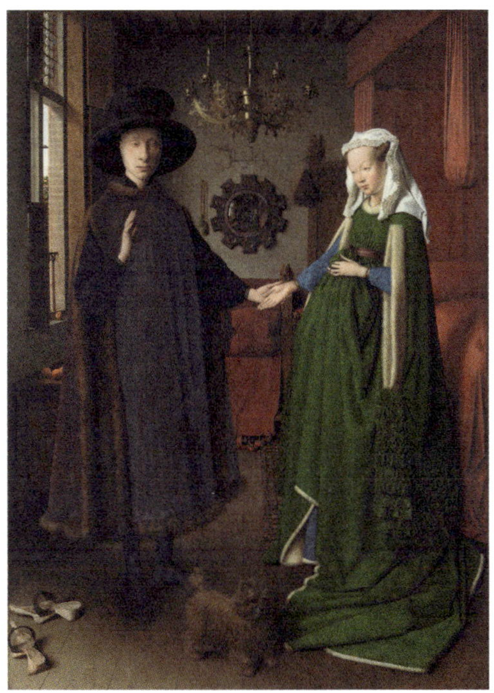

85 Jan van Eyck, *The Arnolfini Portrait*, 1434
Oil on panel, 82.2 × 60 cm
The National Gallery, London, INV. NG186

TC I think that is something I see in your work from the last ten years. So here is a question – for those of us who loved the small scale of your earlier work, it is a bit of a struggle to come to terms with your move to working on a larger scale. Does the large scale have something to do with this notion that painting no longer belongs to an image world of miniaturization, of framing and of placing? Current technologies want to collapse, evade and leap over those boundaries. Is the large scale of your paintings somehow in dialogue with this?

LT No, the large-scale paintings are probably the most meaningless of all my works. The two big paintings at the beginning of this exhibition are all about the spectacle of their own imagery. They deal with the concept of a theme park and the obliteration of the utopian by incarcerating fantasy within a physical space. Therefore, they have to have an obvious visibility, which is what makes them totally abstract. In *Wonderland* especially, if you look into the tunnel, you see Cubist elements. When it was first shown in the US, the audience was shocked by the fact that a European was using

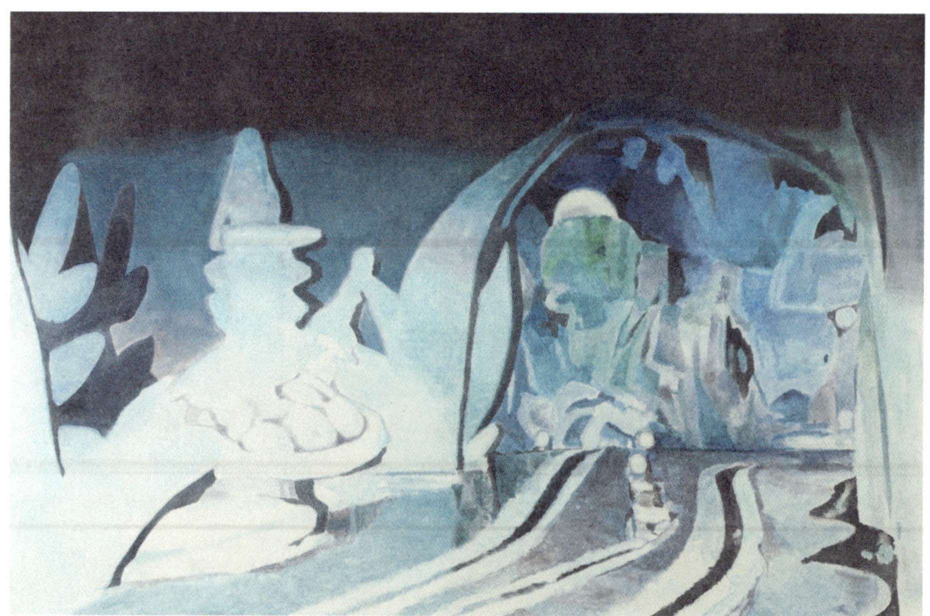

their scale and the Disney Corporation – a long-standing product of their society that claims copyright on its images for eternity. They hated it and reviews were only published after the show had closed. *Still Life* was also about this inflating of the effect and exaggerating the consumability of an image. Scale plays an important part within imagery, which is why I never start working on a stretched canvas, except for with my early works. Many people – especially Americans and Germans – use scale without fully comprehending it. However, a small Caspar David Friedrich painting can be much stronger than a big work by Anselm Kiefer because it is a mental image. My large-scale paintings are, in some ways, a test.

TC I didn't understand this scale when I saw the paintings at the Wexner Center for the Arts in Ohio, although in the current setting it seems to make more sense. It is also a test for the viewer.

LT The Palais des Beaux-Arts in Brussels – the last venue of the touring exhibition – is the best place for these paintings because they look *really* huge, whereas at the Wexner Center and other museums in the US they just seemed large. I wanted to show *Still Life* at the Haus der Kunst in

Munich from the first time I walked through the building, and when it was eventually shown there the effect was shocking. At 3.47 by 5 metres, it already is very big, but hung in an immense space of 40 metres the physicality was amazing. For me, scale is also related to memory. When I would look at El Greco reproductions in books, I was unable to recognize or memorize the colours of his paintings, I thought their temperature was strange and I disliked them. But when I first encountered his paintings as a 19-year-old in Budapest, I was shocked. I saw how an image could be deconstructed and realized that he was not a mannerist painter at all. This has a lot to do with the aspect of scale.

TC I have a very concrete question from the perspective of an art historian. I think I have a general understanding of the kind of processes of discovery that led to some of your earlier works like *Wandeling* [1989], which shows Nazis walking in the snow in Berchtesgaden. I have a notion of the kind of practical thinking that went on between the source image and the paintings. I have a much less clear idea of how you investigated the world of Disney. Were these still images that popped up, or did you immerse yourself in a moving image flow and wait for the moment when something occurred, which you thought could be stopped and worked with?

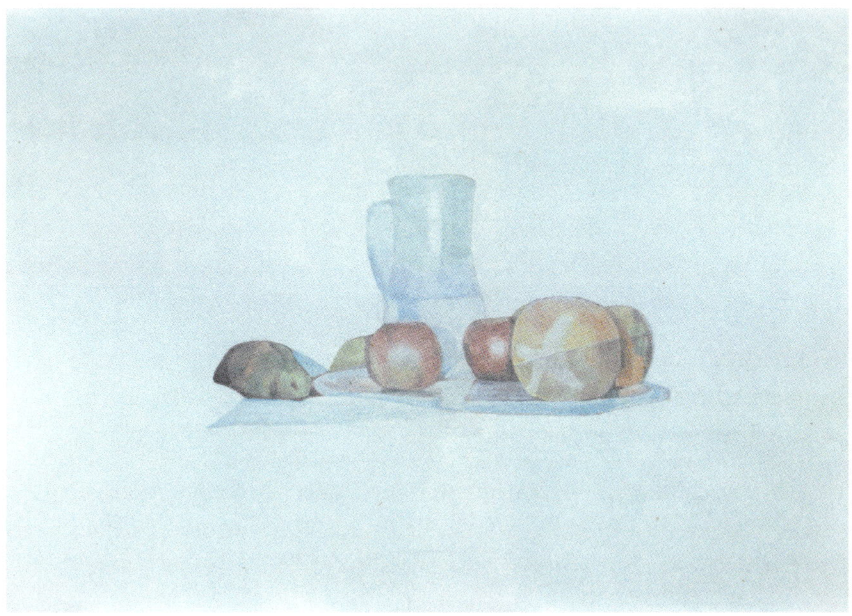

<u>87</u> Luc Tuymans, *Still Life*, 2002
Oil on canvas, 347.8 × 502.5 cm
Private collection

LT The first *Wonderland* image was actually found on the Internet by my assistant, the artist Tommy Simoens. I had just finished an exhibition, *Les Revenants* [Antwerp, 2007] and *Restoration* [Tokyo, 2006], which had examined the role of the Jesuits in the Belgian education system and their influence on the formation of the country's political elite. Moving from a topic as loaded as the Jesuits to the image of *Wonderland* – with its fake, animated fairytale décor – made sense to me and was a seamless transition. The exhibition about the phenomenon of Disney, *Forever: The Management of Magic* [2008], was also one of the most abstract shows of my work, which is probably why the audience reacted negatively to it. I thought the show was strong because it was so tightly knit in terms of palette and light, and it reverberated. The paintings never addressed Goofy, Mickey Mouse, or any of Disney's products. They addressed the surroundings, like a barrier that you had to confront and where you were continuously cast out. It is a similar break as when I first showed *The Diagnostic View*. Before that, my imagery was more akin to *Die Zeit*. So people were shocked because they thought there was an enormous, quite difficult jump in terms of the imagery. The Disney work is the first time that I applied paint to the canvas horizontally, in order to create a grid. Its flatness is opulent and stops you from entering the image. The work totally sidesteps the real because it is symptomatic in its essence and in its depiction. Those jumps are always important for me because they allow for a certain detachment that makes it possible to move forward. We should also note that it is impossible to go back in painting. Technically, I suppose I could repaint everything I've ever painted, but *intentionally* I simply cannot, which is why painting has an essence. It's borne out from this *fact* that you cannot go back – that there is only one, forward-moving trajectory – or you risk losing it, which is a constant fear.

TC I find it very interesting that Tommy Simoens found the image. I would love to talk more about the interaction between artist and studio.

LT Imagery is born from conversations. Before an image is made, it is contemplated. It has already been validated (or not), and I do this with my wife, or with Tommy – a certain group of people within my close circle.

TC Do you think that, even though your subject becomes increasingly a certain picture of a new culture of the image, this culture of total image flow? In her essay in "Painting the Banality of Evil", Helen Molesworth uses a very good metaphor to describe your work. In your works, instead of a cinematic frame or photograph, we have the sense of an image being on pause, as if someone had pressed the pause button. That was tremendously helpful for me and spoke to something that has happened to us, and has happened to your art. In light of that, it seems interesting to me that your starting-point was a still image from a webpage. Do you often work from still images, even if they are part of an image flow, and do they bear some trace of this?

LT Yes. The third exhibition in the series, following the work on the Jesuits and Disney, was called *Against the Day*, taken from the title of a Thomas Pynchon novel. It included two important paintings, *Against the Day I* and *Against the Day II*, both of which show the same figure with a shovel in my backyard, like in a nineteenth-century painting by Jean-François Millet. But they show two stages – one where the man is shovelling, and the other where he is not. This is the pause – two lines, or two beats, of the same situation.

HDW There is a notion of pathos, which we discussed both in relation to El Greco and as a certain condition of the image.

TC Although it remains a strong and complex notion in your work, this term is always tough for an English speaker. "Pathos" is a devalued concept in the English language, which, I believe, lost its original meaning in the nineteenth century. It was imported from Germany and progressively became equated with a failure of sentiment, which is a shame.

LT I also think that pathos, and everything that goes with it, is a terrain that has lost its effectiveness. It entered the realm of the souvenir, obliterating itself in the process. This is unfortunate because it is also a cultural loss. I can easily see Hans-Jürgen Syberberg[4] as being full of pathos, German pathos that is, and being completely devastated because Nazism had killed his entire culture. That is how he must understand his lineage, and it's also how I understand it. It is unfortunate that it is no longer possible to discuss this aspect of "pathos" because it was tainted by the negative history that followed.

GB Perhaps, unlike Syberberg, your pathos is connected with pleasure. Your paintings give the viewer a positive feeling. One can see that you

4 Hans-Jürgen Syberberg (b. 1935) is a German film director, whose best-known film is his lengthy feature, *Hitler: A Film from Germany*.

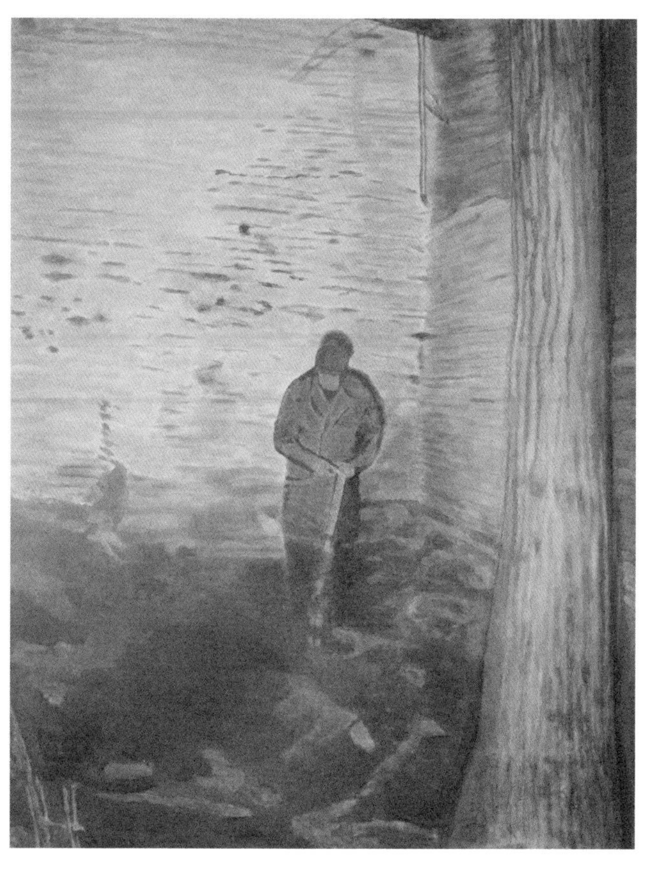

88 Luc Tuymans, *Against the Day I*, 2008
Oil on canvas, 220 × 171 cm
Private collection

89 Luc Tuymans, *Against the Day II*, 2008
Oil on canvas, 232 × 173 cm
Private collection

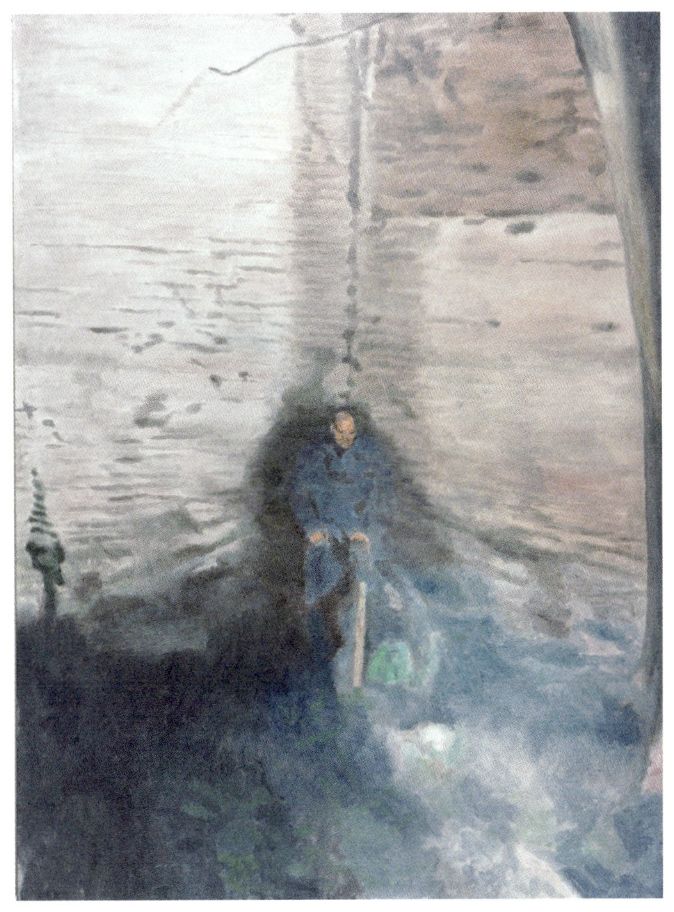

mean what you say as an artist so there's pleasure derived from looking at your work. Would you agree?

LT Up to a point. If I didn't like to paint, I wouldn't do it. The ability to do something has everything to do with enjoyment. But, as you said, it's also important that there is pleasure involved for the spectator. The complexity of an image can never be generated out of a style. It has to remain indelibly *yours* with all the inconsistencies and deficiencies that come with it. For me, painting is about timing and precision. Therein lies the real pleasure. Some will see that, others won't. That doesn't matter, since if I push what I am doing as far as I possibly can, to the very edges of what I can do at any given moment in time, that is sufficient for me. Years ago, I used to be happy for about one week after finishing a painting, now I am only happy for two days. It is very important to respond to the compulsory nature of imagery and of the image world, to try to imagine how people like van Eyck produced images far more slowly, with a different apprehension of reality, and how enormous the pressure now is to produce more and more.

HDW Have you experienced this external pressure?

LT Yes.

HDW What you said brings me to another point, the notion of speed – *Geschwindigkeit* – that scholars have never actually applied to paintings of the seventeenth century. It is fascinating to hear you, as a painter, speak about a painting by Velázquez in relation to speed. And now you bring this idea up again, as if speed was necessary to prevent you from ending up somewhere where you don't want to end up.

LT Artists have their own particular ways of working. Some artists, like Kerry James Marshall, work for a long time on one image. I can't generalize but it is about what feels right within your own attention span. I have always had the ability to work fast.

GB Giorgio Vasari liked speed in painting. He wrote in his *Lives of the Most Excellent Painters, Sculptors and Architects* that a painter who can paint large canvases quickly is the best kind of painter.

TC Fresco painting, after all, depends enormously on being able to work quickly. I agree with you that some painters, like Cézanne, work extremely slowly, although when you look at his paintings, it is obvious that not all of them were painted at a snail's pace. There can be a tremendous speed

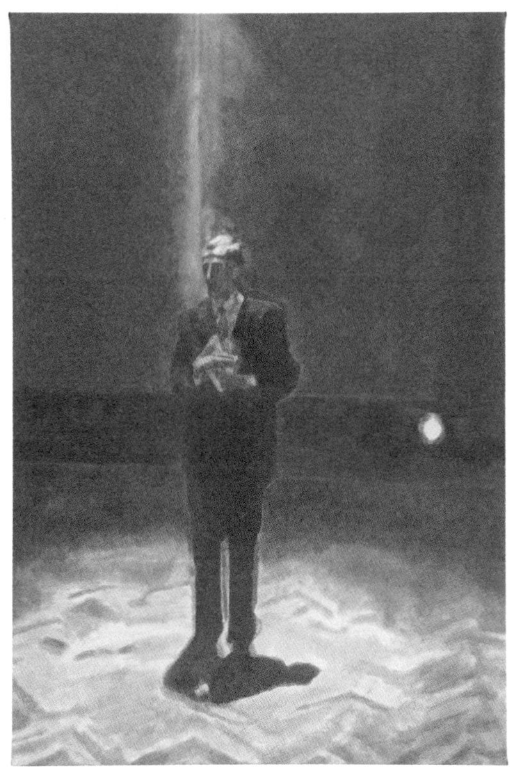

90 Luc Tuymans, *Speech*, 2010
Oil on canvas, 206.1 × 138.8 cm
The Broad Art Foundation,
Santa Monica

to his work. Going back to one of your paintings, *Speech*, the speed of the image is related to the immediacy of apprehension, of not being discursive and lacking the speed of reading or of speaking. It is about dramatizing the difference between the mute and the non-mute worlds. If you compare it with work by artists like Kerry James Marshall, who makes a meal of infinitely going on and on, it is as if there are two dimensions on either side of the normal human dimension of speech – fast or extremely slow.

HDW Let's return to this very particular notion that a picture, and the necessity for the picture, originates with the artist, who makes the decision to make an artwork or a painting. This idea has been crucial in the previous conversations and relates to T. J.'s thinking on art. Then there is the viewer, who has an awareness in front of the artwork that allows him or her to comprehend everything in an instance. This is impossible to explain but is almost similar to what the German language terms *Vorahnung*, an indeterminate feeling, the intuitive sense of something to come.

LT A premonition.

HDW We understood this as a kind of legitimization of the image, as an image in its own right. How would you describe these notions within your own thinking about art, and particularly in relation to Luc's work?

TC I am not sure I have a very good answer, but let me try. One thing that occurs to me – and this is very much the subject of my book, *The Sight of Death: An Experiment in Art Writing* – is this: that we all, including me, believe that the image has an immediacy unlike that of language or music. This idea that an image discloses itself all at once is very traditional. The fact that we actually look repeatedly at images, and images disclose new aspects of themselves, has brought on a great nervousness among art historians. When I realized this, I became interested in writing about the experience and began to look for models of how people have dealt with this in the past. But by and large, they haven't. There always seems to be the unconscious notion that I would betray the very nature of the image if I wrote about a repeated encounter, and the way in which that repeated encounter alters it. Writing about the image must somehow stage the "all-at-once-ness" of its meaning to us. In a way, that is fine. Clement Greenberg, the great master of all-at-once-ness, was probably deleting whole paragraphs that found words for the "all-at-once" impact of a work. That is something that art historians or critical writing can do. But I think it is very bizarre that there is no logical entailment to the idea that one peculiarity of the image in comparison with other forms of human recorded cognition is its "all-at-once-ness", and that therefore we should not talk about the fact that images change over time.

GB It is a different aspect of *Vorahnung*. I think *Vorahnung* is about recognition. In French this is called *tout ensemble*, which is not possible to translate into a distinct proposition, but it has to do with the simultaneous experience or perception of "everything at the same time". *Vorahnung* means "an experience of the whole". It is hard to explain because it is a subjective world, but it's a sense of what is going on.

HDW I would take this a little bit further. Would you not need a very precise notion of the third dimension in order to have such an experience? Because it is not only the picture – there is also a spatial aspect.

TC Absolutely. You must have the capacity to see the *tout ensemble* in order to survive.

LT I agree with Gottfried. On the other hand, let's consider this aspect of premonition, *Vorahnung*. The first word that comes into play is "mood" – an atmospheric word, which fits with any thought, image or language. First there is a mood, then the idea, then the thought. And finally, there is the visual. For the work I do, I think this is the nature of instinct. It is the relationship between mood and intuition. At times I have racked my brain to find something to paint, and then, somehow, I find images by mere coincidence. It could be a matter of light or it could be an image that I almost overlooked, and some of the most important imagery tends to be overlooked because of a lack of distance. Atmosphere is the starting-point of almost any visual. It can be ephemeral, brought on by a vague notion in my head, or an idea that causes tension, or something that I have not yet visualized. But it is there that it gets turned around and stripped down to a particular kind of image. Of course, unlike atmosphere, an image has a beginning and an end – it is a mobilized entity. I think this is the thrust of the idea behind *Vorahnung*.

TC I agree with you, but think the term "atmosphere" is actually easily abused. It can often mean a certain kind of pre-established or prefabricated atmosphere.

LT We've talked about an atmosphere of pathos and that these things are seen as weak entities in our existence. But they stand on the brink, and this element of denial is typical for our culture. That is why the visual is so important – because to visualize something is also to deny it.

TC One of the things I find so tremendous about your paintings is that I am unsure of their atmosphere. I can't tell the affective range of *The Walk* or of *The Diagnostic View*. It is not established and doesn't need to be. This is something that the image does at its best – it puts us in touch with our world, but we don't quite understand how our world is to be sorted under a certain range of concepts. Concepts and, shall we say, knowable states of mood, tone or emotion. I do think that one of the things your paintings do at their best is put me in a position where I don't have an emotion at my disposal to pin onto them. That is a good feeling, but also a weird one!

HDW Would you call it a state of alienation?

TC Yes, although that seems to suggest that you are deliberately alienated. Sometimes it is not quite like that. Take *Body*. I don't know what this picture *feels* about the body it is portraying. I don't know what those two black marks do in terms of emotional tonality. Do they put us in touch? Are they acts of aggression? What are they and what are they doing? They are enacting something between us and the depicted body, but I struggle to find the right word for what this something is. But it's also funny that this isn't actually a struggle – you just accept that this body is being assessed in some kind of way by this painting. That is almost too cold a reading, though the painting is rather cold. I am struggling for words, trying to put into words what seems to me so valuably puzzling.

LT The dark lines are actually a zipper. It is the zip fastener in the middle of the doll's torso so you can open it up to put in stuffing and give it volume. The body looks as though it is injured, and the lines of the zipper suggest the idea of a wound or scars. It is a funny thing that *ma(h)len* in German also means "grinding". The fact that I use an under-painting that makes the subsequent layers of the paint crack and will eventually make the image disappear, forces the cracks and the cloth to interact on the surface, creating the body of a doll. Everyone who sees this image perceives an element of violence, as if there is scarification. Also, the body takes over the face. Later on I made a connection between this work and my fascination with Velázquez's "Infanta" paintings. In these paintings it is not the face that is most important, but the elaborateness of the Infanta's dress, which is, quite clearly, a fetish.

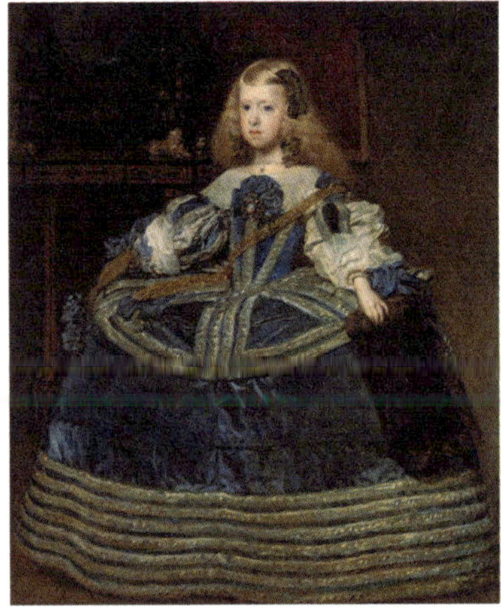

91 Diego Velázquez, *Infanta Margarita Teresa in a Blue Dress*, 1659
Oil on canvas, 125.5 × 106 cm
Kunsthistorisches Museum, Vienna, Gemäldegalerie, inv. 2130

HDW I propose we walk through the whole exhibition beginning in the first room with the earliest works. In Basel we discussed the importance of proportion and scale in relation to the exhibition space.

LT No two shows are ever the same because I always install each exhibition according to the space. I believe it important to work with the existing space rather than altering it too much. For this show in Brussels, we built one free-standing wall, and only out of necessity. Apart from that, we left the architecture as it was. To go back to a point I made earlier, I always hang paintings off-centre, so they work with the space rather than obliterate it. At the Wexner Center the paintings were hung chronologically for the first time ever. We arranged the larger exhibitions in London's Tate Modern and the Haus der Kunst in Munich, where ninety-five works were shown, by thematic pockets instead of a chronological line.

GB I think there is a difference between a painting in a space and a painting working with a space. Could you expand on this? I have the feeling that here, for example, the big paintings are working *with* the space, while the smaller ones are working *in* the space.

LT That is partially true, but it depends on the installation. Here there is a lot of space in between the paintings, so the works act like punctuation marks. In Munich, they were hung closer together as the wall was narrower, and the hall was quite big so they were still visible from forty metres away. Although each painting is singular and was originally painted as part of a group, with specific gallery or institutional venues in mind, when a larger show comes together in a museum for the first time, it becomes its own entity. This is the case both for gallery shows and institutional exhibitions.

HDW Let's return to the early works, such as *The Walk*, which illustrates nicely how the background plays a major role. As Gottfried noted in Budapest, this oscillation between background and motif creates a dynamic play.

LT Some paintings are made on stretched canvas, others are not. *The Walk* was painted on an unframed piece of canvas that had been cut from another previously used canvas. Some paintings have eight or nine other paintings underneath. What also becomes apparent in this room is a certain reductive, graphic aspect that gained ground for me after I had worked with film. *La Correspondance*, my first painting after making films, is more of a conceptual piece. I later began to enlarge drawings, like in *Antichambre*, which

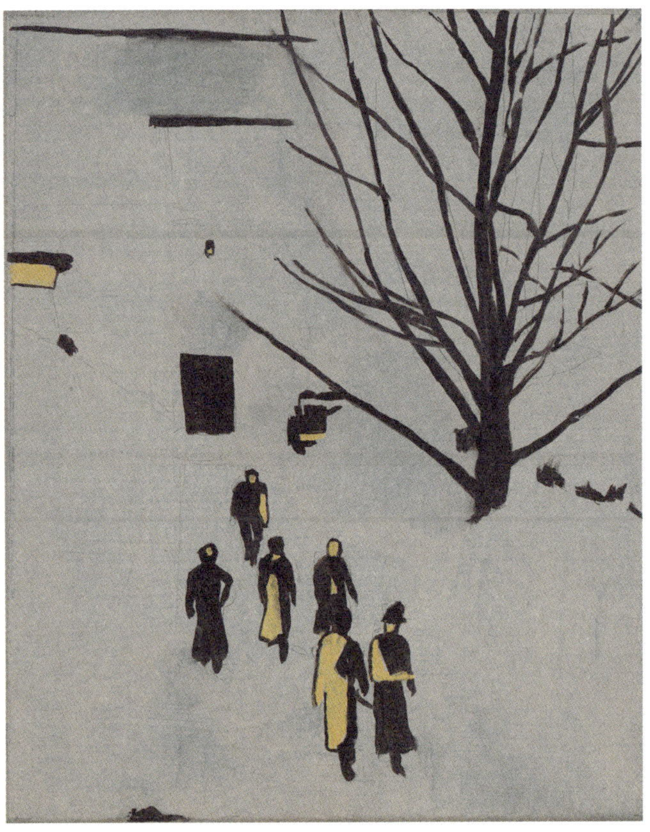

<u>92</u> Luc Tuymans, *Wandeling* [The Walk], 1989
Oil on canvas, 69.9 × 54.9 cm
Private collection

was basically a découpage drawing of a room with a chandelier from a film that I had shot. Nothing was spontaneous – everything was very prepared. Working with film provided a certain distance that enabled me to expand the idea of drawing. There is a huge difference between a drawn and a painted line, which has a contour. A line can be the shadow, such as with Velázquez, or it can be a mental line – something that is not even painted. I was interested in a reductive approach, which is where my fascination with Caspar David Friedrich's paintings and Japanese woodcuts comes from. And then there is the image itself, which in *The Walk* is an image of Hitler taking a stroll with his entourage in Berchtesgaden. We see a car and a house, but in a way the composition is all centred on the figures, which are formed or cast. With this approach the object quality of the figures is introduced, which we find again in the toy paintings and later works.

TC When you were working on the painting of that very charged Berchtesgaden photograph, how faithful were you to the source image, and how much did you eliminate? I think that the tree is key – at first one takes it for granted, but it actually occupies an enormous part of the canvas and, in the end, is decisive in shaping the space. Presumably the tree is in the original photograph?

LT The tree was in the source image, as were the house and car, but I did erase a few other elements. This was because I had two principal ideas in mind there – the woodcut and the photograph. My approach was to think about superimposing one image on top of the other. I wanted to let it be inspired both by a Japanese woodcut – I'd once seen one where yellow and black were used to produce the effect of illumination – and a photograph, in this case a very small one, which is a document.

TC What is decisive for me in this painting is the intersection of the tree's lowest branch with the car that is then strangely petering out into the snow, so that you lose a sense of where it is. Is that something that you invent in the process of painting, or do you notice it in the photographic source?

LT This painting was made quite intuitively, so it was not mapped out beforehand in the same way that some of my other paintings are. *Insomnia* is similar in that respect, although it is based on a piece of linoleum flooring from my studio, that has a dot of paint on top of another dot of paint. I titled it *Insomnia* because it basically has no background and appears bottomless. Although it looks like an abstract piece, it isn't. Its subject-matter is still entirely derived from the "real".

GB There is a difference between a dot and a detail. How much detail do you need?

LT Quite a lot. In my work details become megalomaniacal. I was very decisive early on in my career, because the scale of the works was smaller, so everything had to be very accurate in order to be visible from a distance. The level of detail becomes the subject of the picture and, like in *Insomnia*, takes it over. This is radically different from *The Walk* or *The Diagnostic View*.

HDW "Painting a dot" is almost a contradiction, because dots are marks of chance, aren't they?

<u>93</u> Luc Tuymans, *Insomnia*, 1988
Oil on canvas, 44.5 × 53 cm
Courtesy David Zwirner, New York/London

<u>LT</u> In some cases, yes, but I find the process to be more of a challenge. So actually, there is no aspect of chance, at least not in my work. The same is true for the painting of Himmler, where a very small photograph formed the source image. It is about changing the scale and enhancing something very small by making it bigger.

<u>HDW</u> But in a way, isn't it a found situation?

<u>LT</u> *Insomnia* started with the small piece of linoleum that I cut out of my studio floor, which I then made a painting of. I think I still have the original cutting.

<u>TC</u> When I look at it, I am very sure that what I am looking at is a ground, a solid surface. However, the word choice for your title – "Insomnia" – invites me to think that I am actually not looking at anything or that I am looking into a screen space, which is completely impalpable and associated with hallucination, with looking too hard or looking endlessly. Is that right?

LT Of course. I have consistently given titles to my works, something that wasn't really done much at the time when I was starting out. Sometimes my titles are descriptions of what you see, and sometimes their function changes, creating a very different image.

TC As we're walking through the show, I am very struck by your strange sense of colour. The colours of *Insomnia* are what I typically think of as "Tuymans colours", though I have a hard time giving them a more atmospheric name.

GB "Fading away" perhaps…

TC Yes, fading away, and not fitting precisely into any mood.

LT I refer to it as an idea of tonal "zones". Look at the light outside. Most of the time, the sky is grey but very bright, producing a very even light. If I lived in LA, or in Spain, I would use a completely different range of colours. Where I come from, the idea of the tonal zone plays a role because it creates its own, painterly depth that isn't illusory or perspectival. The painted tone is also difficult to remember. In 1989–90, I painted a seventeen-part series called *Suspended* based on photographs taken from a model-railway catalogue, for which I used very strong colours to depict the plastic of the toys. Before this series, everybody thought of my work as grey. Only from that point onwards, where I had enhanced the colours, was it understood that the earlier paintings also had colour.

HDW In your studio, next to your wall-mounted unstretched canvases, are thousands of paint marks in a vast number of colours.

LT These colours can all be found in my paintings. In order to create a tonal palette like the one in *Insomnia*, you need a lot of colours.

GB Subtractive colour mixing. What is it about the relationship between colour and indeterminacy? I think your choice of colour and tone has to do with this attitude of showing things as being indeterminate.

LT It adds a supplementary space and an ambiguity to the image. And ambiguity is an important theme in my entire oeuvre.

TC For you, that ambiguity and indeterminacy exist in things and in the world. Did you find this extraordinary colour, which is hovering between green and grey, in the linoleum?

LT Yes, it is exactly the colour of that piece of linoleum.

HDW But it is difficult to find a proper name for it.

LT This is true for a lot of floor colours because they are indeterminate and are just there. They are supposed to not disturb, so are often bland colours.

TC They are also colours that don't show dirt. It is important that in *Insomnia* there is a zone that is greyer in modulation than the right side.

LT Since it is over-painted, this could also be because of a previous layer of paint showing through.

TC I find myself thinking, "So, all of this is a painterly effect". For me, it resonates with Modernist colour, but at the same time it is like dirt on something. It can't declare itself to be a straightforward artefact.

LT That is where the triviality comes into play. Although Roberta Smith, in her first article about my work for the *New York Times* in 1994, came to the conclusion that it was compelling, she added that there was an "[air of Conceptual reticence and] rather pretentious humility".[5] Because the works were small, people thought of them as a fluke.

TC Which I see as a defensive reaction on the part of a New York critic that is used to bombastic enormity.

LT She wrote very different articles later on, but I thought this was quite interesting, because the first time you write about an artist is always a significant moment.

HDW How about *Body* [1990]?

LT *Body* is one of the fortunate works that I was about to throw away but then decided to entirely erase instead, and paint a new picture very quickly. When I made a stroke that pushed the paint to the sides and immediately made an outline with the paint, it surprisingly came together. At first I had been trying to model the body much more, but that didn't work. I like this economic component as well as the surgical aspect of the painting – I always work with a flat brush and horizontally, in a way that is reminiscent of cutting. And the black brushstrokes here are, of course, perverse. One can see their texture and how they were applied.

5 Roberta Smith, "Art in Review: Luc Tuymans at David Zwirner Gallery", *The New York Times*, 4 November 1994.

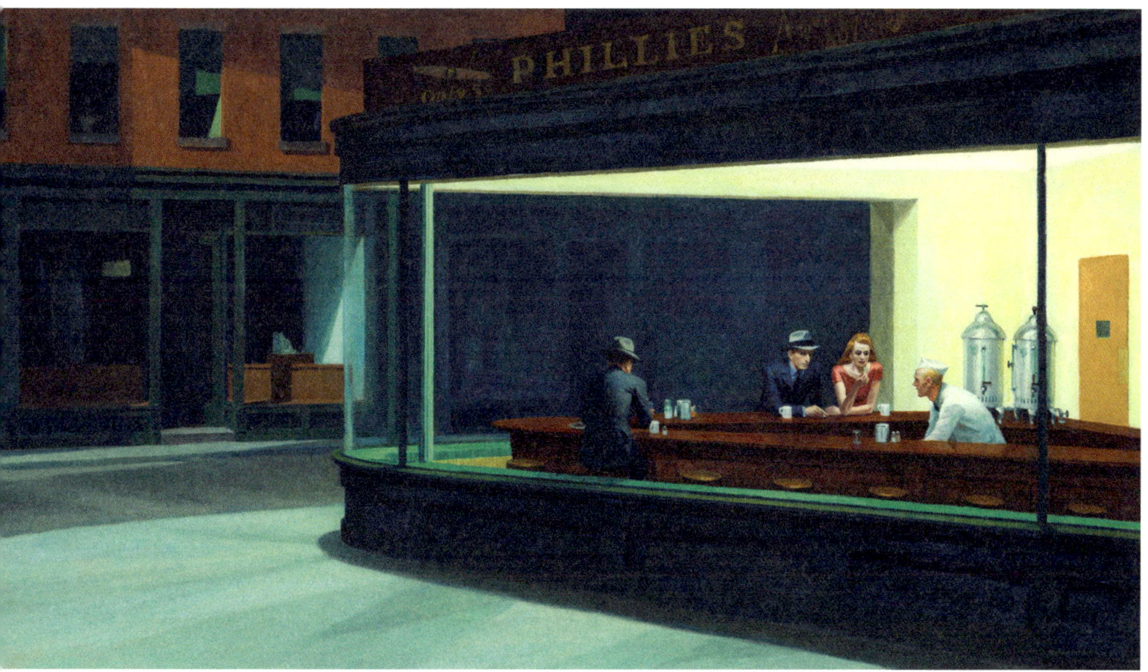

94 Edward Hopper, *Nighthawks*, 1942
Oil on canvas, 84.1 × 152.4 cm
The Art Institute of Chicago, Chicago, inv. 1942.51

TC Did you make those two decisive marks after you had painted the outlines of the body?

LT To create luminosity, the brightest areas actually require less work. First I made the outlines of the body, then I filled in the body area, and the black strokes came last. I always work from inside out, meaning from back to front, like the Old Masters. During my Tate Modern exhibition, it was interesting to see my work next to an exhibition of works by Edward Hopper, who I am very much a fan of. In the case of the *Nighthawks* – a fabulous painting – you could see that he had applied the most paint where there was the most light. This is exactly the opposite of how I work.

TC So you begin where the most light falls, but you begin with the least material.

LT Yes, but it builds up. I never leave blank areas on the canvas, even in the beginning when I am painting wet on wet. I don't project images, so I determine the size of the canvas – even the big ones – by first making a drawing. This is like working blindfolded because there is no contrast when I paint. At least this was true for this particular period, now the process is much more engrained in me.

<u>HDW</u> Did found imagery form the basis for *Body*?

<u>LT</u> No, this image is based on a real doll. It is painted the same size – actually a bit bigger – but without the head and the genitals, and is a recurring image. It returns, for example, in the form of the insect-like creature in *Superstition* [1994]. These paintings are derived from things that come and then recur. For *Die Zeit*, a slightly earlier group, I started searching for found images only after finishing the first two panels. All four panels – painted on four sides of a cardboard box because I had no money for canvas – were made in one day. The first two panels came easily – I painted the first one, then the second one, which could actually be a stand-in for the first panel. I then started to look for photographs for two more paintings. I found a photograph of the compressed vegetable tablets that were specifically developed for German troops during the Second World War, and which is what the third painting refers to. The image of Reinhard Heydrich, the Deputy Chief of the Gestapo, is one that I found in the Nazi propaganda magazine *Signal*.

<u>TC</u> Are you saying that the second image, the one that depicts the corner of a room with empty shelves placed above a square platform, is like an insert for you?

<u>LT</u> Yes, it could be a shop in one of these buildings within the urban setting of the first painting. It is clearly derived from the first image and could be a blown-up detail, which makes it filmic. If we read the buildings in the first painting as barracks or a camp, then within the context of the other paintings, the second image might refer to the empty or abandoned bunk beds of camp internees.

<u>HDW</u> It is like a sequence of disjointed film stills.

<u>LT</u> It is intentional, although intuitive, for this group of four paintings to form one image, creating a kind of non-existing narrative. It is also important in terms of silencing the imagery, as if you were to put a lid on it.

<u>GB</u> Is it true that you avoid narratives?

<u>LT</u> Yes.

GB Do you reduce narratives, or are they simply transferred to a different level? For example, is the narrative present through memory – through the story of the Nazis, of Heydrich, and so on? How much of the story do we need to know in order to understand those paintings?

LT I would say that the viewer should initially react to them in purely visual terms, without knowledge of a story. However, since I work with figuration, I have to be aware of the meaning. From the very beginning, I told art journalists what the paintings were about and revealed the source materials in order to avoid discussing the methodology, although this is not necessarily the way one should look at the paintings.

HDW Knowing the source material is just the start – it is where the viewing experience begins.

LT I think when you look at these works, initially they may appear as "holes" punctuating the wall, and then you notice their grey tones. *Die Zeit* is an important marker of change because it's the first time I used cooler grey tones. In earlier works I used colours that still retained some warmth.

HDW One thing we haven't discussed yet is the situation with painting here in Belgium during the 1980s. It basically didn't exist. During those post-Broodthaers years, everybody was making conceptual art.

LT There was the *Neue Wilde* painting movement, but it didn't interest me. And at that point I hadn't realized that Gerhard Richter was not an abstract painter. That only became clear to me when I went to Germany to install my work in my first group show in Cologne, and watched a documentary about Richter on television. I was amazed to discover that there was someone doing something interesting, relevant and unpretentious. I wrote him a letter and invited him to my opening, but he didn't come. He did see later shows, but we never had any personal contact.

TC Let's come back to the idea of narrative. There is a sequence in these four paintings – and human beings want sequences. When you have four images of the same size, and you hang them at equal intervals, you begin to look for some kind of developing story. So the absence of a narrative leads to a deeper question about the necessary conditions for narration. What is remarkable about these particular images is that you really don't understand the scale until you get to the image of Heydrich.

<u>LT</u> Yes, but their size is also turned upside-down. What I found intriguing about the Heydrich painting is that the tonality inside of his face bears a resemblance to the urban setting of the first painting. This creates a kind of loop, similar to winding a watch, and which is why I called the series *Die Zeit*. For me, this group of paintings has to do with time, but also with monumentality and its relation to recognition. How do you recognize monumentality? How do you determine the distance? What is the perception from afar and from up close? All of these questions and ideas are contained in these four paintings.

<u>TC</u> When I looked at these paintings again this morning, I was struck by the fact that the more I looked at the first image, the more it looked like a model to me – almost like a Thomas Demand maquette. Are the various elements actually part of the same world?

<u>LT</u> The first two images stem from my imagination, but by painting them in the same manner as the paintings of real objects, like the pills, I created a sense of unity and sequence. This also applies to Heydrich's portrait, which is constructed using a cut-out from an actual magazine page. He is standing in his fencing outfit and I positioned him in front of a painterly setting, a bookcase.

<u>TC</u> This might be a rather corny art critic's remark, but when I look at this series I am interested in the visual rhyming going on between the various frames, the fact that the bookcase refers back to the shelves, the two black circles to the two white circles, and so on. When you are working, do you think explicitly and formally on that level? How much conscious awareness of formal processes do you want or do you allow yourself?

<u>LT</u> As I mentioned earlier, I believe it is important to lose the intentionality so there is an element of the unconscious preserved in the process of painting, or mark-making. When I made a work like *Body* or other earlier works, it was clear to me when the painting was finished. The beauty of the Heydrich work is that it is actually just partially painted, so that it is perceived as a painting, but is not really a painting. Rather, it is a collage, so technically it's mixed media. The diptych *Reparations* is interesting because the canvases are about the same size as the television set on which I saw the rarely broadcast 1987 documentary *Die Wiedergutmachung* ["The Lie. 'Compensation' for Gypsies (Sinti) in Germany"] by Katrin Seybold and

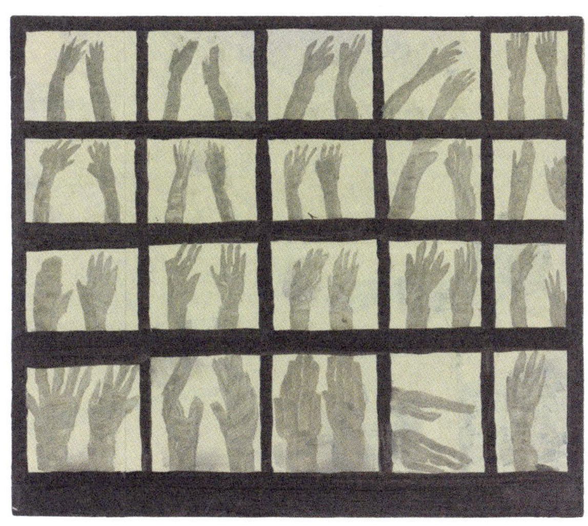

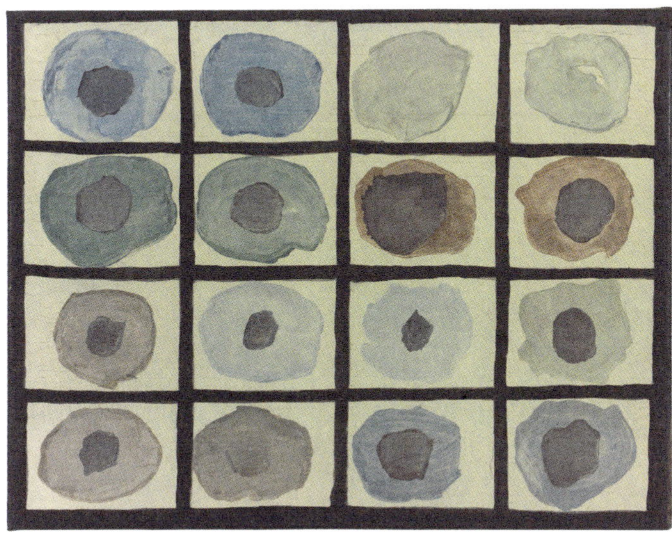

<u>95</u> Luc Tuymans, *Die Wiedergutmachung* [Reparations], 1989

Oil on canvas, oil on cardboard mounted on plywood,
part 1: 36.6 × 43 cm; part 2: 39.4 × 51.8 cm

Private collection

Melanie Spitta.[6] The victims were never compensated because the man in charge of reparations had actually performed experiments on the Sinti. The documentary revealed the names and families who were involved, which became problematic for the filmmakers because of the trials and eventual de-Nazification of these people. Katrin Seybold was married to Thomas Harlan, the son of Veit Harlan, who had directed *Jud Suess*.[7] She came to the opening of my show at Haus der Kunst and thanked me for using the two images that she considered key from the documentary – newspaper articles, pictures, documents and material assembled by the "racial researchers". The paintings are based on contact sheets with eyeballs and hands that were found in the office desk drawers of the same man who was responsible for the reparations, after his death in 1983. Of course I altered the images and made them more abstract, but the grid and the suggestion of genetics are there. The original contact sheets are now owned by a doctor who immediately bought them after they were found. The hands have a gruesome element to them, similar to *Our New Quarters*. When the work was shown at the Bern Kunsthalle I asked a group of visitors during a tour to describe what they saw without any prior explanation, and most of them mentioned words like decay, death and prison – so these aspects are quite clear.

GB While this is contrary to narrative, it's very revealing.

LT The grid helps you relate to the imagery that is multiplied. What also intrigued me about this image was how it isolates the individual images within it. What was interesting about the photograph on which I based *Die Wiedergutmachung* is that there is a repeated colour scheme.

TC This is the actual thing that was discovered in his drawer?

LT In 1976, John Schlesinger directed the film *Marathon Man*, in which Dustin Hoffman's character, Thomas "Babe" Levy, is tortured with a dentist's drill by Dr Christian Szell who is in New York to sell a large cache of diamonds that he had confiscated from Jews later killed at Auschwitz. Dr Szell repeatedly asks Babe, "Is it safe?", which is the title I later gave to one of my publications [*Luc Tuymans. Is It Safe?*, Phaidon, 2010]. Szell is

---

6 The film deals with the persecution of German "gypsies" during National Socialism and the reparations after 1945. It proves that the persecution of Sinti (and Roma) began as early as 1936, and after the war evidence was intentionally hidden to prevent reparations.

7 Joseph Goebbels appointed Harlan as one of his leading propaganda directors, and *Jud Suess* (1940) was his most notorious anti-Semitic film.

played by Laurence Olivier whose performance as the "Weisse Engel", or "White Angel", of Auschwitz, is so precisely delivered that his evil becomes even more horrific and unfathomable. Dustin Hoffman is a history PhD candidate, and at the same time he is part of history. Although it's a documentary, *Die Wiedergutmachung* is somewhat similar to the film. The iconic aspects of the two contact sheets were engrained in my memory. We received the actual photographs much later, when Chris Dercon was able to get them for the show in Munich.

HDW I remember that you presented the source material in vitrines in Munich.

LT Yes, I did that at the MCA in Chicago as well, but not at the Wexner Center, SF MOMA, or in Dallas. In this show, I think it would have been a mistake to include the source material. It's such a beautiful space and it would have disrupted it. I also rejected making an audio guide for the show because I wanted people to think for themselves about what they were seeing.

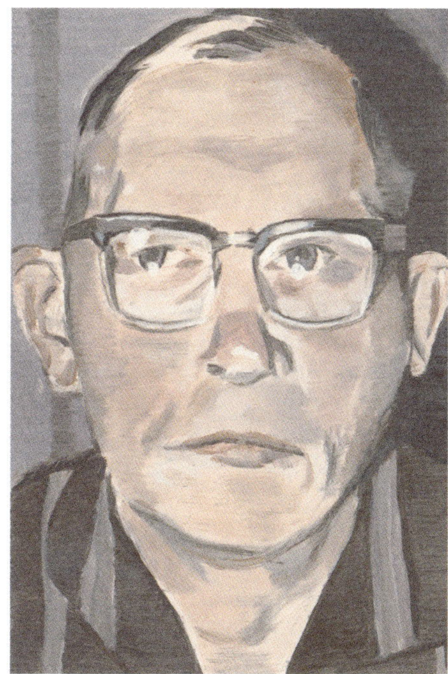

96 LUC TUYMANS, *Der diagnostische Blick II*
[The Diagnostic View II], 1992
Oil on canvas, 58.2 × 39.7 cm
Kunstmuseen Krefeld

LT I returned to a horizontal brushstroke with *The Diagnostic View II*. I had been painting objects, toys or empty spaces, but around 1993 I started to paint people again, although not in the sense of psychological portraits. I wanted something more detached and so I started looking for medical handbooks. When I met a psychiatrist at the opening of my exhibition in Bern in 1992, I asked him if these handbooks still exist and he sent me *The Diagnostic View*. I made cut-outs from this book, which form the basis of the series. Except for one image, they are all portraits or body parts. This portrait [#5] really makes eye contact with the viewer – the others look directly out as well, but I shifted their eyes slightly, so the viewer is unable to feel empathy or sentiment. And so, despite being in some ways very naturalistic, they are somewhat unreal and instead reveal the symptom. Everything is thrown back at the spectator. This is what I wanted to achieve in 1989 with the hands in *Die Wiedergutmachung*, but it didn't work because it was too existential, too tormented, too close to the original photograph.

TC Can you speak a little more about why you wanted to paint people again, but with a certain detachment?

LT I have painted quite a lot of portraits, but unlike other artists such as Lucian Freud, I am not interested in their psychology. What I find fascinating in portraiture ranges from the sturdiness of Velázquez – where you almost feel the *dédain* – to the vacant portraits of Manet, which are almost abstractions or an erasure of the figure. All of the works in *The Diagnostic View* are intentional. The point comes back at you, and I find this harsh, confrontational aspect very interesting. Rather than empathy, the images bear a matter-of-factness.

TC It is extremely hard to get to the outside of a person when looking at them, because you are always reading the inside into it.

LT But of course these portraits are not painted from real people – they are derived from existing images.

HDW I like that those photographs used to have a medical purpose and you've repurposed them for a painterly purpose. Something happens in this process that involves empathy.

TC Yes, it does seem to me that somehow you reconstruct empathy. In the end, this is not the original handbook, *The Diagnostic View*. Even though you are working with that material, it is ultimately a painting of a person.

LT Yes, and that is the ambiguous part. Size here matters again. The heads are larger than lifesize whereas in a much later painting, *The Nose* [2002], the head is almost lifesize. In those later works, psychology emerges in a different way, but it was first important to make this in-between step. In *Wrapping Paper* I worked with the idea of painting something insignificant on a very large scale. The work, which measures 1.82 by 1.20 m, is a painting of wrapping paper from the former GDR [East Germany], and I found its reddish colours and tonal zones appealing – it looks like something familiar, yet it's an abstraction.

HDW Although it is completely different from the kinds of abstraction we find in Malevich or Kandinsky.

LT Yes, there is a completely different intention. You cannot repeat Malevich or Kandinsky. It is also a sort of comment, or joke, like the towel that I painted once. I noticed it while doing the dishes and it reminded me of a Modernist painting, with its superimposition of colour planes. *Wrapping Paper* is similar. The gaping space at the bottom, for example, might suggest erotic connotations.

TC Well, there are definitely overtones. When I think about the grid paintings, *Die Wiedergutmachung* and *Wrapping Paper*, together I inevitably think, "This is how colour stripes occur in the real world, this is what grids are for". So there is a dialogue happening – a critical dialogue with an art that thinks of the grid or the stripe as self-sufficient, formal categories.

LT I still remember the time I saw my first Mondrian. I was twelve years old when I saw one of the diamond-shaped paintings with my uncle in The Hague. I was impressed because it was so simple, yet so monumental. I have always been struck by the simple, spare quality of a work, such as Malevich's *Black Square*, and the concept of reverence this kind of imagery inspired. Without Russian icons, this kind of work could never have existed. From a young age I was also interested in Russian Constructivism, much more than in the avant-garde, because it existed for such a short but intense period of time. Those fabulous paintings by Rodchenko were part of the vocabulary when I was in art school, but I resisted it in order to develop something I could appropriate. The question consisted of how to redo it. That is the perversity of it, how "to redo it".

TC And to bring it down to earth... because of its size, *Wrapping Paper* is quite grandiose.

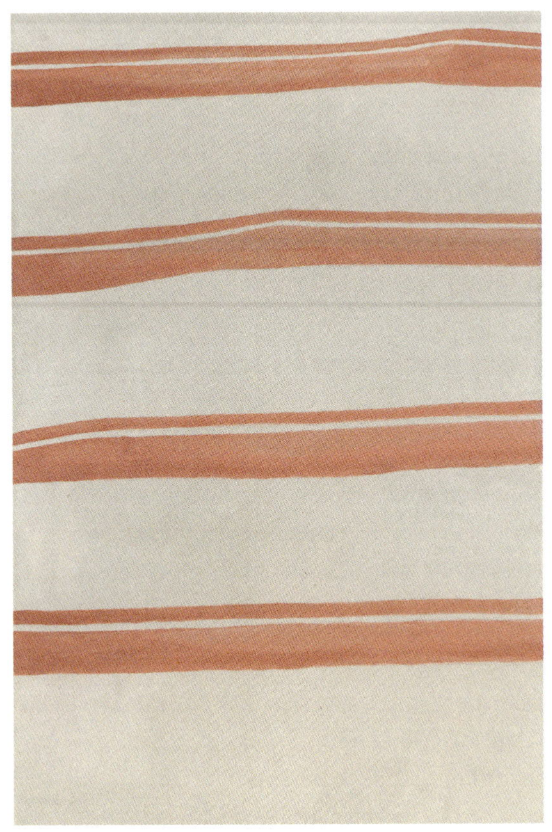

<u>97</u> Luc Tuymans, *Wrapping Paper*, 1991
Oil on canvas, 182 × 120 cm
Private collection

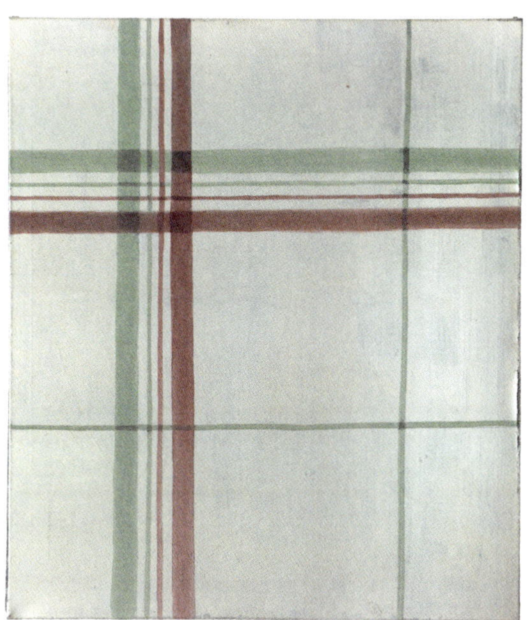

98 Luc Tuymans, *Handdoek* [Towel], 1987
Oil on canvas, 80 × 70 cm
Private collection, Antwerp

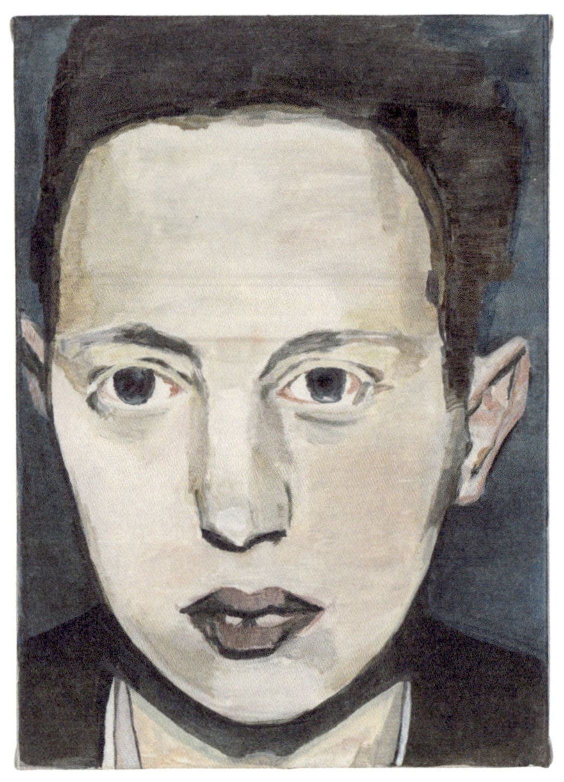

<u>99</u> Luc Tuymans, *Der diagnostische Blick V*
[The Diagnostic View V], 1992
Oil on canvas, 57.9 × 42.3 cm
Private collection

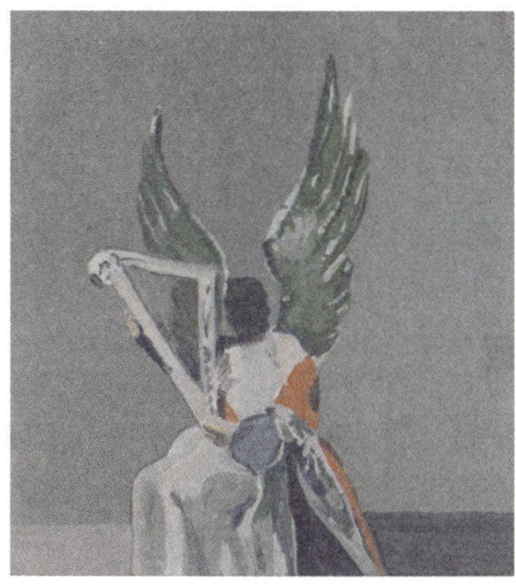

100 Luc Tuymans, *Angel*, 1992

Oil on linen, 65.7 × 61.3 cm

Collection Nancy Lauter McDougal and Alfred L. McDougal, partial and promised gift to The Art Institute of Chicago

HDW When I first saw it, it reminded me of Frank Stella's monumental paintings from the 1970s. Were you thinking of them?

LT Yes, but the difference is that this is just a piece of real wrapping paper that I came across and cut a piece out of. There is an inconsistency, a wave in the paper, which I found interesting, because it acts as the only reference to the real object. I painted both *Angel* and *The Diagnostic View V* in 1992 but they are very different. They were made for a show called *Repulsion* in Berlin that was about façades, or rather, non-spaces. I turned the object around, and the angel became a presence, not by erasing its face, but by placing it in the shadow. Instead of standing upright, I painted it sitting down.

HDW I find the dark line underneath the head of *The Diagnostic View V* surprising. Is this evident in the source photograph?

LT It is probably not quite as strong in the photograph, but I wanted a startling contrast to isolate these elements.

HDW It gives the face a tension.

LT Yes, although *The Diagnostic View IV*, with the blue eyes, is actually the more iconic painting. It looks like a male face but is in fact a woman. The same is true of *The Diagnostic View V*, where we're not sure if the subject is a boy or a girl. If we continue into the next room, *Pillows* was the last painting in my *Superstition* series. With this painting, my interest was in the outline, and the colours are based on an image from a poorly printed porn magazine, where the screens had shifted and created a particular range of colours, a kind of *moiré* effect. It is also one of the first images that is more horizontal than vertical, and is a bit Cézanne-esque, in that it creates another space, and is thus very different from the *Superstition* painting. *Pillows* led to a new body of work, which I showed at Portikus in Frankfurt as *Superstition – At Random* in 1994.

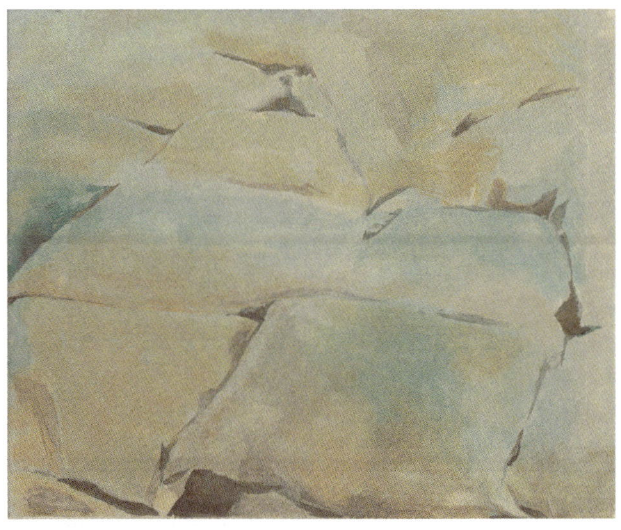

<u>101</u> Luc Tuymans, *Pillows*, 1994
Oil on canvas, 55.2 × 67.6 cm
Carnegie Museum of Art, Pittsburgh; A.W. Mellon
Acquisition Endowment Fund, 1998.1

<u>TC</u> Let me ask you a very naïve question. This piece holds my attention again and again, though I don't have the slightest idea why. What was it about this particular image that you thought would make a painting? What were its qualities? You mentioned that the photograph was badly printed.

<u>LT</u> The printed source image I used was of only one pillow, so I multiplied it. But these dark areas, the shadows and folds, are what really made it happen. This is what happens with a morphological form and image. A pillow is like that – it has no real shape of its own, but takes on any form that is put on it. It is a nameless, relatively formless object, without an identity. But the shadows become holes in between that define the space and create a kind of landscape.

<u>GB</u> That is what you call Cézanne-esque?

<u>LT</u> Yes. And this is what I was talking about – the outline is also the shadow at the same time. There is a cavity that is painted.

<u>TC</u> So you multiplied the one pillow, and you created a landscape?

<u>LT</u> Yes, but the colours are taken from the print.

214

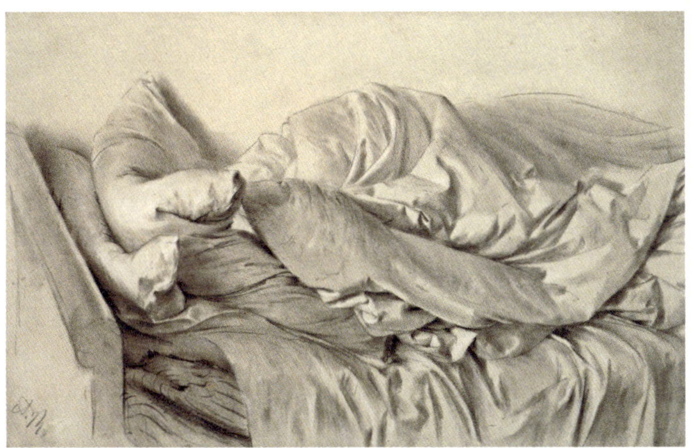

<u>102</u> ADOLPH VON MENZEL, *Unmade Bed, c.* 1846
Black and white chalk on paper, 22.0 × 35.5 cm
Staatliche Museen zu Berlin, Kupferstichkabinett, Berlin, INV. SZ MENZEL N 319

TC There is a wonderful drawing by Adolph von Menzel, the *Unmade Bed* from 1845, which I am sure you know and is full of physiognomic connotations from the traces of the body that was in the bed. The pillows show the imprint of bodies that might have been on them, or they may even take on the shape of a body. I am even kind of toying with the idea that a part of your *Pillows* is a face in a Mantegna-esque perspective. But in contrast to the Menzel, which is all about "you can't look at the world of human objects without anthropomorphizing", your painting is in argument with that, saying that our human world is full of us, yet it has nothing to do with us.

LT There is a form of alienation. In order to acquire this painting for the collection of the Carnegie Museum in Pittsburgh, the curator Madeleine Grynsztejn had to go all the way back to Albrecht Dürer in her presentation to the museum board, and point out that Dürer had also painted pillows.

GB There is something like a Rorschach effect here, which I think is different from Menzel. In Menzel's work bodies would be imaginable, whereas you leave room for free associations.

TC Yes, I think I was trying to say that we inevitably anthropomorphize – in a way we are Rorschach machines. We are looking for ourselves. So what

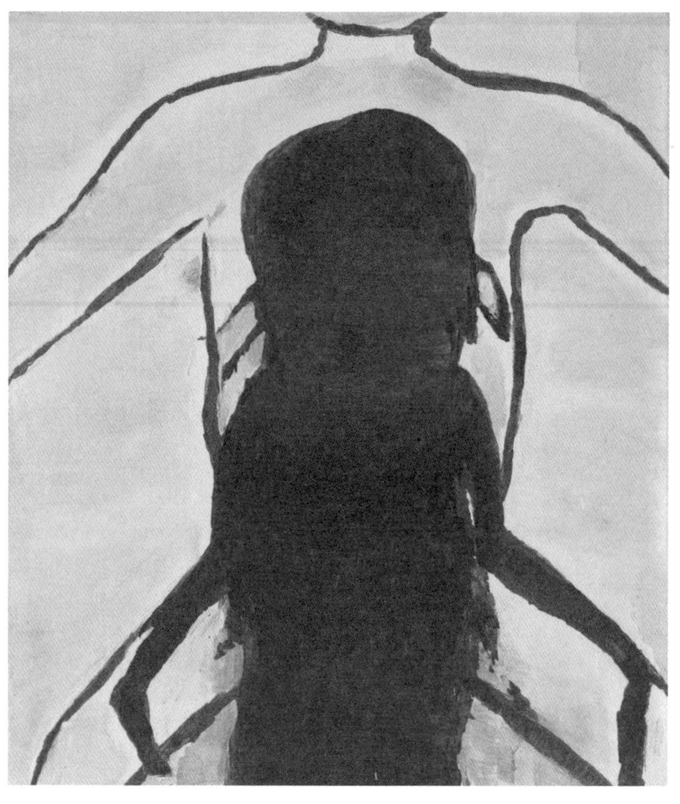

<u>103</u> Luc Tuymans, *Superstition*, 1994

Oil on canvas, 41.9 × 36.8 cm

University of California, Berkeley Art Museum and Pacific Film Archive;
Museum purchase. 1997.32

fascinates me about this painting is that it quietly resists that. It doesn't resemble the great anti-human still-life painters, like Cézanne in a certain mood, where he says, "Look, these objects are not yours". Cézanne's painting suspends the habits of thought and reveals the base of inhuman nature upon which man has installed himself.

LT They are also barely human. What I really love about Cézanne – not in his weak, early paintings, but in the late paintings, when his most important work begins – is the fact that you see an analytical element as if it was made up of superimposed layers of glass. For this reason Cézanne is relevant for *Pillows*. Supposedly this had something to do with his vision problems, the fact that he was myopic and probably later suffered from retinopathy and refused to wear glasses. Whether this is the reason or not doesn't really matter. What matters is the sheer superimposition of planes in his paintings, and how he is trying to look at the world through a different dimension. One could say that Cézanne tried to paint what he saw with both eyes open simultaneously. Usually, when you apply perspective to drawing, you close one eye and use the other like the lens of a camera. In Cézanne's drawings and paintings, you can recognize how the contours of his motifs – for example, an apple – break open and become multiplied. Seen from a greater distance, the objects in his paintings can be recognized better than they would be in a "realistic" painting made according to the laws of one-point perspective. He had a sense of "wandering perspective".

TC I think it is wonderful that we are talking about a comparison with Cézanne, to which I think the painting invites. And yet it is very unlike him. Cézanne is almost implacable that here is the object world. This, on the other hand, is not implacable. It is very quiet.

HDW Let's take a look at *Superstition*.

LT This is what I meant about the body, about how things recur. In *Superstition*, there is an outline of an adolescent body as well as a poltergeist, insect-like element. Once again, the initial image is important – something that you can see from very far away which pulls you in, and then throws you out again. A pulsing image, but very different from the pillows.

HDW A tension exists between *Pillows*, a painting of a material object, and *Superstition*, an idea.

LT Yes, the word "superstition" is a good word for art and other forms of belief.

TC This brings us back to Roberta Smith and her description of your paintings as "pretentiously humble". She must have been nonplussed by the difference between this kind of work and the large-scale Georg Baselitz heavily Expressionistic paintings at that time. This seems to be in a sardonic dialogue with the Baselitz, in the sense of, "I'll show you a vision."

LT I also think that it was tied to being from Europe. I thought the United States was pretty straightforward, which of course it isn't, as I found out the hard way. So I think that was the first cynical reaction I encountered in New York and realized how New York is actually quite European and different from any other place in the States. I think Roberta Smith's reaction was double-sided. On the one hand she was intrigued, on the other hand she was sceptical.

TC Let's just go back to the idea that this is in dialogue with, or in opposition to, a certain kind of myth-making, large-scale, heavily impastoed, Anselm Kiefer–Georg Baselitz universe. Were you aware of this? Did that matter to you?

LT Yes, of course. In the 1980s I went to see an Anselm Kiefer show at the Stedelijk Museum in Amsterdam. I did not dislike his earlier paintings, but when I saw the large-scale works in this show I thought their totally material quality basically turned them into shit. Kiefer was falling into his own metaphor. When I turned around and saw a Mondrian painting, I thought that it was much better and far more effective.

HDW What I've always wondered about the iconic *Superstition* painting, is why I see the image as a child's body.

LT It is perhaps some kind of state between giving birth and not. This is what I mean by a morphological form that bans part of the imagery. It covers it and, at the same time, devours it. It is interesting to note how this very graphic image is in opposition to *Pillows* and how these two paintings move between these two poles.

TC *Superstition* did not start with a found image?

LT No, it began with one of my drawings and you can still see the outline. *Pillows* was based on a found image. What is also important here is that the backdrop is like a graphic outline, whereas the centre of the body has volume. It bears affinities with the Himmler painting, where you see a frame and the shadow in the frame. It is similar in its obsessiveness – even in the case of the ballroom dancers, around whom you can almost put your hands. That is what fascinates me.

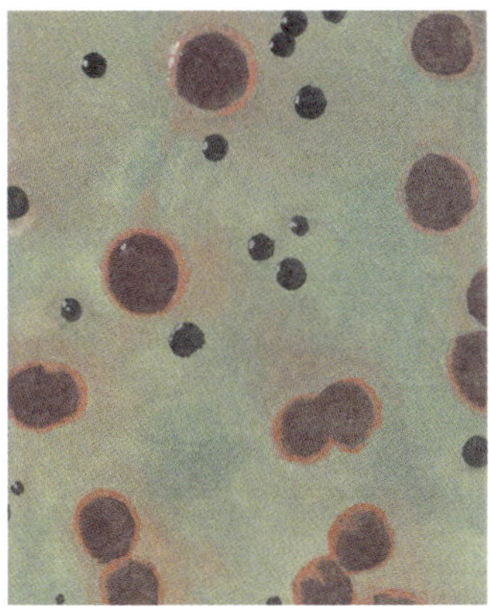

104 Luc Tuymans, *Bloodstains*, 1993
Oil on canvas, 57.5 × 47.5 cm
Jenny and Jos Van den Bergh

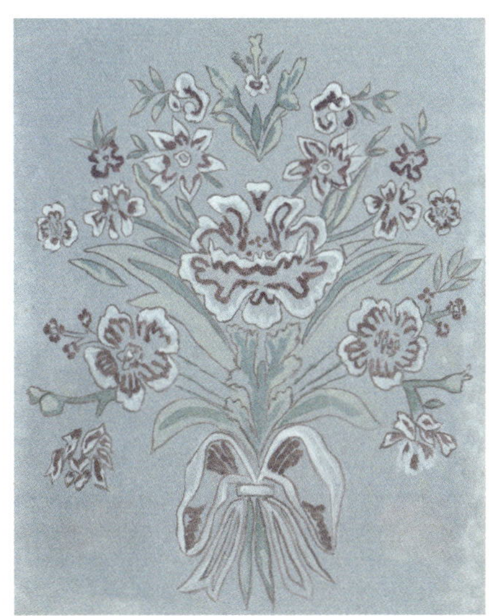

105 Luc Tuymans, *Tracing*, 1994
Oil on canvas, 101 × 82 cm
Private collection, Switzerland

Moving on, *Bloodstains* shows a drop of blood through a microscope. Again, there is a kind of multiplication but it is also about the highlights. What is important in this painting is the way in which the drops of blood are isolated and constantly moving. The embroidery pattern of *Tracing* was taken from a chair in which someone was murdered. I changed the colours of the embroidery to a deep red, similar to bloodstains. It was important for me to turn a banal, decorative pattern into something very violent. Decorative elements can turn into ornamentation, and ornament encompasses the world – this then represents a circular notion that everything eventually returns to the same source.

TC It also has something of a Rorschach test about it.

LT Yes, because the image unfolds.

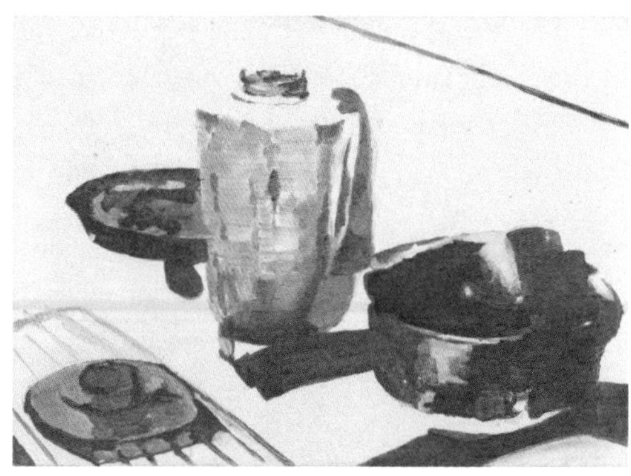

106 Luc Tuymans, *Peter*, 1994
Oil on canvas, 53 × 75 cm
Courtesy Jarla Partilager Private Collection

LT *Peter* was painted from a forensic police photograph of the kitchen of a serial killer who murdered animals and people, then cooked their blood and drank it. Of course, this back-story is not evident from the painting, but I liked the very graphic qualities of the photograph. I copied it, but shifted this almost abstract line that crosses the background and indicates space. Without the line, the painting would not be finished.

HDW That line organizes the space.

GB If we're speaking in more general terms, how and when have you used Polaroids?

LT I painted my very first work from a Polaroid, *The Flag*, in 1995, out of disgust with the right-wing Flemish Nationalists – which makes it a relevant painting today. The Flemish political party "Vlaams Blok" [Flemish Block], now called "Vlaams Belang", received one out of three votes in Antwerp that year. So I wanted to look back at the icons of the movement. The story of Flanders is complex and layered, even within my own family, caused by collaboration during the Second World War. On the Dutch side, there was resistance, bad marriages, rows, and the war eventually became quite a phobia. Flemish Nationalism has been appropriated in the sense that it was somehow "acceptable", which is of course the worst possible nightmare scenario. I made *The Flag* by first making a watercolour of the lion flag, the symbol of Flanders, which is black with red claws on a yellow background, on a little piece of paper that I then crumpled and pinned on the wall. Then, following my intuition, I took a Polaroid of it using a very bad camera, which obliterated the image and turned it into something else.

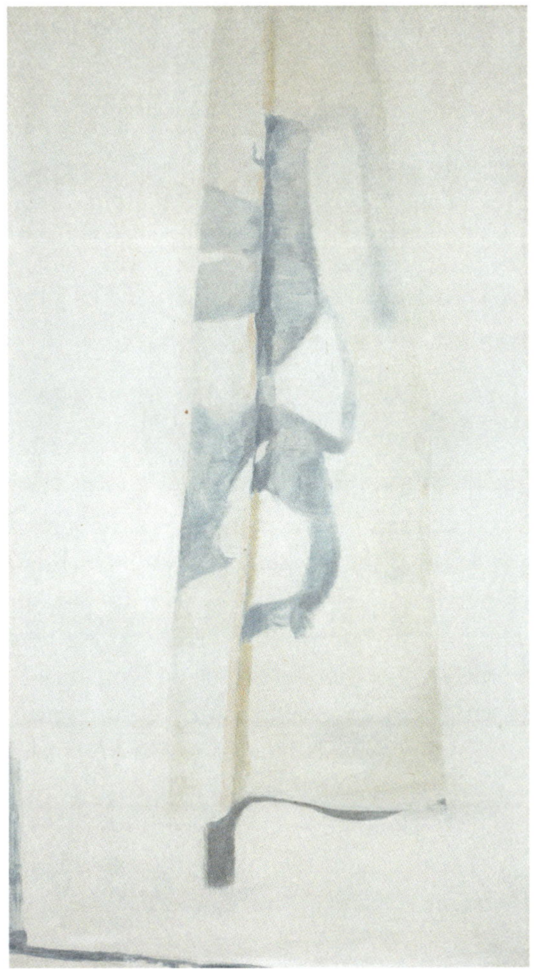

107 Luc Tuymans, *The Flag*, 1995
Oil on canvas, 138 × 78 cm
Private collection

HDW Is that around the same time that you started to paint projections of projections, the empty slides?

LT The empty slides came later, in 2002. But of course there's a connection since those are also about completely obliterating the image.

HDW Would you agree that this was a conceptual approach?

LT The great thing about Polaroids is that they are different from photographs, and the emulsion develops in a similar way to how I paint. When the Polaroid image of the flag developed, it already had this painterly element that intrigued me.

HDW In this case, you are producing your own source material.

LT Yes, here I began working with source material in a different way. Polaroids became part of the toolbox just as websites have. I am not interested in fighting against new media – why should I?

HDW I always found painters who embraced photography in the nineteenth century, like Manet, the most interesting.

LT Here we could add that Gerhard Richter influenced a whole generation of German photographers, among them Thomas Struth.

TC But for me, *The Flag* marks the beginning of your crossing over from the realm of the film still, the photograph or the painting – although, of course, you are still painting – to the Polaroid and to a fluid, emergent imagery. Where it stops is arbitrary, the Polaroid acts like a pause button. So I see this work as the beginning of your painting delineating a new status of the image. It has become very mobile, accidental and impalpable. If you think back to the four images in *Die Zeit*, they are hard as nails and have a tremendous impact. Even *Pillows*, compared to *The Flag*, is an actual "thing". Painting reaches back to this great tradition from van Eyck to Velázquez. It is what oil paint is all about – a materializing. So it is notable that *The Flag* is such a politically charged image, and yet so volatile. The flag is there, but it is part of some impalpable image world.

LT What really interested me was the mistiness of the image and the ornamental aspect of the shadow, similar to *Pillows*, where I applied the same technique but in a different layer. In *The Flag*, the image starts to become transparent. *Pillows* prefigured that, and it was then carried through all the way to *The Rabbit*, which is an image taken from a computer image of a rabbit reproduced in a newspaper. In *The Rabbit*, the light changes for the first

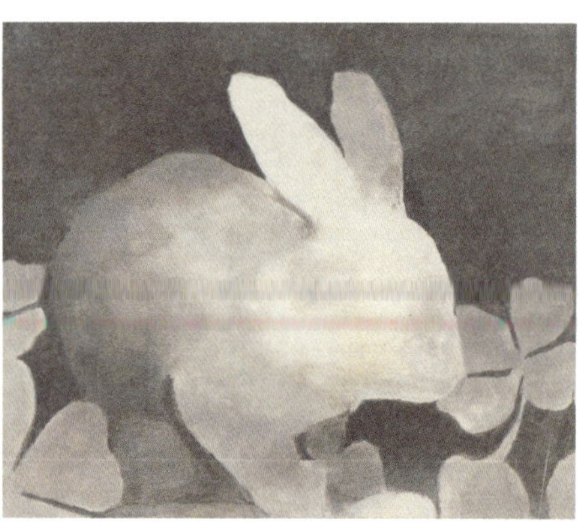

108 LUC TUYMANS, *The Rabbit*, 1994
Oil on canvas, 59.5 × 72 cm
Private collection

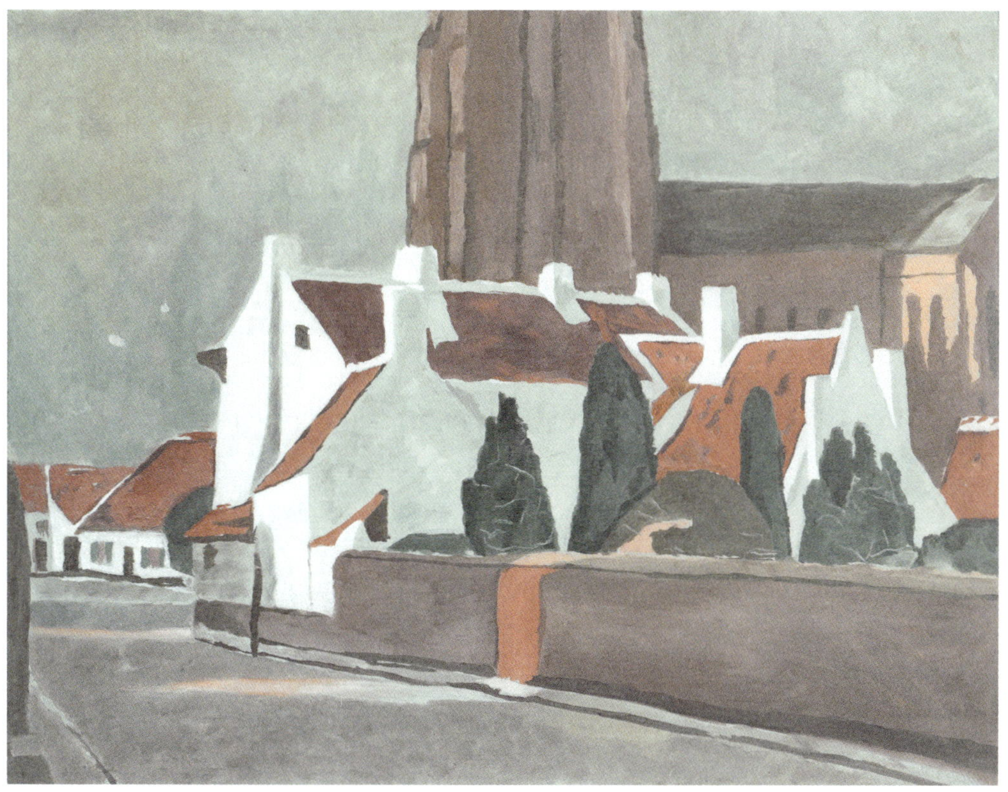

109 Luc Tuymans, *Flemish Village*, 1995
Oil on canvas, 110.7 × 145.1 cm
Collection M HKA – Collection of the Flemish Community

time because it comes from within. While *The Flag*, painted one year later, erases, swallows everything around it and thereby becomes an emerging image.

GB Does this painting work on a political level?

LT When *The Flag* was shown in the exhibition *Heimat*, together with other works that draw on themes of Flemish nationalism – the movement still lobbies for Flemish independence from Belgium – and iconography, like *Flemish Village*, it was pretty clear what the flag would provoke. Reactions were immediate and virulent. This still holds true today, even though the work is from a different moment in time.

TC A virulent reaction? Meaning what? That they resented what you were doing to the flag?

LT No. Rather, they were saying that it should be about national identity, that one should basically portray one's native territory, which is idiotic. One is not supposed to use such symbols in such a literal way.

HDW I think the Flemish government should buy it.

LT The Flemish community bought *The Yser Tower*, which is quite an important monument, and *Flemish Village*, whereas *The Flag* went to a private collection. The works ended up in embassies for a time, and eventually wound up at M HKA in Antwerp.

HDW I think it is wonderful that paintings still produce those kinds of effects, that prime ministers and other politicians are concerned about them.

LT Although I think there is a tenderness too in these works. Violence can be interesting but only when combined with tenderness. One's culture is not exclusively rooted in any region. Cultures may originate in certain regions, but they always spread.

HDW These are illogical constructs that ultimately end up preventing us from having healthy relationships with the historic past.

TC Speaking as someone who is very interested in the intersection of painting and politics, what I find so interesting is that it is very much about the notion of what can painting do in present circumstances to register that range of concerns that you were just talking about. Of course it can't be denunciatory, right?

LT No. It is also a matter-of-fact-like statement up to a point, but with a particular side to it. That side is where the obliteration of the image becomes surprisingly effective because it has the qualities of a disappearing act – it is not particularly informative.

HDW One example would be Courbet, because we know that at one point he was very engaged in politics.

LT Courbet was one of the most aggressive painters ever. He was very acidic – this is part of what was so great about him.

TC But even Courbet is restrained. *The Burial at Ornans*, for example, deals with the political situation but its attitude towards the bourgeois subject is very restrained. Interestingly, it is in these moments where painting most

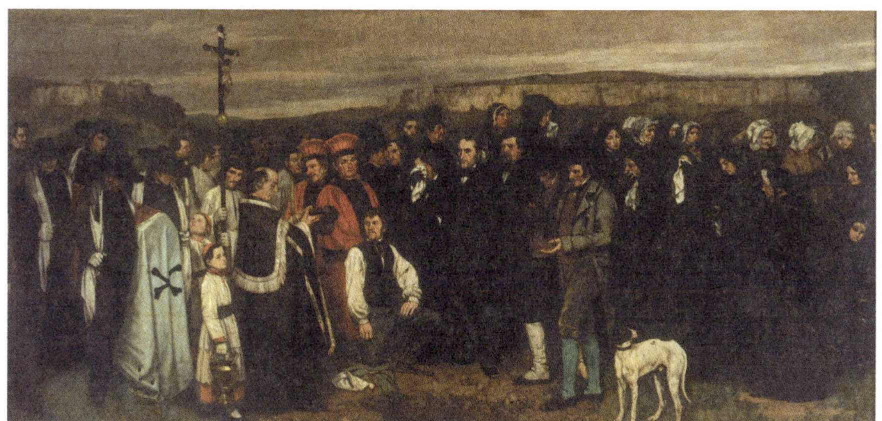

110 Gustave Courbet, *The Burial at Ornans*, c. 1849–50
Oil on canvas, 315 × 668 cm
Musée d'Orsay, Paris, inv. RF 325

seriously engages with the political that there is a deep level of restraint. What is it that painting can show you about the political, about the languages and imagery of politics, about its actors? It shouldn't be offering narratives that are too clear or immediate. Once again, I think we have come back to question the difference between an image and the way in which political language works.

LT Also there is no moral point. It is not about pointing fingers at mistakes that are being made, or about right and wrong. Clearly, my work is much more about the status of an image, how an image is entangled with power, how it comes into being, how it evolves and how it is perceived over time. The flag is actually an after-image because, when it was shown in 1995, the Flemish nationalists wanted to get rid of the flag and all their other icons. Now they've reintroduced them, which is a strange turn of events.

GB The Benjaminian term *Denkbild* might be apt here. Luc's answer to the question about the relationship between painting and politics is about the relationship between different icons, and could be summarized by this word, *Denkbild*. It is neither a commentary, nor a manifesto, nor a reproduction, but it is a space of reflection.

LT And that is where people have to fill in the gaps. Right after the exhibition in Antwerp, I made a show about patriotism called *The Heritage*. It included this group of paintings about the United States, which occupied

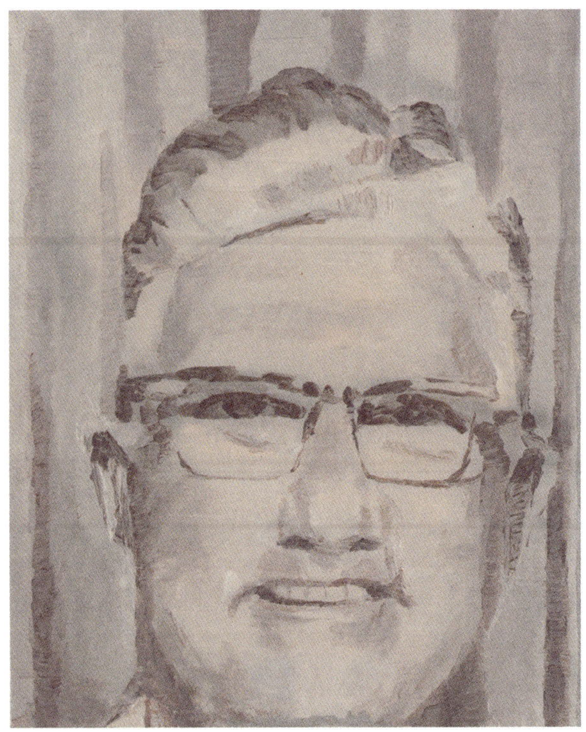

<u>111</u> Luc Tuymans, *The Heritage VI*, 1996
Oil on canvas, 53 × 43.5 cm
Private collection. Courtesy David Zwirner, New York/London

a completely different realm, since it is about a country made up entirely of immigrants. With nationalism no longer an option, another "viable" option has emerged as an extremely populist position – *patriotism*. And that is where this face of a rather typical patriarchal American figure in *The Heritage VI* came from. This simple face with a stupid haircut and enlarged eyes, wearing glasses. But once we discover the kind of person that is depicted, everything about our viewing experience changes, since this painting is a portrait of the wealthy Ku Klux Klansman Joseph Milteer. The way in which the black and white tones in the original photograph became flesh-coloured fascinated me. Something very similar was happening in the "Lumumba" painting that prefigures this work. Aspects of the archive and history are clearly at play here, but within the painting they are manifested in very different dimensions. And while these paintings were made during the same year, in some ways, they are actually opposing each other.

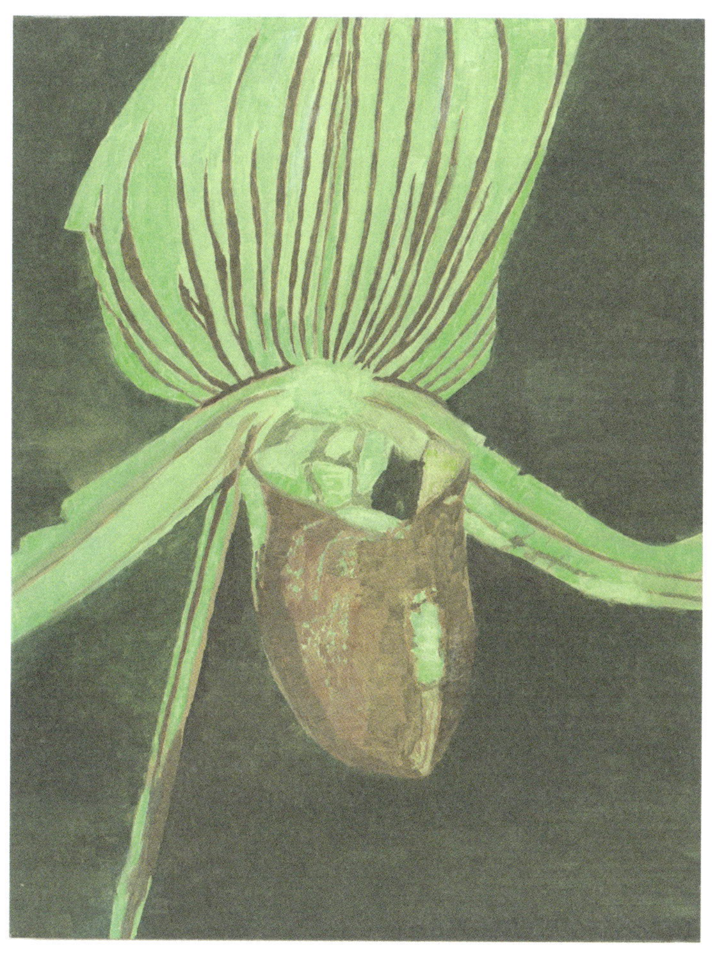

112 Luc Tuymans, *Orchid*, 1998

Oil on canvas, 99.5 × 76.7 cm

Private collection. Courtesy David Zwirner,
New York/London

<u>LT</u> In *Orchid*, the toxicity of the image is important. I had read an article about how plants were changing their gender from masculine to feminine on a massive scale because of climate change. So I took the most feminine and erotic-looking flower – an orchid – and masked it with a poisonous, green foliage. You miss the fact that the subject is organic, because the colour takes over. It contaminates the image as well as the space.

The painting *The Architect* is an example of an image that almost appears to come out of the frame. It is very small and was exhibited on the second floor of an apartment building in Torstrasse in Berlin, not in a white-cube gallery. The painting was partially triggered by a documentary about Albert Speer, Hitler's architect and designer of Nazi offices, camps and monuments. I made this painting in 1998, when the KGB first released written proof of documents and telegrams that revealed how Speer – who was also the Minister of Defence – had prolonged the war. Towards the end of the war, before going on a ski holiday, he sent a telegram to Himmler, describing how some of the inmates in the camps had too much space. Then the documentary cuts to a home movie shot by Speer's wife, which shows him skiing down a slope and falling. This still frame from the documentary served as the source image for the painting. I videotaped the documentary and paused the frame, which is what gives it a bluish glow towards the edges. I painted Speer's face as a blank, white oval so that the white hole in place of his face creates a sense of annihilation. I had the idea of making a group of paintings about architecture and snow, because the term "Der

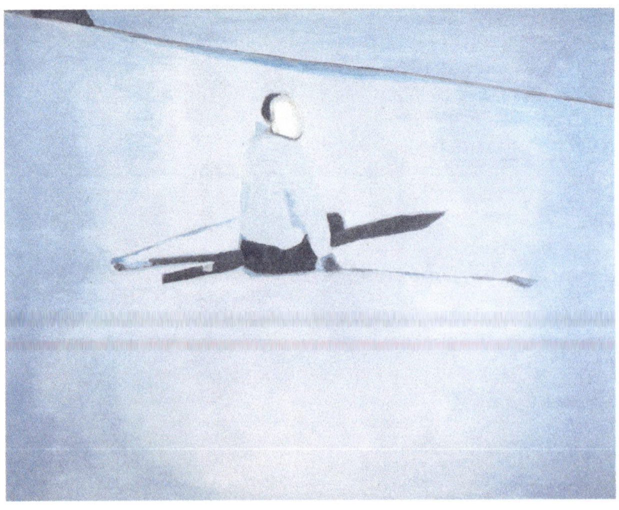

<u>113</u> Luc Tuymans, *Der Architekt* [The Architect], 1998
Oil on canvas, 113 × 144.5 cm
Gesellschaft für Moderne Kunst in Dresden E.V.

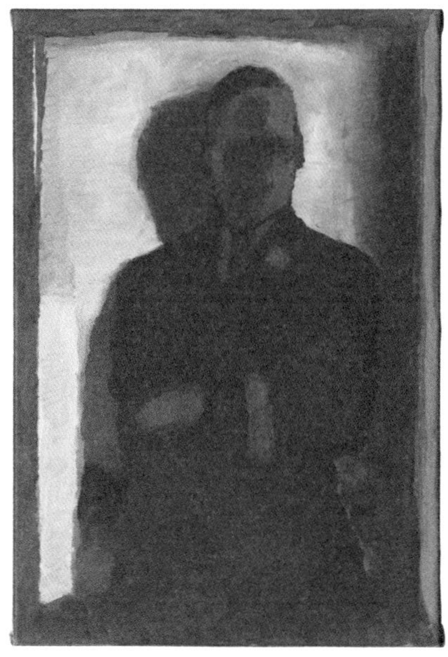

114 Luc Tuymans, *Himmler*, 1998
Oil on canvas, 52 × 36.4 cm
Kunstmuseum Wolfsburg

Architektur des Wahns" [The Architecture of Delusion] is quite important. Speer was asked to create an architecture in which the element of decay was a fact in the building process, as Hitler's megalomania demanded. Rotting and decay were factored into the building process and layout of the whole megalomaniac city, as demanded by Hitler himself.

HDW Those seem like unusual colours for you.

LT That is because it is painted from a paused video, where you get these violet and bluish tones.

TC I have to say that I don't understand the relationship between the three images we just looked at. I need your help here.

LT The exhibition *The Architect* was a show about Albert Speer. Since snow is faint, it is almost a non-existent element, although it is still a field. The image of Heinrich Himmler was painted from a printed reproduction of a photograph, copies of which were hung in most Nazi offices. The size is exactly the same. The original image comes from a book entitled *Topographie des Terrors*. This painting is not the same as that of Speer, of course, but they are both faceless. And the very small painting *Paratroopers*, of Nazi soldiers landing in the snow, was taken from the Nazi propaganda

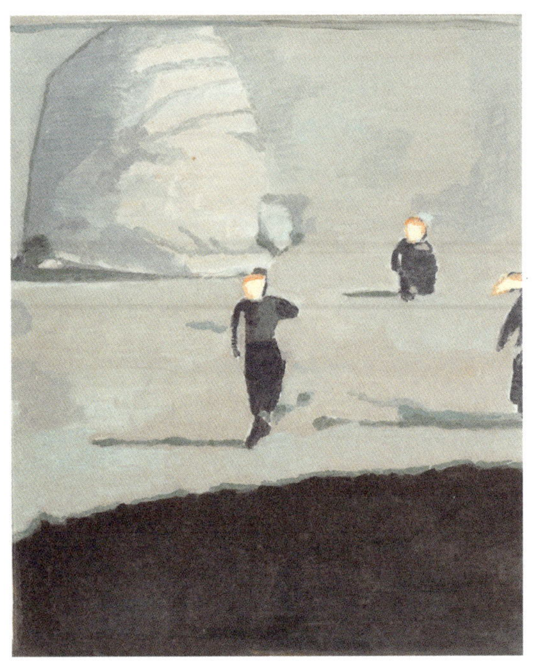

115 Luc Tuymans, *Parachutisten* [Paratroopers], 1998
Oil on canvas, 61 × 50.6 cm
Goetz Collection, Munich

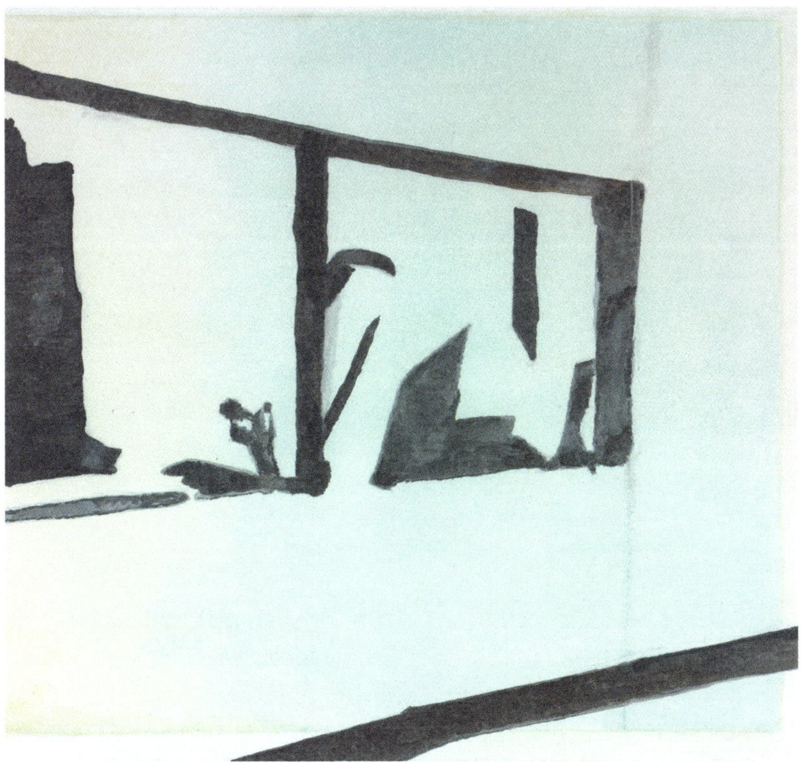

116 Luc Tuymans, *Recherches*, 1998
Oil on canvas, 139 × 151 cm
Kunstmuseum Wolfsburg

magazine *Signal*. Here too, the faces of the soldiers are obscured. I perforated the cut-outs of their heads with pin-pricks and lit them from behind with a flashlight, so that the images of their faces are back-lit, or rather, they emit light. This projected light coming through the image becomes a process of degradation, and renders the physiognomies of the individual paratroopers as worthless objects. This is a remake from a third, much smaller, panel called *Recherches*, which I enlarged. When I first made this drawing in Auschwitz, I used a felt pen, but then totally reconstructed it because it gives off this element of carbonized material.

HDW You made the original drawing during a visit to Auschwitz?

LT Yes, but based on that I made a triptych, which also existed before I remade this painting on a larger scale. The drawings are now in the Kunstmuseum in Bern.

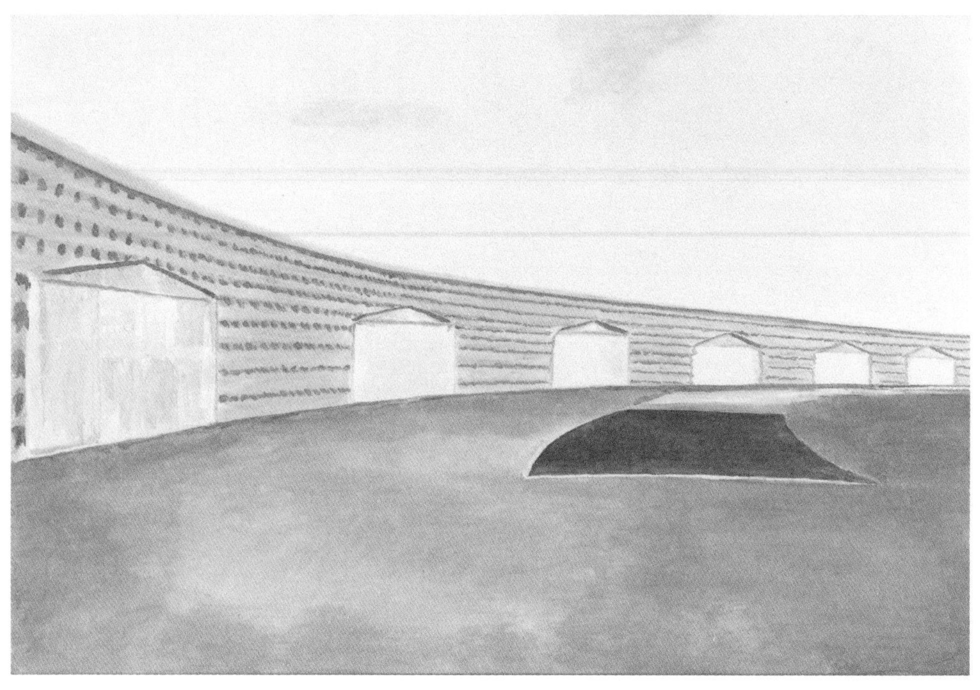

117 Luc Tuymans, *K.Z.*, 1998
Oil on canvas, 112.4 × 167.6 cm
Private collection

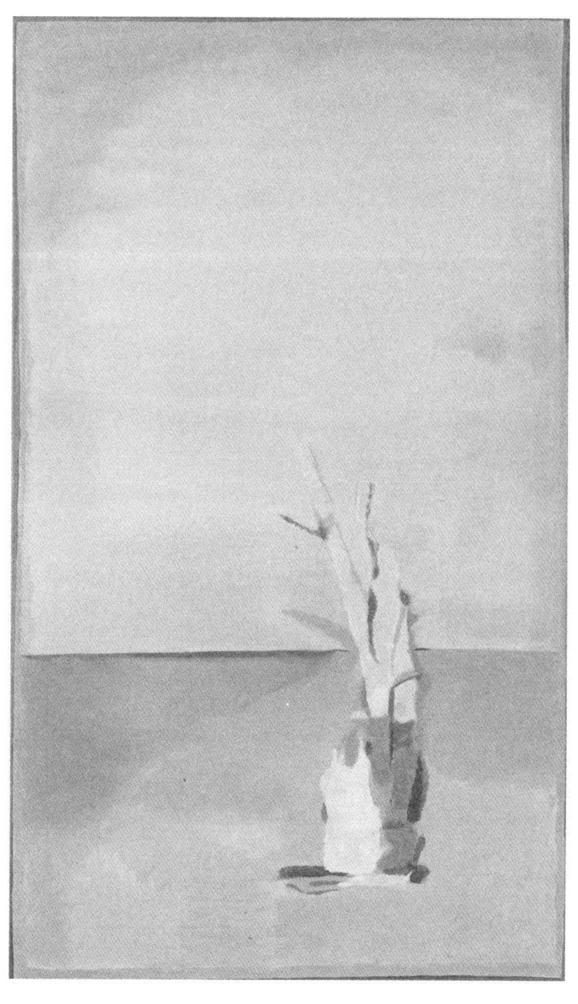

<u>118</u> Luc Tuymans, *Die blaue Eiche* [The Blue Oak], 1998
Oil on canvas, 176.5 × 105 cm
Grażyna Kulczyk Collection

TC *K.Z.* is still part of *The Architect* series…

LT Yes. In this painting, whose title is an abbreviation of the German word for concentration camp, *Konzentrationslager*, we see the sides of barracks, more of a stage than an actual compound. That black shape in the middle is made out of human ashes. This goes back to Caspar David Friedrich, but then strays because the next painting is called *The Blue Oak*. There are visual similarities but conceptually they are different and that's what makes them interesting. This painting of a tree is based on the Caspar David Friedrich painting *The Lonely Tree*. I am fascinated with Friedrich, who was one of the first artists to create a psychological landscape and to reduce it for effect. I cut out the image, placed it on a linoleum floor and took a Polaroid. I then cut into the Polaroid, which immediately corrupts the emulsion and causes discolouration. Friedrich was one of the few German painters who intrinsically knew what scale was, but in a very strange way. For example, if you compare *The Lonely Tree* with other trees he painted later on, you can see that the scale in that first painting is much more effective.

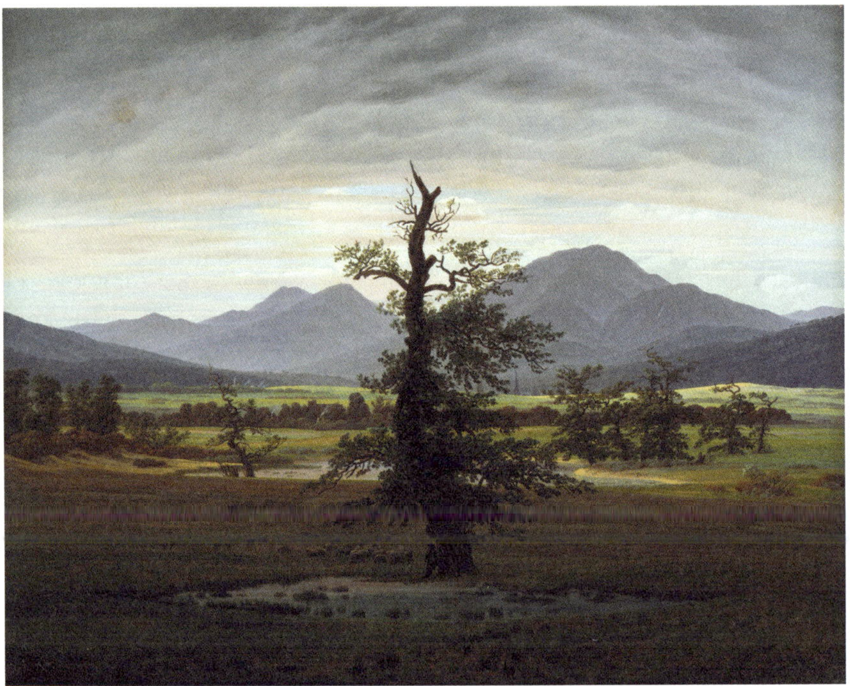

119 Caspar David Friedrich, *The Lonely Tree*, 1822
Oil on canvas, 55 × 71 cm
Staatliche Museen zu Berlin, Nationalgalerie, Berlin, inv. w.s. 52

HDW I always thought Friedrich was aware of the fact that his paintings need space in order to be understood. I don't think that you can have fifty Caspar David Friedrich paintings in two rooms together – they would kill each other. They require a certain distance that allows for thought and reflection.

LT Friedrich always painted in his studio. He made drawings *en plein air*, but his essential work was done within the studio space. That is why it was so important for this work to be shown in the building on Torstrasse where Galerie Gebauer is. The building is from the 1920s – it looks more like an apartment than a contemporary white-cube gallery. Subsequently it was exhibited in Brussels, the city where the establishment basically decided to kill Patrice Lumumba, from *Mwana Kitoko: Beautiful White Man*, which is probably the most journalistic body of work that I have ever made. It was important for me to have both protagonist and antagonist on one wall again, as they were shown in the central space of the Belgian Pavilion at the Venice Biennial in 2001. When I was offered the opportunity to exhibit in the Belgian Pavilion, there was not a lot of time to make a decision. I had two options – either to show a survey of more than twenty-five years of painting, or to create something specific for the space. I found out that the Pavilion had been built by a colonial architect, so in a way it was an ideal space and I decided to do something new. The expectations were high, as if I was going to be on the witness stand, which I hated, because actually the best part of the show was already done with the Pavilion building itself.

TC This brings us back to our conversation about the difficulty of political painting in the present, and how carefully you have thought about the ways in which painting might contribute to political thought. When you say, "This is the most journalistic work I have done", does that mean that you are uneasy about it? What is it that interested you?

LT Let's start with the first painting from the Venice series, *Mwana Kitoko*. The image comes from my memory of a propaganda documentary film made in 1955 by André Cauvin about the first visit to the Congo made by Belgian king, Baudouin I. The king, who is depicted in this painting, was given the rather disrespectful nickname of "Mwana Kitoko" by the Congolese, meaning "beautiful boy". The colonial authorities were quick to turn this into "Bwana Kitoko" – "beautiful master", or "beautiful, noble man". Yet again, the face of power is masked, and I wanted to paint the uniform as an icon. This is what I was referring to when I said that this

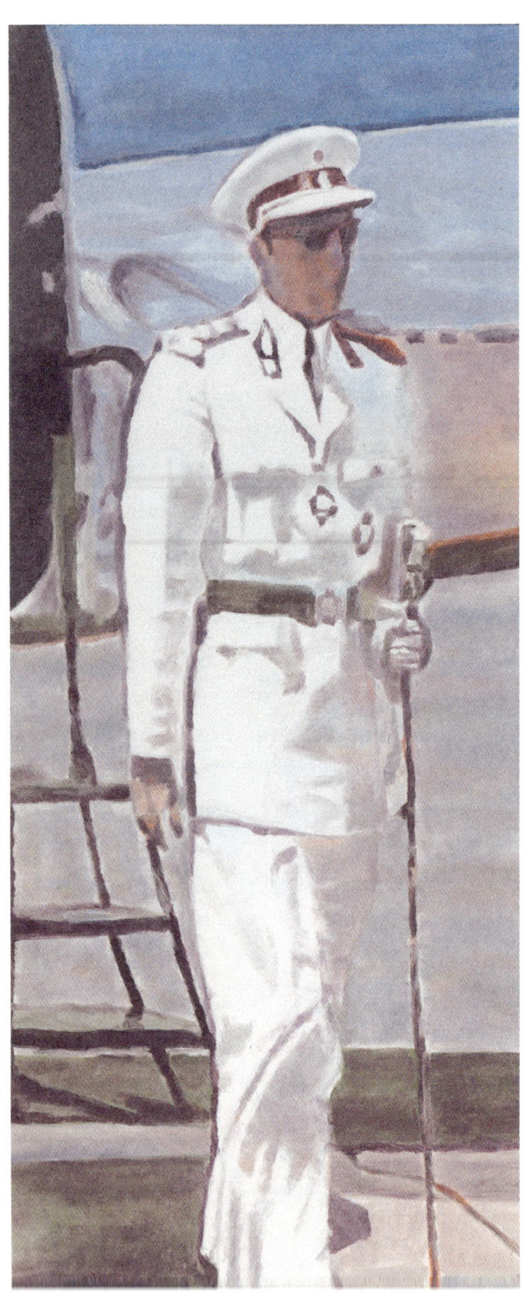

120 Luc Tuymans, *Mwana Kitoko*, 2000
Oil on canvas, 208 × 88 cm
Collectie S.M.A.K., Stedelijk Museum voor Actuele Kunst Gent

work is about "journalism". The two images *Mwana Kitoko* and *Lumumba* come straight out of that Cauvin film.

HDW To understand that Belgium has a very hard time coming to terms with its colonial past, one must only pay a visit to the Royal Museum for Central Africa in Tervuren. At the same time, there is a kind of imaginary aspect to these histories that comes with it. Is that what your series is about?

LT Well, yes. It was born out of my visits to the African museum. Even kids who visit this museum are struck by its exoticism. I also had memories of the film, which led me to do further research and to have a more critical way of looking at the subject. For example, the leopard skin is not a symbol of ultimate power in the Congo. At that time, the Congo was organized into different tribes, and while some chiefs wore leopard skin, it was not a universal symbol of power. Yet the Belgian colonialists brought it out and installed it as such. Only the chief, who is at the feet of the king, could walk over it. The way in which the spots are dispersed give the painting a certain heat, and the holes are basically like a map with blind spots.

HDW Perhaps it contains a global idea of common memory?

LT Common memory, yes, but a funny, coincidental thing, was that while I was making this work, Ludo de Witte published a book about

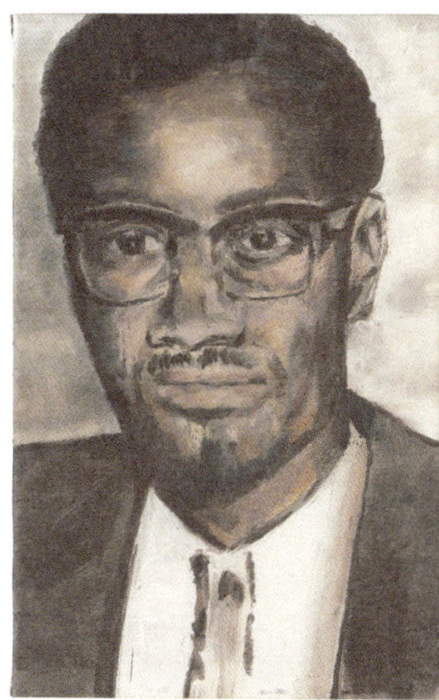

121 Luc Tuymans, *Lumumba*, 2000
Oil on canvas, 62 × 46 cm
The Museum of Modern Art, New York, fractional
and promised gift of Bettina and Donald L. Bryant, Jr.

the assassination of Lumumba. This then led to the formation of the "Lumumba Committee", charged with investigating the extent to which Belgium was involved in his assassination. The critically acclaimed feature film *Lumumba* by Raoul Peck came out in 2000 – so all of this was happening at the same time. This painting ended up in the Belgian Pavilion, which is like an anachronism. One year later, I was invited to participate in a discussion at the Centre for Cultural Studies in London, and Raoul Peck's movie was screened. I was also invited to listen to the conclusion of the Lumumba Commission, which of course was triggered much more by the book than by the paintings, but nevertheless everything was happening simultaneously. It was like a coincidence, a momentum. And that had far more of an impact outside the country than in Belgium. What happened in Belgium is that the protagonist and antagonist were put on the front page of a newspaper in order to kill the story. We Belgians don't assess much of anything – we tend to shut it down.

TC Did you know from the beginning of this project that you were going to make a portrait of Lumumba?

LT Yes, it began with that portrait, but I already had all the other imagery lined up before I started painting. *Mwana Kitoko* was donated to the S.M.A.K. in Ghent and I had wanted to donate *Lumumba* to the Museum of Modern Art in Brussels, but it was refused. The director at the time had a colonial past, and therefore didn't accept it. Finally, in 2002, it ended up in the collection of MOMA in New York. Lumumba was one of the first pan-African thinkers. He was an idealist. He wasn't a great politician, and he certainly wasn't a power-monger, whereas Baudouin was a very patronizing king. The speech Lumumba gave when the Congo gained independence sent shock waves through the entire African continent. Never before had anyone been so blatantly outspoken about the sheer gruesomeness of the colonial system, and from a strategic and political point of view, this was not very smart. The fact that he put Mobutu – an officer who constantly created chaos – at the top of his army, was astonishing. Of course, it was Mobutu who was the real power-monger. He started the nationalization of foreign-owned firms and, ultimately, he could never be controlled by the Americans. This is also why the Congo became independent overnight, because the Belgians were there during the Cold War and afterward, and the Americans were waiting at the door to access uranium and other natural resources. We know that people with university degrees were at the centre of things during this time, so the best thing was for everyone to accept the chaotic status quo, but to keep a foot on the ground – which they did. And Lumumba did not really fit into the picture. He was strangely – and ironically enough – the head of *les évolués*, the urbanites who mostly conformed to the colonial rule.

TC It's strange, I do not remember seeing *Lumumba* at the Wexner Center. It is an astonishing painting and it strikes me that, time and again, you return to portraiture. The portrait and self-portrait are key markers for you in your oeuvre, and often you seem to be constructing a way to renew the portrait. For example, *The Diagnostic View* series in some ways offers the most powerful kind of portraiture, through a distance between subject and portrait. It is full of complex empathy.

LT Yes, this is true, for the portrait of the king too, but with a totally different position and point of departure. There is a psychological factor at play in *Sculpture* as well, which is a sculpture from a bar in Antwerp. Since it is not a real figure, the exoticism is thrown back.

HDW Do you mean to say that the eventual tragedy is already manifested in that picture?

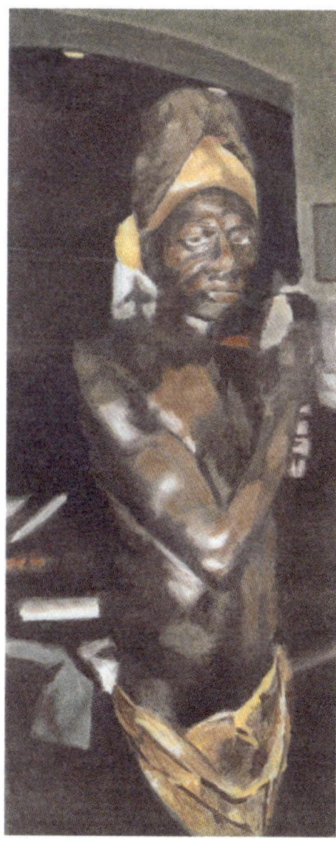

122 Luc Tuymans, *Sculpture*, 2000
Oil on canvas, 155 × 64 cm
Private collection

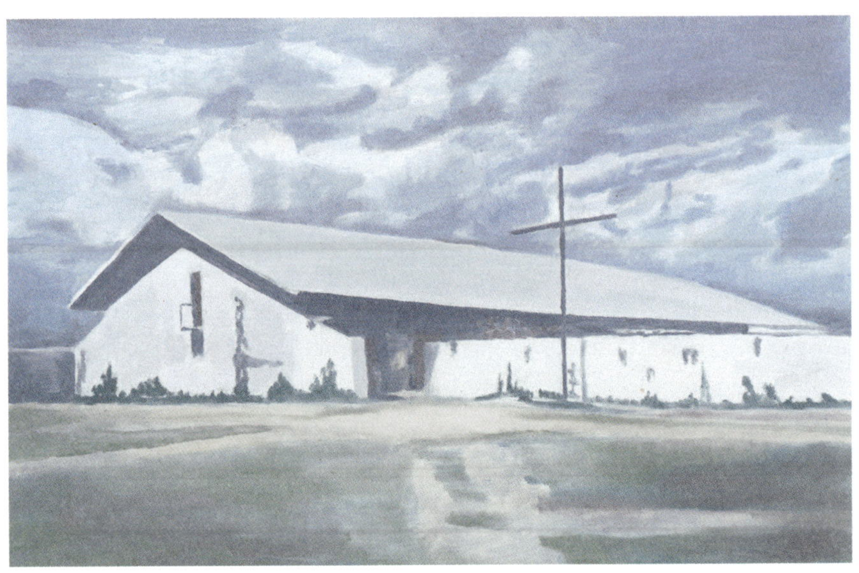

LT Yes. It is already part of history, so cannot be denied. And of course this feeds into an idea of the heroic – for example, what would have happened if the figure had survived? There began to be an emerging admiration of the African intellectual, which at that point was imminent. Therefore it also failed. There is a painting, *The Mission*, of the mission schools where both Mobutu and Lumumba were educated, and this is one of the last paintings. While I was painting *Lumumba*, an article was published about a colonial police officer who had just died. He was one of the officers that had dissolved the bodies of Lumumba and his Cabinet in acid baths, but before doing that, he pulled the last teeth from the jaws of Lumumba and kept them right until he died, when he threw them in the sea, the same year I was working on this series.

HDW That is what he says... There is another Belgian artist who is convinced that he knows where the teeth are. He meditated every day near a tree where he thinks that they are buried.

LT Then I painted *Chalk*. These are the hands of my wife wearing black gloves.

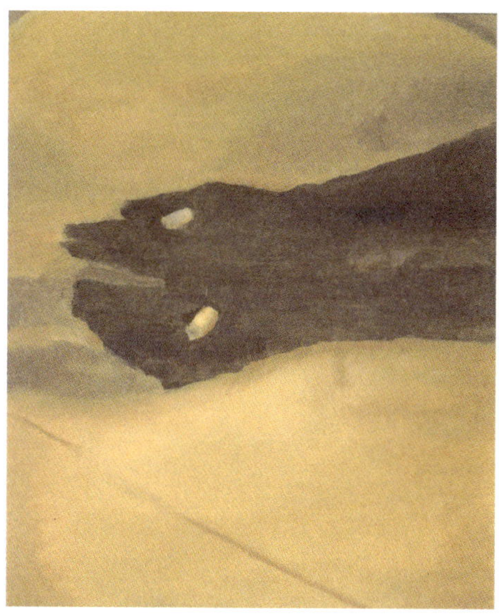

124 Luc Tuymans, *Chalk*, 2000
Oil on canvas, 72.5 × 61.5 cm
Private collection, Promised gift to the San Francisco
Museum of Modern Art

TC What interests me quite a lot about this series is that it is full of a productive reminiscence of your previous work. It takes me right back to your first paintings, which I think are very inspired – those paintings from the 1980s where you are inventing a space, and there is a lack of focus, but also a kind of intimacy. This is quite unlike the others.

LT This is due to the convergence of "recollection" and "recognition", and the way in which these familiar objects function within their constructed, painted environments. *Reconstruction* is based on a re-enactment. The place and circumstances of Lumumba's death can only be reconstructed from incomplete information – there is no certainty whatsoever. A friend [Karel Schoeters] made a documentary about the night he was murdered, which

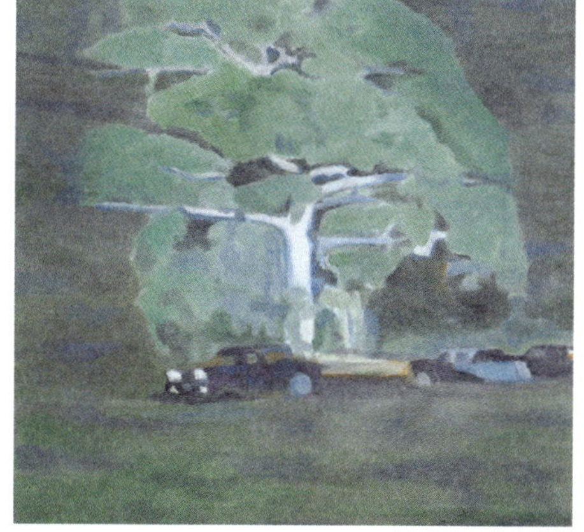

125 Luc Tuymans, *Reconstruction*, 2000
Oil on canvas, 113.5 × 124 cm
Friedrich Christian Flick Collection

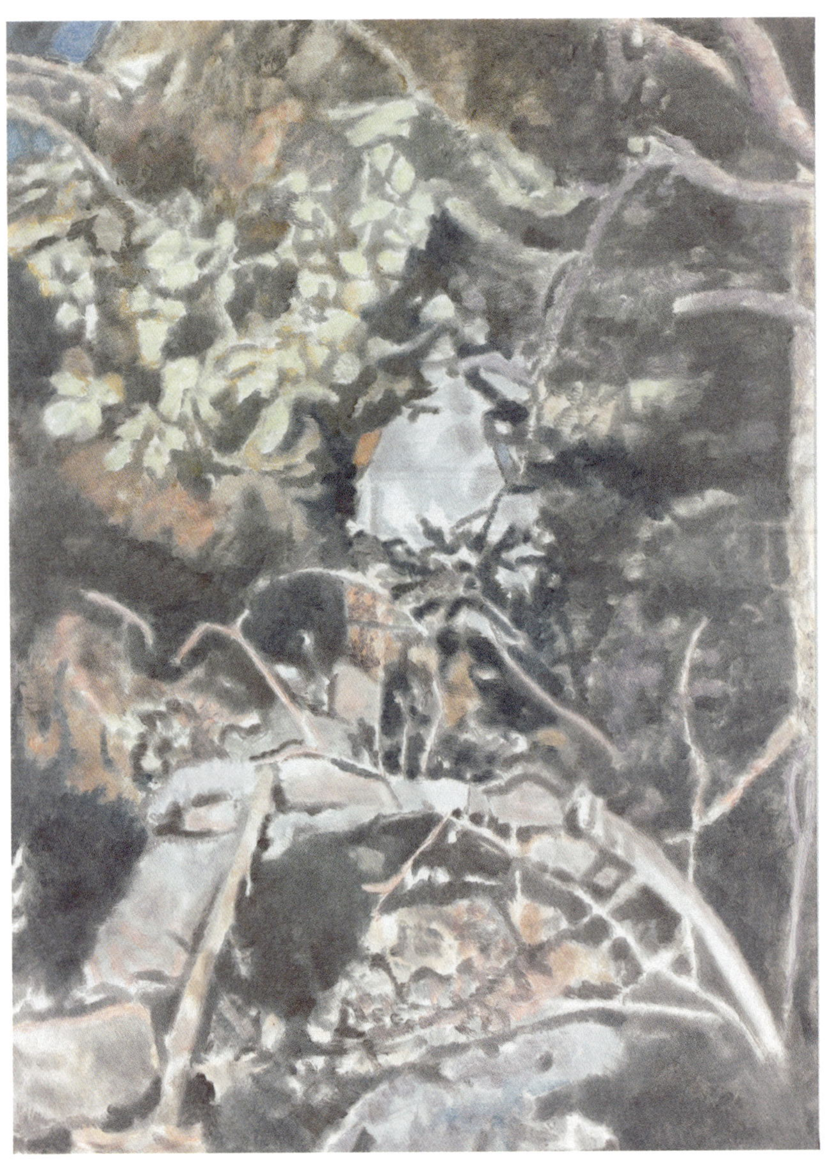

126 Luc Tuymans, *Diorama*, 2001
Oil on canvas, 296 × 285 cm
Rubell Family Collection

was shot in Cuba because they still had American cars from that era. The cars are driving away from underneath an enormous tree. The nocturnal scene with the white trunk of the tree forces the spectator into the role of voyeur who is witnessing a secret operation. The painting of the rhinoceros – *Diorama* – is where I brought the Royal Museum for Central Africa into the series. I went to the museum but couldn't get close enough to the diorama, so I bought a toy rhinoceros and made my own diorama. And from there, I could take the image from the top. You can feel the awkward, immense size of the image. At that point, it was the largest canvas I had ever made.

HDW Can we speak about the films?

TC I saw some of them at the Wexner Center, but there seem to be so many more now?

LT Yes, we've produced a different compilation, and included excerpts from television, such as the documentary about the Congo and part of the films by Hans-Jürgen Syberberg. This was an important inclusion because Syberberg is one of the first Germans that I identify with from a cultural perspective. I think that this was one of the only ways to do it. It was not very well received in Germany because the premiere of the film *Hitler* had to go to Paris. Nevertheless, it was shown on television very late, spread over two evenings.

TC Some of the material is from films you made in the 1980s. I was looking at this yesterday, an extraordinary sequence with the woman and the bird that was at the Wexner Center. It seems that early cinema was very much on your mind at that point. Is that right?

LT Yes, it's true. The Palais des Beaux-Arts, where we are now, had one of the most important cinemas when I was studying here in Brussels, and I came here to see films at least three nights a week, including silent movies. There were small Art Deco viewing rooms, which are now all destroyed. Systematically, I worked from the 1928 French horror film *The Fall of the House of Usher*,[8] all the way through, to more recent films. Silent movies had an enormous impact on me, especially the way they tell the stories visually. For example, in *Nosferatu* you see the way in which Murnau already

8 *The Fall of the House of Usher* (1928), directed by Jean Epstein, is based on Edgar Allan Poe's Gothic short story, "The Fall of the House of Usher" (1839). Luis Buñuel worked on the film adaptation with Epstein.

understood how to use animation to convey something horrific in the way he speeds up the imagery. So, yes, I was very influenced by early cinema.

TC It is an interesting move on your part in the early 1980s, although you don't seem to have the same interest for recent avant-garde cinema.

LT No, I was totally taken by Sergei Eisenstein and Fritz Lang – lots of light, hard shadows, a very graphic way of dealing with film. That is also why it is quite juvenile, in a sense.

TC Yes, but it resonates in your painting. When you returned to painting, it seems that early cinema and montage were absolutely fundamental.

LT Because there is an enchanting quality in silent movies that you don't get in a movie with sound. The imagery has a different magnitude because there is no sound, only the image. And the image moves, but the narration changes when sound comes into play.

HDW If we think of cinema now, we think of the Hollywood model, where something is written, images are filmed based on what's been written, and then it is all put together in the editing process. This work represents a different way of thinking about cinema, where a filmed archive or bank of images is created and constructed by the author, who then begins to establish what belongs together.

LT It started out as a kind of journal and, for years, I tried to make sense of it but never could. We eventually made this compilation to show that some of the ideas in the paintings were formed from it.

HDW So how many hours are in the completed version?

LT Too many, and it is also not even really meant to be seen. One has to make something out of it, but now everything has been digitized, so we can go through it again from different angles, which is maybe work for a later time. But in the end, I did want to make a film and to construct a scenario.

TC And did you have an idea?

LT Yes, the idea was about my doctor, who looked exactly like one of my favourite Dutch writers, Jan Jacob Slauerhoff. Slauerhoff was a poet and novelist, as well as a naval doctor for JCJL, the Java–China–Japan shipping line. This was a guy who had learned Chinese, and some of the most beautiful prose written in Dutch comes from him. He died in 1934 at the age of 38.

HDW He is almost forgotten now.

LT His work was a precursor to the *nouveau roman* since he was writing about different times, places and so on. My story was about a found boat in the middle of a harbour. The boat was chained up because its owners could no longer pay their dock fees, but the captain and the whole crew were still on board. They and the shippers were broke and owed back pay to the captain and crew. This all took place sometime around Christmas, and I placed my doctor character – who was based on Slauerhoff – on the ship. The plan was for the boat to be filmed, and then emptied out, so that the traces of people, instruments and food would remain. I intended to present a transitional space – that of the harbour – as an immobilized space, in need of a presence. Of course, in real life, the boat was eventually disassembled. But anyway, that was the idea. It was called *Life on Earth*, which started to seem like it would be a bit too much like a Jim Jarmusch film.

HDW So you didn't do it?

LT No. It is not that I would never want to do it, but it is quite difficult to combine painting with film – impossible, actually – because they are too similar.

GB Too similar?

LT Yes, I mean I am a very bad photographer, because I am always too late. Painting is also time-based – working with time, through time, over time. But my experience of filming with handheld cameras is that you can edit in-camera, which works for me in the same way as over-painting a painting. It is much more of an image-based approach, whereas with photography, the ultimate moment is the release of the shutter, the very instant of capturing the image.

GB But is this material still inspiring for you?

LT Some of the imagery does resonate, yes. As I said, imagery can be obsessive, based on things one cannot fully explain. Images can recur, the same way as fears do. The painting *Ballroom Dancing* is a commentary on the Bush administration. The idea first came about during a time when the US was completely ruled by fear. It is no coincidence that there was simultaneously a resurgence in the popularity of ballroom dancing – an inherently antiquated and conservative anachronism that harks back to the economic turmoil and war of the 1930s and '40s. My initial idea was to depict a

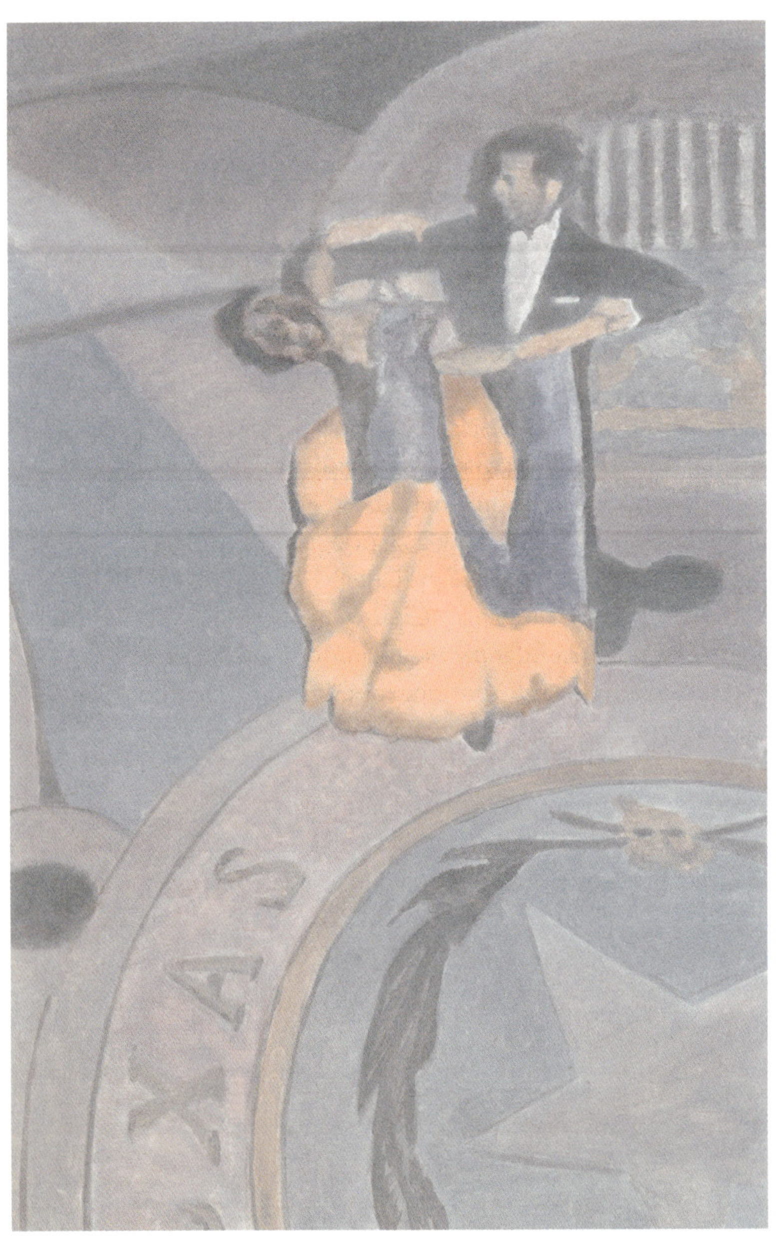

127 Luc Tuymans, *Ballroom Dancing*, 2005

Oil on canvas, 158 × 103.5 cm

Private collection. Fractional and promised gift to
the San Francisco Museum of Art

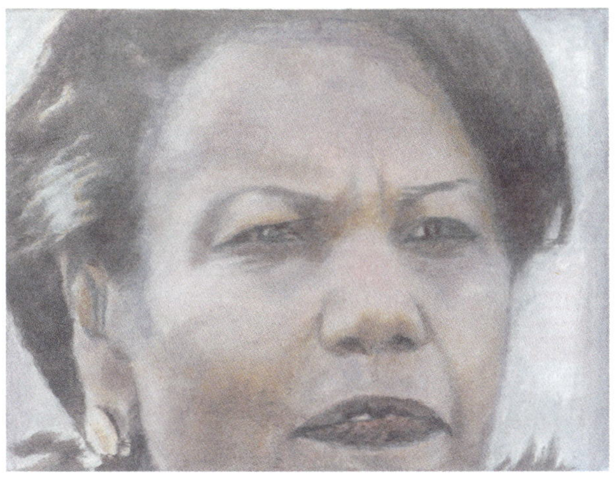

<u>128</u> Luc Tuymans, *The Secretary of State*, 2005
Oil on canvas, 45.5 × 61.5 cm
The Museum of Modern Art, New York.
Fractional and promised gift of David and Monica Zwirner, 2006

classic Hollywood musical scene, such as Fred Astaire and Ginger Rogers,
an artificial rose-coloured view of the world. My wife and I were browsing
the Internet, and found this image of the 2005 Governors Ball, and it was
the exact image that I needed. The dancers are located between the seals of
Texas and the United States. *The Secretary of State* was inspired by a friend
of mine who, at the time, was the Minister of Foreign Affairs. He made a
remark about Condoleezza Rice when she visited Belgium on a state visit,
saying "She is actually quite smart and not un-pretty." And there I had the
two components: Condoleezza Rice and ballroom dancing, because there
is the aberration, but also an aspect of irony from the beginning, because
it is not the Democrats that abolished slavery, but the Republicans. And
there is also the fact that to paint this woman, about whom we still do not
know what it added up to, I had to reflect her determination. She after all
replaced someone like Colin Powell, who accepted the stigma of racism
in order to get somewhere. And I did it on the size of a flat screen, which
is a reflection of her media image. Luckily Glenn Lowry, the director of
MOMA, was actually smart enough to take it in, and said "the painting has
to be public", because actually its presence in a private collection could be
misunderstood. Here, I found the difference in skin colour interesting, as
well as the shape of her face and physiognomy. If you painted the entirety

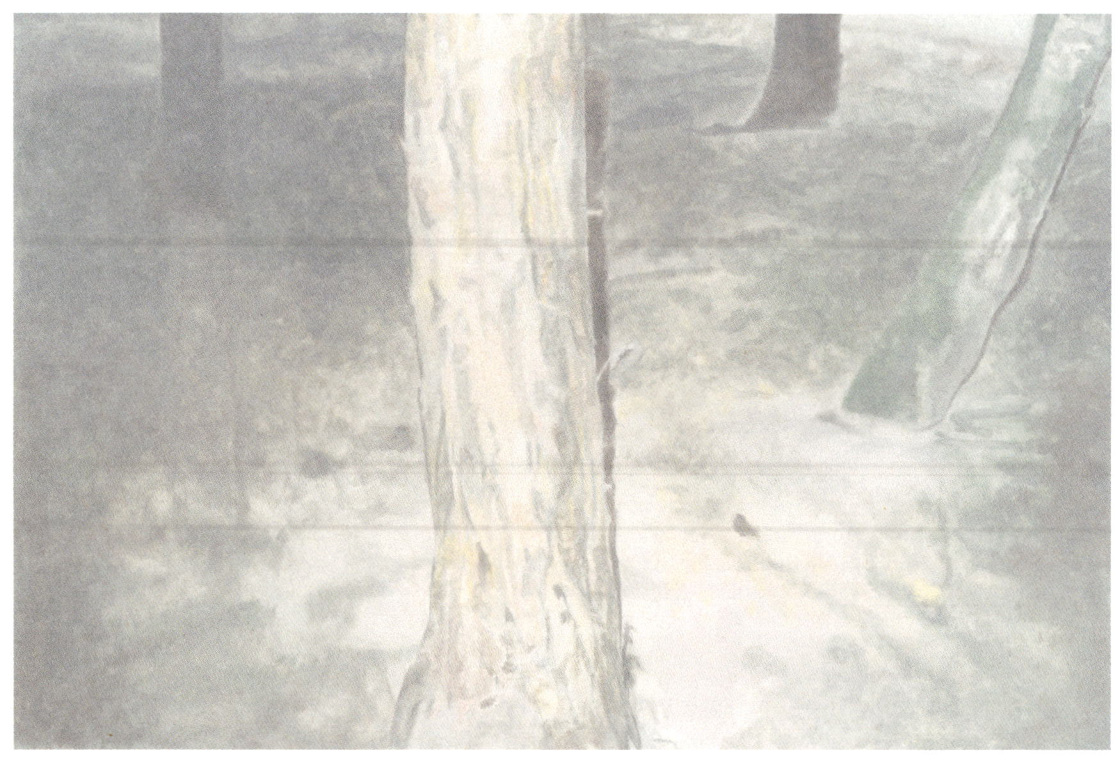

<u>129</u> Luc Tuymans, *The Parc*, 2005
Oil on canvas, 160 × 246.5 cm
Private collection. Courtesy David Zwirner, New York/London

of Condoleezza, in a manner that approximates the scale of her *as an image*, she would be humongous, a monstrous woman, just enormous. But I like the tint and the bleeding of the imagery.

HDW You know what I thought when I first saw it? I thought of Socialist Realism, where a beloved leader looks to the future.

LT Well, sure. It has all of that, of course. One of my collectors was once seated next to Condoleezza Rice at an embassy dinner, and asked if she had seen "her" painting? Rice, without turning, replied, "Yes."

TC It is very striking to me that this and the *Lumumba* picture are two high points in your work – these moments in which you create a framework to look directly at a face again. Portraiture is very important, and it never occurred to me before that these are two portraits of black intellectuals. Rice was the Dean of Stanford University. So this is a complicated image. It comes back to what we were talking about earlier – how political painting has to be very careful not to come on too strong or too directly with its opinions.

LT Exactly, because then it does become not only too opinionated, but also too confrontational. And that is what politics is not about.

The Parc is also from the *Proper* series, but it's an exception. I took this Polaroid in a park near my home, and the odd vantage point has something to do with the height of an animal. It's a murky and slightly paranoid image, with no horizon and a grim section of bare dirt. At the same time, there is an aspect of surveillance and control. The harsh white light suggests an artificial source, like that of a searchlight.

HDW There is something claustrophobic about it.

TC In my opinion, we are not too far away from the world of the *Pillows*. It is another strange vision of a landscape surface.

LT Three quarters of these paintings were painted in an apartment – a small, interior environment – whereas my more recent work was painted in a larger studio.

TC *Seal* is an inspired painting. You manage to capture the space and colour of Internet mediation. Did it come from the Internet?

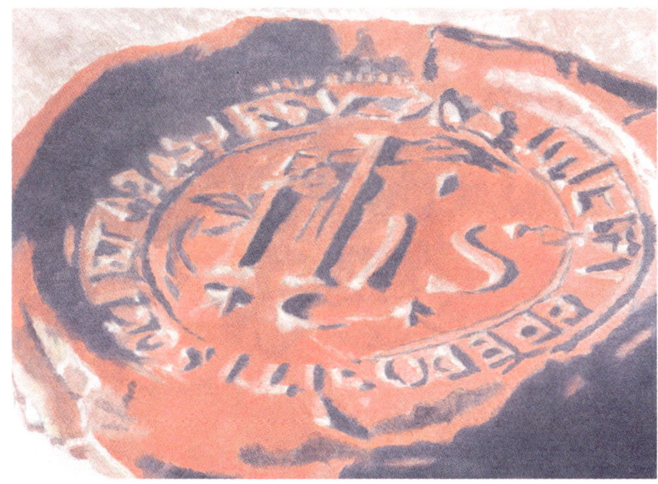

130 Luc Tuymans, *Seal*, 2007
Oil on canvas, 50 × 70 cm
Private collection, London

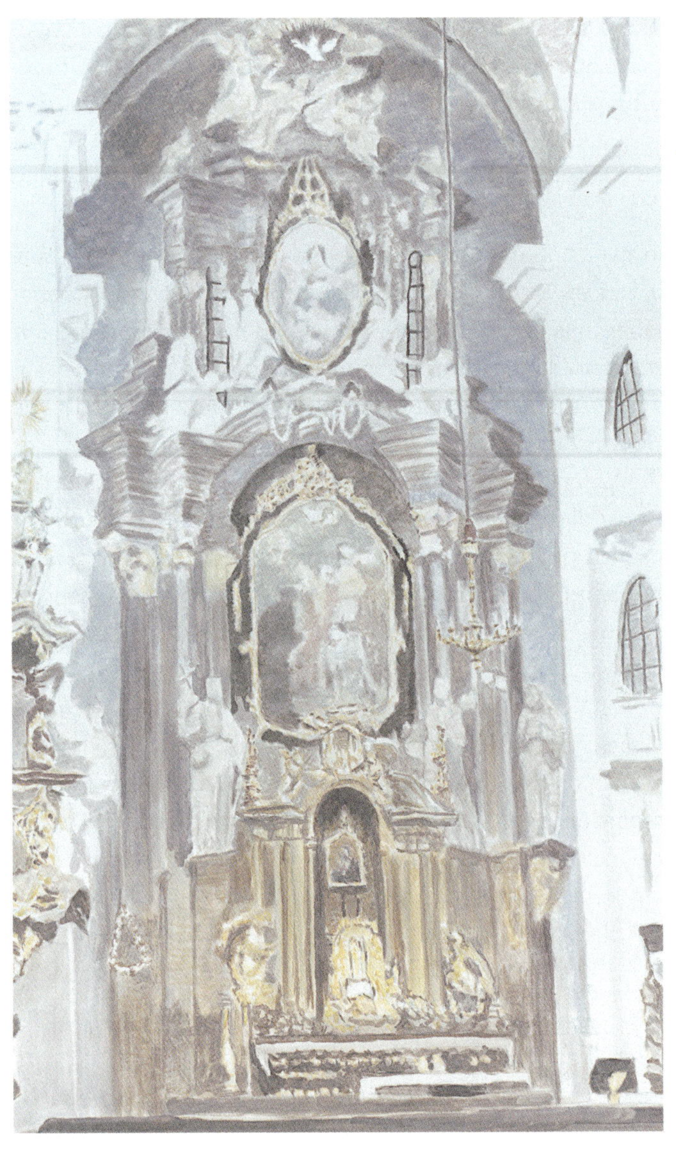

131 Luc Tuymans, *Church*, 2006
Oil on canvas, 235.5 × 142 cm
The National Museum of Art, Osaka

LT Yes, this is an image of a Jesuit seal that I found on the Internet. The purple renders it hazy and feverish, and the text is unintelligible.

TC Somehow your paintwork captures this strange interim, indeterminate state of the Internet, which is very uncanny. It is horrifying in a way.

HDW Was this painting also in the *Proper* show?

LT No, I made it for an art fair. This is important, as paintings for art fairs are solitary.

We know what *Church* is about, right? It shows a Baroque altar of an Eastern European Jesuit church whose interior includes a number of *trompe-l'oeil* images. There's an ambiguity in what is real and what is an illusion… This particular church in Slovenia is by no means an important Jesuit church. I never liked Baroque painting – it felt like there was too much information. But once you start analysing it, it is quite fascinating because of how complex it is.

HDW What did you find so interesting about this Baroque way of reflecting?

LT First of all, the painted inside of a church. That was intriguing because of the double act of the *trompe-l'oeil*. I actually repainted it in the Zachęta

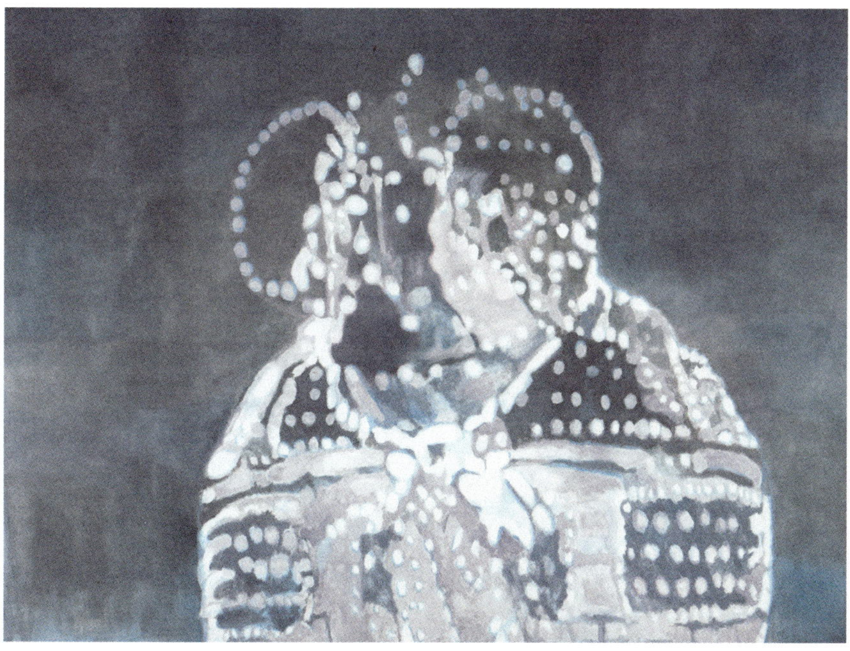

132 Luc Tuymans, *Turtle*, 2007
Oil on canvas, 368 × 509 cm
Private collection. Courtesy David Zwirner, New York/London

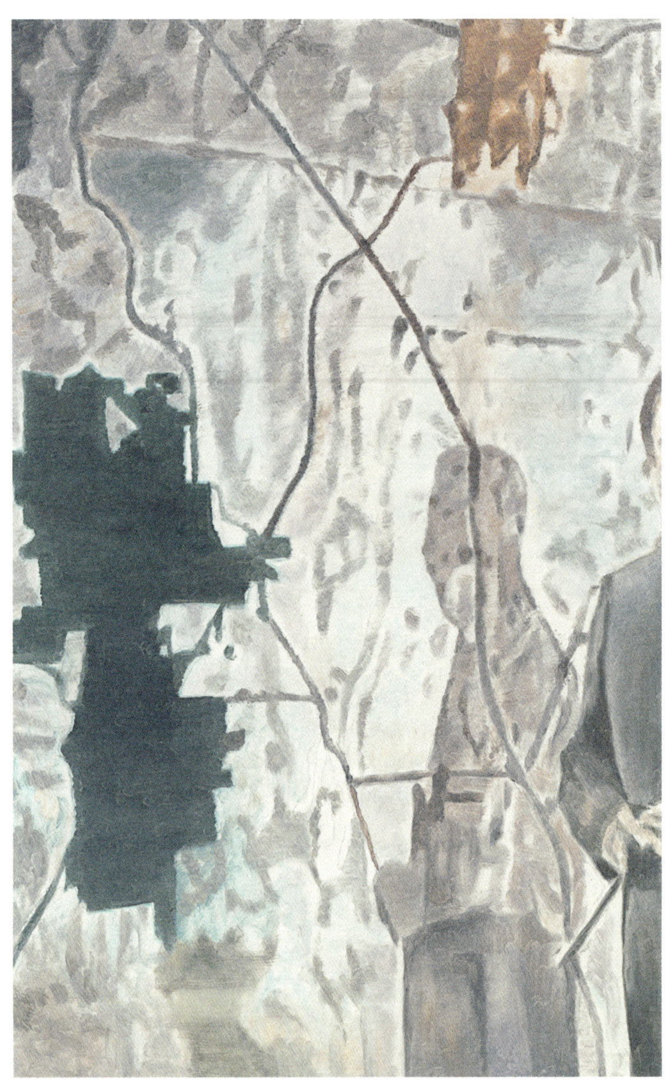

133 Luc Tuymans, *W*, 2008
Oil on canvas, 188 × 119.4 cm
Private collection, New York. Courtesy David Zwirner, New York/London

National Gallery in Warsaw as an 8-metre-high wall painting that was there specifically for the show. After the exhibition closed, it was destroyed. Then again, it was already painted from a painted image, no longer from a photograph. This is another step. It all deals with this element of representation. Of course there is a hidden agenda, for sure…

TC As we move to the final series about Walt Disney, I find *Turtle* to be a truly frightening painting. And I think the Disney series would not make sense without it.

LT And this is our *W*, Walt himself, chain-smoking.

HDW Really, was he a chain-smoker?

LT Yes, and also manic-depressive. He invested all of his money in every project, like gambling. This is based on a photograph of him just before he died, when he was working on EPCOT [Experimental Prototype Community of Tomorrow], a utopian city of the future that he was luckily unable to build. He flew over the United States to find the exact location where he was going to build it. And this time he didn't make the same mistake as he made with Disneyland. He bought everything around that land, so that there would be no brothels or bars.

HDW This must be something that is deeply connected with American capitalism. Ford had the same kind of obsessions with Fordlândia. He wanted to make the ideal town for his workers in Brazil. It is still there but falling apart.

LT The Disney story is very intriguing to me. How did Disney perceive himself? As an artist, a creator? I think he actually saw himself much more as an organizer. But nevertheless, he started with a silly drawing of a mouse. It is fascinating how he built a huge empire from something that small. And to this day, there is an eternal copyright that is closely monitored. Two days before my show opened, we received a notice that the Disney Corporation knew we were going to do this show, and they were watching us. Strangely enough, we had been in contact with them to agree part of the *Snow White* authorization that was included as part of the source material and in the documentary. There was no problem with that and they were actually helpful.

TC Well, you know, repressive tolerance. They have a very intelligent outfit and know that they don't want a scandal. It is not an attack on Disney, of course. It is just reflecting on what the Disney-fication of the world amounts to.

<u>LT</u> The Disney work emerged from a line of thought that began with a utopian starting-point. It started with my interest in the Jesuits and evolved from there, however disjunctive this may seem, towards ideas about Disney and the topography of fantasy. The following exhibition, *Against the Day* at Wiels, Brussels, in 2008, with its title taken from a Thomas Pynchon book, dealt with the triviality of the present, insofar as the source images often came from websites that were still under construction, and dealing with virtual reality, surveillance, technology, Big Brother and YouTube. These three exhibitions, if we reflect on them together and in context, actually constitute a strong example of the working framework for my paintings.

<u>HDW</u> Why was it important to have Loyola appear in such an isolated manner, almost as an isolated, skull-like orb?

<u>LT</u> Because he was an icon, and it is an iconic image taken from his death-bed. They actually reopened the eyes because his eyes were, of course, closed, and then they built and constructed the whole square behind it. That is how it is kept in the Vatican, where you can see it. The Jesuit order is such an amazing force, the enormous impact they had on knowledge and on education.

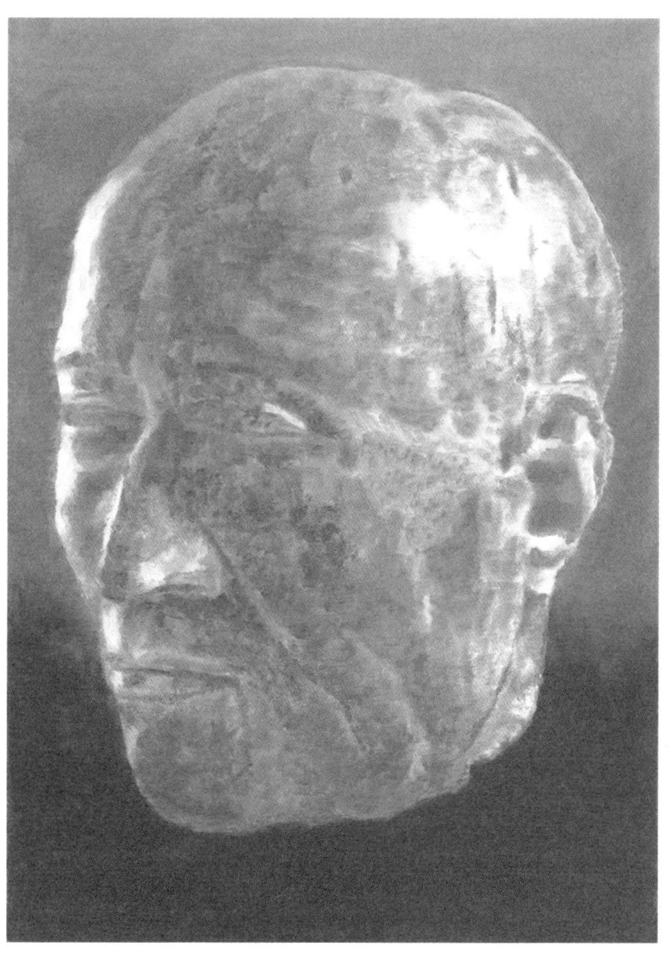

134 Luc Tuymans, *Ignatius de Loyola*, 2006
Oil on canvas, 113 × 81.5 cm
The National Museum of Art, Osaka

Basel: The Conclusive Conversation

The conclusive conversation of this project between Gottfried Boehm and Hans M. De Wolf took place in Basel at Boehm's home on Saturday March 10th 2018. It is in fact the second conversation after the recording of an earlier one was accidentally erased.

Gottfried Boehm (GB) | Hans M. De Wolf (HDW)

HDW Luc once told me a very good story: he was on a train, dozing, returning from somewhere to Brussels, when suddenly he saw a very clear picture in his head. He became excited, hopped out of the train in Brussels and took a taxi to Antwerp. Once in his workshop, he took a canvas and started painting this picture that he held in his mind. This took him about fifteen minutes. At the time, he could not quite believe that it could take him such a short time, so he spent another quarter of an hour working on improving it. After those additional fifteen minutes, the original picture was kind of destroyed, which angered him enormously. It took him the whole of the next day to repaint the original picture, and yet it still wasn't as good as the first one he had made.

GB Interesting, but why are you recounting this anecdote now, at the beginning of our conversation?

HDW Because I believe that the essence of our talks with Luc is related to the question of how and what a picture is communicating.

GB Indeed, that makes a lot of sense. We can also add that what this story illustrates, in addition, is the importance for an individual to listen to his or her intuition, and to know how to (re)act: Luc knew that there was something in the image he saw in his mind. He jumped in the taxi, went straight to Antwerp to hammer it out and promptly made a mistake, which he was able to fix afterwards. This is a very clear illustration of the way in which mental and sensual productivity, both from an intellectual as well as artistic standpoints, are linked to the fact that individuals receive and grasp opportunities unhindered and unlimited by any institutional regulations. Let's leave it here for the time being. With respect to art academies, the Bologna Process calls for more attention to be paid to administrative rules and standards, and to the content that is taught, rather than to the development of individual talent, which is seen as being outdated and old-fashioned. Ultimately though, it is the old European idea of a person. This humanist dimension is still the strongest one we have.

HDW Certainly, and we have to protect this! That's also why the Bologna case is such a deeply sad one. It is constructive if an artist misuses the situation to make with it a project of his own, but this then becomes somehow corrupt.

GB Additionally, with the Bologna Process, an administrative regime takes over, which might be useful for the management of big industrial companies, but I cannot be a judge of that. It is as if you were in need of a CEO that can organize. But within the context of an art institution, above all in art academies, schools, or even universities, the administration's power is, ultimately, a dangerous one.

HDW And its power was able to reach such levels because of the lack of objective criteria against which we can assess this kind of artistic research. It is almost an act of cruelty that there can be so many people out there – some of them with good intentions – who are acting in this grey zone, without any university or even administration having clear criteria to evaluate this "research" in terms of its content. This is our current reality.

GB True. And actually, you also have to ask why the Bologna Process was set up and why it has been so successful. By this I do not mean successful from the content point of view, as this has definitely not been the case. But how has it happened that it spread throughout Europe like a storm? An autumn, winter and spring storm. For the reasons we have not yet spoken about, but they are certainly interesting as they throw light on the situation in which we have to live. It was an initiative that came into being after 1989, at a moment when a certain type of economics and neoliberalism were equated with democracy, and which has resulted in a kind of global dominance. We know that this is an illusion, but the aftermath of these decisions truly exists. And the constraints on cultural institutions are atrocious, because if politicians can decide who money is afforded to, they also want to maintain control of it. In addition, if you want control, you need an administration, and the administration wants to feel confident so it takes the power instead of offering it to more productive or creative forces.

HDW I couldn't agree more. A friend of mine, a sociologist, has looked up those statistics since the 1980s. Belgian universities have 20 % more employees, but 19 % of them are working in administrative positions – hence they are only employed to control us. This obsession with control and the forms with which it is executed is wholly counterproductive.

GB Moreover, the growth in the evaluation of institutions speaks volumes. I remember a number of very active years when the art history seminar here in Basel formed part of the university, and alongside it we had the research institute Eikones, as an additional body. There I was evaluated four times within one year! Four times! Absurd!

HDW But who is doing the evaluation?

GB Interestingly enough, the evaluators are not experts. I am not claiming it would have been any better if they were, but at least there would have been somebody who understood something about the issue he or she was there to evaluate. But if these people are externally recruited and have no inside expertise, then it is obvious that the evaluation process is only there to ensure that the administrative structures are maintained and that the programme requirements are fulfilled. And then something different is revealed: this new idea and reform is based on outlined programmes and syllabuses, a regime that sets and defines what is thought, how and when. And for a free academy, be it affiliated with art or with the sciences, this is not helpful.

HDW This has also led to a separation. In the beginning, when trying to implement the Bologna rules, Luc and other artists were willing to participate. They thought, "Why not? It could be interesting working together with 'intelligent people'. It might lead to something new and interesting." Like our example has shown. Nowadays this has become impossible. No real, free and independent artist would be interested in such a thing. This also demonstrates how much the negative effects of the Bologna Process have spread. There are now so many different working groups that are not really connected, even though they are theoretically, and on paper, supposed to be doing the same thing. This is my opinion, but I would like to know yours. Has this also contributed to the current "administration" crisis in Europe, which, in a greater sense, is also an identity and utopian problem?

GB Those are interesting and important points you're bringing up. In response to the first one, I think there is a difference, at least a subtle one, between an art academy and a scientific or philosophical institution. Art is a cultural force which, as we have known for a long time, cannot just be learnt. It can only be practised. You can be introduced to it, but you cannot learn it.

HDW Art and science have nothing in common.

GB Indeed, and art cannot be taught either. There cannot be any instruction books or manuals; you cannot construct teaching based on how good art is to be produced. Nevertheless, there are art academies that bear their own particularities, an idiosyncratic type of living and interaction between experienced artists and younger people who are studying and testing themselves, seeing whether they too are able to become artists. This type of schooling needs to be protected. Yet the contrary has happened. The art academy has been regarded as an antique in need of refurbishment – and has been substituted by a strict didactic programme, where artists are trained in the most scientific way possible. And there are doubts as to whether this scientification makes any sense.

HDW It is frightening that there exists now an entire generation of young people who believe that what they do attests to some kind of research. Whereas it is clear as daylight that it is not about research. Of course, an artist is always conducting some kind of research. I remember for instance an experience I had with Frank Theys. I wanted a free-hanging screen for an exhibition on which a film could be projected on both sides. I went to a specialist company in Belgium, but they could not provide this and claimed that if they could not, nobody would. Two months later in Beijing with Frank, he spent half a day experimenting with different filters on Plexiglas – and one day later we had our screen with a wonderful projection on both sides using just one beamer. This is research, you see! A very particular kind of research, one that is not interested in knowledge but in experience.

GB And your example shows very nicely that it is not about students and artists bidding farewell to the world of knowledge, but it is about accumulating enough knowledge. They should not walk past the world, but learn to use this knowledge with their imagination in a confident manner.

HDW Exactly!

GB The term "imagination" is very important to me. You talked about utopia. Imagination is a little less projectively conceived, but in the end it is all about cultivating the unprecedented importance of that curious capacity of the imagination. Today this is done, at the most, via so-called "creativity research" in order to find out how creativity works instead of just letting people that are creative or have a talent to be so, use their imagination as it used to be done.

HDW To this end, you simply have to accept that there will never be a script telling you how to do such things.

GB Absolutely, and, by the way, if you are interested in a criticism of this so-called "creativity research" as it has been conducted for the last twenty years, we can round it up here. This research failed every time when it should explain how to become creative, when a prescription should be made out on what I should do to become creative

GB All right, artists would die laughing if they knew that this kind of research really exists.

HDW But let's come back to Luc. How did you experience this one-on-one exchange with the artist about painting?

GB It was about building a connection. This is pertinent in relation to our discussion about the basis of what should be encouraged within art academies: a learning from one another through conversation. This process allows you to reveal something about yourself and to develop an individual practice by way of asking questions: "How do I do that? How can this materialize or develop in(to) a drawing? What kind of prerequisites from a visual point of view can I bring into play?" This core activity of teaching in academies is analogous to the process we undertook when we first started talking to each other.

Together we visited a museum in Budapest and, while looking at the target paintings in the collection, we tested our minds in this shared dialogue about our relationship to these works, what feelings and ideas they brought up and what these latter were grounded in. Is it a question of what we see, or whether we are even able to find the right words to convey these questions? It was this mutual exchange standing in front of the paintings that proved to be the best way forward. Luc was completely right that this is the best way to engage with art. The speech around reception is only fulfilled when this kind of "participation" really takes place. What brought us together is the engagement with things that we saw with our own eyes.

HDW Right, and also the impromptu form of participation is, in my opinion, a very important element. I also realized and actually saw the willingness of the two of you to open up and discuss the culture that has formed your experiences – and this needs some courage.

GB Indeed, it takes courage and also experience. But if you are prepared, it is not too demanding, especially if you can rely on the strength of the situation. I believe that "situation" is a very important keyword for cultural practice. This was a very classical situation that we engaged in when we stepped in front of those paintings together. Situations always gain momentum when they include people. A situation only exists if there are individuals within it. If you're outside, you're not in the situation.

This means that a mere observer isn't part of the situation, which of course consists of many coincidences and circumstances that can also be negative ones. There's also a power in the notion that something enters your mind when you're confronted with something that you did not know before. Maybe our minds are tickled simply because we hear something that we would not have heard under normal circumstances.

HDW Let's return to the "zero schedule", so as not to reveal how matters should run.

GB This was, above all, your idea when you stated: "Let's get going, without a fixed notion of what we will do and how it will go". You wanted a project based on mutual trust, implying that it would soon build up and keep growing steadily, which it was very nice to see happen.

HDW Again, this shows that our intuition wasn't bad! If you had selected the Bologna Process in order to make similar exchange projects around it, I strongly believe that the world would have been a better place now. But we didn't achieve that. We didn't have this strength and power because of the institution. Institutions do not foster an approach that builds energy and encourages collaboration between individuals.

GB Exactly!

HDW Hence this idea couldn't get any institutional funding, couldn't get institutionally evaluated and also couldn't be brought under an institutional system. But all of this was my aim from the beginning, because I knew who the enemy was.

GB It's curious that you're bringing this to my memory right now, as there exists, on some level, an incredible, almost mythological, appreciation for the great artist-individuals of modernity. There are the Picassos, the Van Goghs, the Seurats, celebrated as those unfathomable people who were only following their imagination and nothing else. This is what makes them the heroes of our time. On the other hand, there is also a deep mistrust in young people and very little confidence to allocate them just a few years to test out their potential. Because then, you might have to leave open the possibility for failure. And it might so happen that, during that process, people realize that this is not for them. However, a society that no longer allows opportunity for trying and testing individuals is a society which will kill itself in the long run. I remember that during our university debates, there was a discussion to shorten the length of study time, because the Bachelor's and Master's degrees were being introduced – and in order to introduce the BA, the so-called "Grundstudium" had to be shortened from eight to six semesters. In those six semesters the curriculum needed to be completed with all the prescribed classes and exams. The first time I heard that, I thought back to the time when I was a student, and asked our rector what they would be doing here? "You're taking the young people that are coming here – who are almost all still teenagers and, since in urban societies, adolescence takes longer to grow out of than in rural ones, far into one's twenties – you're taking away their opportunities to live out their adolescence. You are preventing them from turning their adolescence into something productive and forcing them immediately into a pattern of success by saying that they have six semesters during which they have to do this and that exam, otherwise they're forever out of here." This deadly move to eliminate freedom was also introduced through the Bologna Process.

HDW I always refer to the example of the Venetians. They were smart because they didn't set up their university in Venice, but in Padua, so that the young people could enjoy their freedom, but when their studies were over, this period came to an end and they had to work for the Republic of Venice. I think this is an essential part of youth, to give them room to manoeuvre, to allow them freedom for experimentation. How else can you take on responsibility at a later stage?

GB When this way of doing things was established, it was clearly set against a background of economic efficiency, since there was always the idea to train people up to fit in with operating processes, so that they could be employed by companies. By the way, the initial result of the first Bachelors who had completed the curriculum was that nobody wanted them! They didn't know anything and especially had no knowledge of what the companies needed. So then the natural thing happened: companies trained their employees up themselves and gave them the knowledge they needed. So although the Bologna model completely failed in its goal, it continues to exist.

HDW But it had even further negative impacts, as I wrote in the introduction of this book. Every good and authentic artist who is doing interesting work has turned away from that model, including Luc. Yet nevertheless, or despite this, there are now hundreds of people who are undertaking "research in the arts". This is extraordinarily expensive, but for every PhD, universities are afforded government funding. This is a grey area and one where there is very little that you can do about it.

GB It would be very interesting to talk to those people. I can imagine that someone with real artistic talent wouldn't lose this talent entirely through such an "education". Such a person will develop the ability to safeguard this talent. On the other hand, people who fail this system, meaning that they don't finish their study programme, might still be successful later in life and achieve important stature, be it as artists, curators or museum staff.

This means that the importance lies less in the success of the curriculum, but in protecting your individual talent.

HDW There is still the possibility that great artists don't need to work with knowledge in the same way. For example, you saw the work we're doing for Duchamp's "Infra Mince". It bears many similarities to the logic of Wittgenstein, in the sense that Duchamp says similar things as Wittgenstein but in a different manner. I cannot imagine that Duchamp had actually read "Tractatus", although he might have had the book lying around and had maybe even sniffed it. Luc, on the other hand, has studied art history. He holds an intellectual claim on his work, with references to certain texts he says to have read and the understanding he's taken away from them. What do you think about this particular intelligence that he has as an artist but also as an intellectual?

GB I think that Luc makes a very interesting and special case study of an artist, who needs intellectual material for his imagination, which he gets through studying and reading. The point of our discourse shouldn't be that artists aren't allowed to or should not be intellectually occupied. They should do whatever makes sense and is best for them. If this is intellectual work, so be it! If getting a PhD in philosophy is the right thing for an artist, let it be, but you should never tell an artist what to do, or make him or her talk about things they aren't interested in, or try to convince them of something that is not relevant to them. Anyhow, it clearly strengthens Luc's confidence in the situations we were in together. And he definitely has a big intellectual repertoire which you immediately become conscious of when talking with him.

HDW What did you think about the idea of opening up the talks in the last two sessions in Brussels? Let me first explain what gave me this idea. I really enjoyed the Basel sessions, especially the second one. You could see there that the two very complex "knowledge constructs" were in complete unity with one another and, in the end, there was only the shared understanding of how the paintings work, what they signify and so on. I thought that perhaps that was all it was, but then had the idea of including a third person in the conversation, someone from a completely different background. This ended up being an art historian with a sociological background and approach. Was this a surprise for you?

GB In a way it was a surprise because I didn't know T.J. Clark personally and my perspective on his research was always affected by his Marxist leanings. But when we were talking to each other he was way more flexible than I expected, and my prejudice was conquered. Later, both of us met again in Los Angeles at the Getty Foundation where we were both fellows. He gave a talk about Cézanne, which was split into two parts. The first part was really brilliant, there he really gave a close analysis of the picture, but in the second part, he was trying to use Karl Marx as a way of reading Cézanne, and I found this approach trivial and absurd. Of course, Marx is describing situations of alienation in which Cézanne also existed, but it simply didn't work to use this as an interpretation of the paintings and I found this almost abhorrent. Nevertheless, he has a great analytical ability. And, by the way, he said at the conference in Los Angeles that he is not giving a classical talk, because if he were, he would have spent every day of the last three weeks in the museum in front of that picture of Cézanne taking notes, and then he would have been presenting from those notes, so to speak. He was essentially improvising as we did in Budapest, yet differently. The background against which we were still able to communicate rather well in the end, is that we all came to the point where we were going to check what criteria are needed for an artistic work or for the production of paintings. And how those requirements are linked to the imagination, which was the keyword here. How do they relate to other cultural symbolic forms? Artists mostly express themselves non-verbally, at least when they paint, draw or make photography. But how is this related to the verbality or acoustics of others? This is the dimension on which we all agreed and were trying to make progress, and even constitutes the intellectual base for this project. This wasn't our topic, strictly speaking, but this was the requirement that ensured we could go through with it.

HDW To conclude, I would like to confront you with another question that is very important for me. When I talk with students, I often use the example of how Russian filmmaker Sergei Eisenstein almost randomly discovers a new and revolutionary method for cutting and mounting his masterpiece, *Battleship Potemkin*. This film becomes a worldwide success in 1926. One year later for the 10th anniversary of the revolution, Eisenstein is offered the chance to make a film meant to commemorate this historic event. For weeks he locks himself up in his office trying to understand what exactly he had been doing in his previous film, turning it into a kind of aesthetic manual. When the film *October* finally comes out, it becomes rapidly clear that Eisenstein had produced a dragon. Maybe this idea can also count for this project. The director of BOZAR, Paul Dujardin – fascinated by our exchange – had set up something similar with another Belgian artist and an architect; however, it failed completely.

GB And why did it fail?

HDW It simply didn't work out in the end. It did not fly. Maybe it is that this exercise can only be completed the one time.

GB What you were telling me about your experiences with your students and university work is the essence under which we all work: to have the courage, the seriousness and the intellectual openness to find something and engage in a search for something you are not looking for. That is the point. You undertake to find something, but in the end, it is altogether something different than what you were looking for. This is the structural figure that works best to describe this mental communication, and to distinguish it from other mental processes that stick to ordinary forms of prescribed knowledge. There is nothing to say against a lawyer who needs to learn certain things in his studies, and acquire a set canon of knowledge. There is nothing that can be said against it. We only want to protect the specific conditions under which the intellectual artistic productivity functions. This is very old European.

HDW That is who we are and who we will be.

GB However, please, we should not be considered old Europeans because we were not interested in pushing our learning further! I would presume that I adopted this idea of an old European in the moment that I took some provocations about modernity seriously and went through them. I then think that this position isn't simply about being conservative, but it is more a position through which we can find out what others before us have learned, and what needs to be redeveloped again today and under contemporary conditions.

Index

Page numbers in bold refer to illustrations.

Ai Weiwei 170

Artschwager, Richard 109

Baldessari, John 149

Baselitz, Georg 218

Bosch, Hieronymus 100–102, 107, 111
Last Judgement (Workshop or Follower) **107**

Broodthaers, Marcel 203

Bruegel the Elder, Pieter 40, 72, 100–106
The Battle between Carnival and Lent **106**

Capa, Robert 172–173
Loyalist Militiaman at the Moment of Death, Cerro Muriano, September 5, 1936 [*The Falling Soldier*] 172, **173**

Caravaggio 32, 36–37, 52, 123
Supper at Emmaus 37

Cézanne, Paul 48, 54–55, 85, 128, 159, 190, 213–214, 217, 267–268
The Buffet 54–55, **54**

Chagall, Marc 129

Courbet, Gustave 40, 44–50, 96, 114–116, 123, 130, 172, 224–225
The Artist's Studio, a Real Allegory Summing up Seven Years of My Artistic and Moral Life 115–116, **115**
The Bathers 44, **44**
The Burial at Ornans 224–225, **225**
Cedar Tree at Hauteville 48, **49**
L'Origine du Monde 48, 114, **114**
The Wrestlers 44–47, **45**, 52, 130

Dalí, Salvador 114

David, Jacques-Louis 126, 172
Madame Récamier 126, **126**

de Chirico, Giorgio 64, 145

del Mazo, Juan Bautista Martínez 33–35
Infanta Margarita Teresa in a Green Dress 35, **35**
Portrait of a Noble Youth 33–35, **33**

Demand, Thomas 204

Douglas, Stan 149

Duchamp, Marcel 48, 110–116, 121, 127, 142, 144–145, 162, 181, 266
Boîte-en-valise 112, **112**, 115
Bottle Rack 142
The Bride Stripped Bare by Her Bachelors, Even (The Large Glass) 110–111, **110**, 162
Étant donnés 111, 113
Nude Seated in a Bathtub 111, **111**

Dürer, Albrecht 177, 215

El Greco 10, 14–30, 32, 39, 41, 55, 87, 95–102, 105, 124, 140, 172, 185, 187
The Agony in the Garden **16**, 17, 19–21, 23
The Annunciation 19, **19**, 20, 22–23, 140
The Baptism of Christ 27, **27**
The Burial of the Count of Orgaz 24, **24**
Holy Family with Saint Anne (Workshop) **28**, 29
The Martyrdom of Saint Maurice 100, **101**
The Penitent Mary Magdalene **22**, 23, 25–26
Portrait of Cardinal Niño de Guevara 102
Saint Andrew 20, **21**, 22
Saint James the Less 24–25, **25**
View of Toledo 22, **98**, 99

Ensor, James 54

Freud, Lucian 208

Friedrich, Caspar David 124, 184, 196, 234–235
The Lonely Tree 234, **234**

Géricault, Théodore 40, 89–90, 125
A Man Suffering from Delusions of Military Rank **125**
The Raft of the Medusa 89–90, 125, **125**

Goya, Francisco 37–42, 48, 128
The Knife-Grinder (El Afilador) 41–42, **41**
La maja desnuda 128
La maja vestida 128
Scene from the Spanish War of Independence 37–42, **38**
The Second of May 1808 in Madrid (The Fight against the Mamelukes) 37–42, **37**
The Third of May 1808 in Madrid (The Executions) 37–42, **37**
The Water Carrier (La Aguadora) **40**, 41–42

Hals, Frans 44, 107

Hopper, Edward 79, 82, 159, 201
Nighthawks 201, **201**
Sun in an Empty Room 159

Judd, Donald 144

Kahrs, Johannes 109

Kandinsky, Wassily 129, 209

Kelley, Mike 112, 149

Kelly, Ellsworth 134, 154
Two Panels: Yellow with Large Blue **134**

Kiefer, Anselm 184, 218

Klee, Paul 129

Kliun, Ivan 129

Koons, Jeff 114

La Tour, Georges de 31
The Hurdy-Gurdy Player 31, **31**

Lloyd Wright, Frank 138

Malevich, Kazimir 129, 209
Black Square 209

Manet, Édouard 11, 39–40, 46–47, 49–55, 121–128, 140, 146, 154, 160, 172, 208, 222
Berthe Morisot with a Fan 51, **51**
The Dead Toreador **122**, 123
Le Déjeuner sur l'Herbe 46, 123–124, **123**
The Execution of Maximilian 39, **39**, 124–126
The Fifer **122**, 123, 125
Lady with a Fan 50–53, **50**
Olympia 50–51, 121–123, **121**, 127–128

Mantegna, Andrea 132–133, 215
The Death of the Virgin 132, **133**

Marshall, Kerry James 190–191

Matisse, Henri 85

Millet, Jean-François 172–173, 187
The Sower 172, **173**

Mondrian, Piet 129, 209, 218

Morandi, Giorgio 60

Morisot, Berthe 51

Munch, Edvard 120
Frieze of Life 121
The Scream 120–121, **120**

Newman, Barnett 108, 134, 154
Voice of Fire **134**

Patinir, Joachim 102

Piano, Renzo 138

Picasso, Pablo 55, 90, 112, 120, 265
Guernica 90

Poussin, Nicolas 176

Redon, Odilon 85

Reinhardt, Ad 154

Rembrandt 179

Ribera, José de 50

RICHTER, GERHARD 61, 71, 87, 140, 152–155,
    174, 203, 222
    48 Portraits 155
    Dead (October 18, 1977) 152–155, **154**
    S. with Child 155, **155**
RODCHENKO, ALEXANDER 129, 209
RODIN, AUGUSTE 90, 128
    The Gates of Hell 90
ROTHKO, MARK 67, 128–129, 159
RUBENS, PETER PAUL 17, 25, 36, 43–44, 89,
    97, 99, 106
SANDER, AUGUST 59, 143–144, 149
SEURAT, GEORGES 265
STELLA, FRANK 213
STILL, CLYFFORD 107–108, 119
STRUTH, THOMAS 222
TANIGUCHI, YOSHIO 138
THEOTOKÓPOULOS, DOMÉNIKOS
    see EL GRECO
TINTORETTO, JACOPO 18
TITIAN 18, 34, 89, 100
    The Assumption of the Virgin 89, **89**
    Portrait of Gerolamo (?) Barbarigo 34, **34**
TOULOUSE-LAUTREC, HENRI DE 126
TUYMANS, LUC
    Against the Day I, II 187, **188**
    Alice in Wonderland 139
    Angel 207, 213, **213**
    Antichambre 61, 80–82, **81**, 87, 195
    Apotheek [Pharmacy] 67, 151, **151**
    Der Architekt [The Architect] 228–229,
       228, 234
    The Arena 61, **61**
    Ballroom Dancing 219, 245–247, **246**
    Die blaue Eiche [The Blue Oak] **233**, 234
    Bloodstains 219, **219**

Body 180, **180**, 194, 200–202, 204
Chalk 240, **241**
Church **250**, 251, 253
Cif 157
Cinq Anneaux [Five Rings] 77–79, **77**
La Correspondance 79–80, **80**, 82–83, 195
The Cry 135, **136**
Der diagnostische Blick I, II, III, IV, V [The
    Diagnostic View *I, II, III, IV, V*] 64,
    81–84, **83**, 86, 141, 186, 193, 197,
    207–208, **207**, **212**, 213, 239
Diorama **242**, 243
Drum Set 74–75, **74**
Dusk 78–79, **78**, 139
Exhibit #3 67–71, **67**, 159
Flag 220–224, **221**
Flemish Village 223–224, **223**
Gas Chamber 140
G. Dam **58**, 59, 80, 143
Handdoek [Towel] 209, **211**
Heillicht [Curing Light] 55–59, **57**
The Heritage VI 226, **226**
Himmler 198, 219, 228–229, **229**
Ignatius de Loyola 254, **255**
Incest 55–59, **57**
Insomnia 197–200, **198**
Intolerance 84, **84**
K.Z. **232**, 234
Lumumba 226, 237–241, **237**, 248
Mayhem 72–73, **72**, 79
The Mission 240, **240**
Mwana Kitoko 86, 235–238, **236**
The Nose 209
Orchid **227**, 228
Our New Quarters 79–80, 145, 151, 153,
    175–176, **175**, 206

Parachutisten [Paratroopers] 229, **230**

The Parc **248**, 249

Peter 220, **220**

Pillows 213–215, **214**, 217–218, 222, 249

Plant **70**, 71, 75, 151

The Rabbit 222, **222**

Recherches 231, **231**

Reconstruction 241, **241**

Resentment 73–74, **73**

Rome 139

Sculpture 239, **239**

Seal 249, **249**, 251

The Secretary of State 247–249, **247**

Secrets 61, **61**

Skin Cancer 83

Slide #1, #2, #3 67, **68–69**, 159, 221

The Smell 55–59, **56**

Speech 191, **191**

Still Life 184–185, **185**

Suicide 60–61, **60**, 80

Superstition 202, 213, **216**, 217–219

Suspended 199

Swimming Pool 135, **136**

Tracing 219, **219**

Turtle 139, **251**, 253

W **252**, 253–254

Wandeling [The Walk] 185, 195–197, **196**

Die Wiedergutmachung [Reparations] 204–209, **205**

Wonderland 183–184, **184**, 186

The Worshipper 75–79, **75**

Wrapping Paper 209, **210**, 213

The Yser Tower 224

Die Zeit [Time] 61–66, **63**, 131, 145, 151, 156–158, **156**, 173–175, 186, 202–204, 222

VAN DER WEYDEN, ROGIER 176

VAN DE VELDE, HENRY 130

VAN DYCK, ANTHONY 42–44, 71, 97, 156

    Portrait of a Man 43–44, **43**

    Saint John the Evangelist **42**, 43–44

VAN EYCK, JAN 8, 97, 176–177, 182–183, 190, 222

    The Arnolfini Portrait 8, 182, **183**

van Gogh, Vincent 129, 265

van Meegeren, Han 37

Vasari, Giorgio 190

Velázquez, Diego 18, 25, 30, 32–33, 35–37,
    52–53, 84, 100, 104, 106–107, 121, 127,
    160, 172, 182, 190, 194, 196, 208, 222
    Los Borrachos 32
    Infanta Margarita Teresa in a Blue Dress 84,
        194, **194**
    Las Meninas 182
    Peasants at the Table (El Almuerzo) 36–37, **36**

Veronese, Paolo 23, 89

von Hildebrand, Adolf 118

von Menzel, Adolph 215
    Unmade Bed 215, **215**

Warhol, Andy 108, 114

Zurbarán, Francisco de 29–33, 36–37,
    100–101
    Saint Andrew 30–33, **30**, 36, 40, 100

Photographic Credits

Every effort has been made to contact copyright-holders of photographs.
Any copyright-holders we have been unable to reach or to whom inaccurate
acknowledgement has been made are invited to contact the publisher.

The Art Institute of Chicago / Art Resource: ill. 94

The Barnes Foundation, Philadelphia: ill. 55

Bayerische Staatsgemäldesammlungen, Munich / bpk: ill. 57

Bridgeman Images, London: ill. 51, 59

The British Film Institute: ill. 71

Robert Capa / Magnum Photos: ill. 82

David Zwirner, New York/London
    Ben Blackwell: ill. 47, 83, 84, 92, 93, 96,
    97, 100, 101, 103, 104, 105, 106, 108,
    111, 112, 113, 115, 117, 118, 120, 121,
    122, 123, 124, 125, 127, 128, 129, 139,
    131, 134
    Dan Bradica: ill. 133
    Tim Nighswander / IMAGING4ART:
    ill. 43

Jürgen Doom: ill. 88–89

Hamburger Kunsthalle, Hamburg, Germany /
    Bridgeman Images, London: ill. 78, 79

Paul Hester: ill. 34

Kunsthistorisches Museum, Vienna: ill. 56

Mark Menjivar: ill. 76

The Metropolitan Museum of Art / Art Resource /
    Scala, Florence: ill. 52

Mondadori Portfolio / AKG Images: ill. 65

Musée d'Orsay, Paris
    Bridgeman Images, London: ill. 62, 67
    RMN / Hervé Lewandowski: ill. 61, 64

Museo Nacional del Prado, 2017 / Scala, Florence /
    Photo MNP: ill. 15, 72

The Museum of Contemporary Art, Los Angeles: ill. 73

Museum of Fine Arts, Boston / Scala, Florence: ill. 81

The National Gallery, London: ill. 12, 85

National Gallery of Art, Washington DC, USA /
    Bridgeman Images: ill. 66

National Gallery of Canada, Ottawa: ill. 74

The Oskar Reinhart Collection "Am Römerholz",
    Winterthur: ill. 69

Philadelphia Museum of Art / Gift from the estate of
    Katherine S. Dreier, 1952 / Bridgeman
    Images, London: ill. 58

Scala, Florence: ill. 27, 53, 63, 68, 70, 110
    De Agostini Picture Library: ill. 23
    Photo MNP: ill. 7
    White Images: ill. 18

Staatliche Museen zu Berlin / Kupferstichkabinett / bpk /
    Jörg P. Anders (Menzel): ill. 102

Staatliche Museen zu Berlin / Nationalgalerie / bpk /
    Jörg P. Anders (C.P. Friedrich): ill. 119

Studio Luc Tuymans, Antwerp: ill. 30, 31, 33, 35, 36, 38, 41,
    42, 44, 48, 49, 50, 75, 77, 80, 86, 87, 90,
    95, 98, 99, 107, 109, 114, 116, 126, 132

Szépművészeti Múzeum / Museum of Fine Arts Budapest,
    2018: ill. 8, 9, 11, 13, 14, 22, 26
    Jozsa Denes: ill. 1, 2, 3, 4, 5, 6, 19, 24
    Razso Andras: ill. 20
    Scala, Florence: ill. 10, 16, 17, 21, 28

Joshua White: ill. 45

Zeno X Gallery, Antwerp
    Felix Tirry: ill. 32, 37, 39, 40, 46

Colophon

With many thanks to Cornelia Tietz for her help
with the transcription of the conclusive conversation.

CONCEPT — Hans M. De Wolf

EDITING — Michele Robecchi,
with the assistance of Anya Harrison

TRANSCRIPTION — Donna Wingate

LAYOUT AND TYPESETTING — Dylan Van Elewyck

COORDINATION — Ruth Ruyffelaere

PRODUCTION — Emiel Godefroit

PRINTING — DeckersSnoeck, Ghent

ISBN 978-94-9181-979-7

D/2018/6328/4

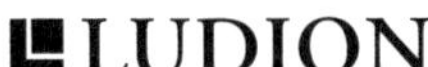

WWW.LUDION.BE